726.50942

B96

Date Due

DEC 20 '78

D1156987

CELLARERS

BUILDINGS

GARTH

PASSAGE

CLOISTER

CHOIR
ROOM

FONT

GREAT
WEST
DOOR →

N A V E

CONSISTORY
COURT

S.W.
PORCH

ORY

TER.

0   50   100 feet

ENT

Lincoln Christian College

KEY TO PLAN OF THE CATHEDRAL

a. ye body of the C. and great square steeple

b. the quier

c. La Mary Chapp

d. the sid iles of quire

e. the uestri

f. parish church

g. the trough ile

h. the chancell

i. Mary Magdalen chapp

k. St. Nich chapp

l. the screene

m. steeple doore

n. south doore ending (?) p.c. [parish church]

o. the 2 buttr's whereon steeple stands

p. turning stares over La Ma Chap

q. dore into green church yard

r. broad ile

s. singing schoole porch

t. the old steeple now consistory C.

u. Weste doore

w. side iles to the broad ile

x. cloister doores

y. the cloisters

z. Sprise garden

2. maidens ile

3. archflemings temple now Chapter house

4. the entrance

5. passage and staires to dormitory

6. ancient priests cellers

7. the preists kitchens

8. cellars

9. munkes hall or fratry now free schoole

10. munks celler

11. passage from abby court throw celler into cloisters and so to the dining hall

12. Bishops gate or porch of his pallace

13. the kitchen now questerers houses

14. the pantry now the consistory office

15. the passage

16. east gate of abby court

17. backhouse with 2 ovens, the one 19 foot diameter

18. St. Tho Chapp; now the deans house

19. brewhouse and storehouse

20. great well

21. the great kill and drying floors

22. abby gates

23. St. Tho Court

24. porters lodge

25. abbats kitchen

26. the tower and larder

27. serving mens hall over wh. is great dineing roome

28. strong beare cell. over it darby chamber

29. the pantry over it the stone hall

30. the wine seller

31. the gallary

32. bishops garden

33. abbots well

34. the great celle over it the great hall and green hall

CHESTER CATHEDRAL

Aerofilms

AERIAL VIEW OF CHESTER CATHEDRAL

CHESTER
CATHEDRAL

From its Founding by Henry VIII
to the Accession of Queen Victoria

By

R. V. H. BURNE, M.A., F.R.Hist.S.
Canon of Chester Cathedral
Archdeacon of Chester

LONDON

S · P · C · K

1958

First published in 1958
by S.P.C.K.
Holy Trinity Church
Marylebone Road
London N.W.1

Printed in Great Britain by William Clowes and Sons, Limited
London and Beccles

© R. V. H. Burne, 1958

TO MY WIFE

726.50942
B96

CONTENTS

37376

v

CONTENTS

LIST OF ILLUSTRATIONS

For the purpose of recovering authentic contact with the past, we must return to the jungle of details and complexities . . . return to the elasticity of ordinary narrative history. In the last resort the student of the past is dealing with nothing less than the irrepressibility of human beings and the unsleeping flow of life itself.

H. Butterfield, *History and Human Relations*, p. 67

PREFACE

THIS book originated in a series of lectures which were recently delivered to the Chester and North Wales Archaeological, Architectural, and Historic Society, and which, after being revised, were eventually published in the Journal of that Society. I am very grateful for permission to use them here.

They are based on the Cathedral Treasurer's Accounts, which have never before been carefully studied. They begin with the founding of the Cathedral in 1541 and although some years are missing they form a valuable record, and the only one we have, of the life of the Cathedral until 1664 when the Chapter minute books begin.

My reason for seeking a wider circle of readers is the fact that no one has yet written the post-Reformation history of any of our cathedrals, or so I am informed, and therefore it seemed to me that there might be a place for this book, even though some of it must necessarily be of local interest only. In writing it I have tried to make it sufficiently interesting to hold the attention of the ordinary reader and at the same time to provide the historian with some fresh material, however slight, for the social and ecclesiastical history of the country. I have therefore aimed throughout at setting the doings of the Cathedral against the larger background of our national history, hoping that the former will illustrate the latter and that the latter will help to explain the former.

I am afraid that the picture of the Church of England and its clergy presented in these pages is not a very favourable one, and the reader may get the impression that the clergy—or at any rate the Cathedral clergy—were very worldly-minded and intent only on adding benefice to benefice. There are three things to be said on the other side. One, it was an age when pluralism was rife and was taken for granted, and we must not judge the clergy of those days by the standards of our own times. Two, in many cases the only information we have of a clergyman is a record of the different livings he held, and that may give the impression that he was interested only in preferment. Three, a quiet conscientious ministry passes unnoticed and unrecorded, for indeed there is little to record. It has no news value. It is the back-slider who gets all the limelight, for it is a sad but true fact that the sinner is more interesting than the saint.

Among the many kind friends who have helped me in writing these chapters there are three to whom I am specially indebted. They are Mr W. Fergusson Irvine, editor of the *Cheshire Sheaf* since 1896, who has generously placed at my disposal his vast store of knowledge collected during a long life spent in the study of local history; the late Mr J. H. E. Bennett, his fellow-editor, who has been equally generous and whose knowledge of the City of Chester was unrivalled; and the late Mr Fred H. Crossley, who has been my guide, philosopher, and friend in all things archaeological and architectural ever since I came to Chester eighteen years ago. My thanks are also due to Professor V. E. Galbraith at Oxford and to Professor E. C. Ratcliff at Cambridge who have always been ready to answer my questions; to the Reverend Dr J. S. Purvis who sent me a copy of a manuscript in the Diocesan Registry at York; to Miss Heather Peek, who did the same for me at the Public Record Office; to the Reverend P. C. Moore, who has allowed me to quote from his unpublished thesis on cathedral choirs; to Mr J. W. Clarke, who has helped me with the reproduction of the seventeenth-century plan of the Cathedral; to Mr F. Brown, F.R.I.B.A., who has kindly provided the modern plan; and to Canon F. L. M. Bennett, whose book on Chester Cathedral with its very full references is invaluable to anyone who tries to follow in his footsteps.

Chester,   R.V.H.B.
19 *March* 1958.

I

UNDER HENRY VIII AND
EDWARD VI

1541–1553

S T WERBURGH'S MONASTERY came to an end on 20 January 1540. In July 1541 Henry VIII made a progress to the north and from 24 to 28 July he lay at Pipewell Abbey with an enormous retinue. During that time—on 26 July—he sealed with his Privy Seal the writ for the letters patent reconstituting the monastery of Chester as a Cathedral, and forwarded it to his Lord Chancellor, Sir Thomas Audley, who was at Walden in Essex, for him to add the Great Seal, which he did on 4 August. Thus was Chester Cathedral founded.[1]

What happened to the buildings in the interval, and whether any services were held in the church we do not know.[2] There are three reasons for thinking that a skeleton staff was maintained. One, that at Peterborough, which was in exactly the same position, the services were carried on during the interim[3]; two, the fact that the new Chapter seal was made a month before the letters patent were signed, which shows that there were people on the spot who considered themselves qualified to act for the Dean and Chapter which were to be; and three, the fact that the last Abbot, Thomas Clarke, seems to have remained in the Abbot's lodging until he became Dean, and death overtook him there before he had time to move out. He died in September 1541, and

[1] W. T. Mellows, *The Foundation of Peterborough Cathedral*, Northants Record Soc., XIII, p. 16.

[2] There is the same lack of evidence at Westminster: "Whether there was any kind of continuity between the old and new foundations cannot be determined. It is not even possible to say if services were being carried on in the cathedral church. But that the Dean and Chapter had some kind of existence before the date of the patent is clear from the fact that Chapter meetings were being held, but there is no record of these until March 3, 1542." (Westlake, I, 217.)

[3] W. T. Mellows, *The Last Days of Peterborough Monastery*, Northants Record Soc., XII, p. 92.

as his last will[1] is dated 14 September 1541, he must have made it only a few days before his death. Attached to it is an inventory of his goods. It reveals amongst other things that his funeral cost £20 12s. 2d. and that the legal charges for the "erection" of the Cathedral amounted to £141. The reason why I think the Dean was still living in his old (abbot's) house which the new Bishop had not yet taken over is that in his will he gives the Bishop first refusal of "my best bed on wch. I lye and the bed wthin the second chamber wth hangings aboute the same".[2] Also there was a chapel in the house, which would be the present St Anselm's Chapel. Its walls were hung with "coverings", one with two images, one ornamented with "stories", and one with "conies and briddes". There was also "a patched covering wth a unicorne" and a carpet of "deyseyes".

It is unfortunate that all the rooms are not mentioned, though probably all the furniture is. We are however permitted to peep into the Dean's bedroom and see the feather bed upon a wool mattress on the four-poster hung with curtains of sarsenet. On the bed are a bolster, two pillows and two blankets. The sheets, when the surveyor made his inventory, were in a chest in the bedroom. The walls are hung with arras and a hanging of green sey, much worn, together with three painted cloths. An "old worse carpet" is on the floor. The furniture consists of two folding tables, a press, a cupboard, a looking-glass and "2 formes with 2 bankers" (? benches). Noting that there were some-where on the premises "xxtye score of coles" as well as firewood, let us now go and rummage in a black chest in the second chamber. At the top of it are two grey amices, a rochet and "a greyt surplese", then come a couple of towels, a pair of sheets and "a shurt", twelve yards of linen cloth and another pair of sheets, old ones this time. But between the "shurt" and the linen cloth we find reposing "an English bibel". Whatever can it be doing there? I suggest that the Dean bought it for the Cathedral as ordered by Cromwell in 1538, an order which was repeated on 6 May 1541, but delayed putting it into the church until a chain and staple had been procured. The chain was bought on 19 November 1541[3] and the plate and staple on 25 November, but there is no mention in the Accounts (which begin in October of that year) of the purchase of the Bible, which suggests that it had been already

[1] Piccope, p. 115.

[2] In the letters patent the rooms in the house which the Bishop was to take over are enumerated and among them are "another chamber lately the Abbot's there, with two *nausalia* and a more private chamber adjoining". (Ormerod, I, 95.)

[3] St Mary's, Chester, bought "a cheyne to the byble" in 1545 (J. P. Earwaker).

bought and put away safely in the chest in the Dean's inner bedroom. Be that as it may, the English Bible lying mixed up with amice and rochet is an eloquent symbol of the transitional period upon which we are now entering.

The inventory also throws some light on the Dean's friendship with Hugh Aldersey and William Goodman, two friends who conspired to hold some manors for the Abbot during the crisis and return them if the Abbey was not dissolved. Goodman was one of the witnesses of the will, and Aldersey was entrusted with a coffer in which was packed "a box containing evidences" and a set of vestments, which he took away to his own house, no doubt for safe keeping in case the worst came to the worst.

The Abbot's farm at Ince must be briefly mentioned, for the contrast with modern farming is interesting. It was stocked with 506 sheep and lambs and *one cow*. It was worked with five horses, not counting "2 old horses one wth a broken leg and another blind", valued at 6s. 8d. the pair. It should be noted that the stock on the farm was the Abbot's private property.

DEAN HENRY MANN 1541–47

Thomas Clarke's successor was Henry Mann, D.D. Born in Lancashire about 1500, he was admitted a scholar of Corpus Christi College, Oxford, in 1520, but left it in 1521 to become a Carthusian monk. He rose to be Prior of the Monastery of Sheen in 1535 and took his B.D. and D.D. degrees in 1539. In the same year he surrendered his monastery into the King's hands and received the enormous pension of £166 13s. 4d. This was the man who became Dean of Chester on 8 October 1541.[1]

The Sub-Dean was not, as we should have expected, the Prior of St Werburgh's, but Dr William Wall, D.D., ex-Warden of the Grey Friars in Chester, whose house had been dissolved in August 1538.[2] He did not die until 1574, so that he must have been quite young when he was made warden. He is famous in local history for having begun to build a conduit in 1536 to supply his convent with water from some springs in Boughton. According to the Harleian MSS.[3] he "began the conduit at Boughton, which came to the Bridge Gate, against Mr Brerewood's house, along the Dee side, in pipes of lead".

[1] *Sheaf*, 3rd Ser., II, 11.
[2] Ormerod (I, 268) must be mistaken in saying that Wall was ever a Canon of St John's, Chester. A Franciscan would not have been a secular canon.
[3] No. 2125 quoted by Morris, 282.

The senior Prebendary was Nicholas Bucksey, who had been Prior of St Werburgh's. He became Treasurer of the Cathedral, a proctor in Convocation and later on Archdeacon of Chester. Thus the first three members of the new Cathedral body were all either ex-monks or ex-friars. And what a mixed lot they were—Mann the Carthusian, Wall the Franciscan, and Bucksey the Benedictine. Bucksey and Wall, agreed, however, in this, that "whatsoever king might reign" they would keep their stalls in Chester Cathedral, for they managed to conform to the régimes of Henry VIII, Edward VI, Mary and Elizabeth.

The remaining four prebendaries[1]—Thomas Newton, John Huet, Thomas Radford, and Roger Smith—were all, except the last-named, ex-monks of St Werburgh's, and we know nothing of their academic qualifications except that Thomas Radford was a scholar of Queens' College, Cambridge. The King went on the principle that the more jobs he could find for the monks the fewer pensions he would have to pay—for all those who did not take up parish work received a pension —and for that reason five out of the six minor canons were also ex-monks.

We learn this from the Treasurer's Accounts, where their names are given, and it is on these Accounts that we have to rely for the next three years, for the statutes were not issued until 4 June 1544.

The petycanons, as they are called in the Accounts, were six in number and whereas the prebendaries were designated "Mr", the petycanons are always designated "Sir", that being the inferior title in those days. The choir was composed of six lay clerks or conducts and eight choristers. One of the former, Sir Richard Davis, seems to have been a priest, for he appears as "Vyker of St Oswald's" in the Survey of 1540 and drew a pension from the Abbey of 33s. 4d. The deacon and sub-deacon, called also gospeller and epistoler, are also designated "Sir", though they would probably be only in minor orders as their title implies. The office of gospeller survived at the Cathedral until the late 'seventies and at Durham until 1884-5, and under the name of "deacon" was mentioned in Bishop Jayne's Visitation of 1899.[3] It is interesting to notice that in April 1542 the Gospeller was Sir John Mayre, who must surely be the monk, John Mayer, returned to his old home with a pension of £6 p.a. in his

[1] The number was cut down from six to four by Act of Parliament (3 and 4 Victoria) and at the same time the name was changed from prebendary to canon.
[2] Ormerod, I, 268.
[3] He asked, "How do matters stand with regard to the Office of Deacon of the Cathedral?"

pocket. From 1544 onwards he appears in the list of petycanons. As he was still drawing his pension in 1547 he seems to have been more worldly wise than his brother monk, William Milner, who worked it the other way round, beginning as a minor canon and leaving the Cathedral to take a pension.

The organist was John Bircheleye, formerly schoolmaster in the monastery. He too had a pension of £6.

What we may call the domestic staff of the Cathedral consisted according to the Statutes of two vergers, two porters (one of whom was to be a barber), one butler, and two cooks. But the Accounts show that in 1541, three years before the Statutes were issued, there were three butlers, one for the Dean, one for the Canons, and one for the Petycanons, and no fewer than five cooks, one for the Dean and two each for the other two bodies. There was also a baker (Robert ap Willy'm) and a water carrier.

> (Dec. 24, 1541) to Hughe Hey wattercarior for s'ving the Deane and Canons of water   10s.
> (March 31, 1542) to the Smythe for shoeing the water horse this dim. yer paste   5s. 4d.

One of the porters was Edward ap Gryffyn who kept the gate of the monastery and carried on there during the interregnum. The Petycanons' cook was another link with the past, for he was Thomas Goose or Gose, formerly servant of Abbot Clarke and tenant of Cellarer's Meadow "with all the tithe of hay and corn in the Bache".

Last of all must be mentioned the six bedesmen who were to be nominated by the Crown and assist the Vergers in the Cathedral. "They must be poor and indigent persons, or who have been disabled or mutilated in battle, or otherwise disabled and reduced to poverty and wretchedness." In the Accounts they are entered as "almsmen", and sometimes as "King's almsmen". They received £6 13s. 4d. a year and were appointed by the Crown.

THE CHAPTER SEAL

The first business of the Dean and Chapter was to devise and make a seal, without which no business could be done. They produced two, a seal and a counter-seal, so different in design and execution that some explanation is called for, but has not hitherto been forthcoming. I must therefore treat the subject in detail.

The brass matrix of the seal "is from the hand of a superior, perhaps even royal, medallist; for there is much feeling and character in the

THE CHAPTER SEAL

THE COUNTER-SEAL

design and the execution is both vigorous and artistic".[1] The matrix of the counterseal, on the other hand, seems to be of copper and is of very inferior workmanship, while the inscription round the edge of it is lacking except for one word. It is evidently the work of a different hand and of a different date. The seal proper depicts the Virgin Mary kneeling at a desk with an open book before her, a house with pillars in the background and a figure of a man holding a cross appearing to her. Above her head is a scroll with the words SALVE · SCT · PARENC. The inscription round the edge of the seal is SIGILLU · COMMUNE · CATHED · ECCLESIE · XPI · ET · BEATE · MARIA · CESTRIE · 1541. XPI must be the Greek capitals CH, R, I, as we find on the sixth-century font in the Cathedral, and the translation of the inscription is "The Common Seal of the Cathedral Church of Christ and the Blessed Mary of Chester 1541". The scene depicted on the seal has long been a puzzle, but inquiries made at the British Museum have revealed that it represents a medieval legend and is not Scriptural at all. The subject is Christ appearing to His Mother after the Resurrection, and the words on the scroll . . . "Hail, Holy Mother" . . . are the opening words of an introit in the medieval Mass. It is easy to see how the Dean and Chapter reasoned. As the new Cathedral was dedicated to Christ and the Blessed Virgin Mary they would require a seal containing both these figures, but being unable to find one in the New Testament, would fall back on one which though un-Scriptural was probably very well known.

The counter-seal is even more puzzling. It depicts Henry VIII sitting on a throne under a canopy, holding in his right hand a sceptre and in his left the orb. A saint stands on either side of him and at his feet are two kneeling figures. Above the King are the letters HR and the figure 8; below him are D and C, and between the two kneeling figures are the letters HB. There is also a V against the saint on the King's left. The only words of the inscription which are extant look like DEI GRACIE. Some light is thrown on the problem of this seal by the discovery that it is not the same as the one at the British Museum. The wax impression which they have there has the inscription nearly intact, there is an O against the saint on the King's right, instead of D and C there are the letters T and D and there is no HB. The explanation seems to be as follows.[2] The impression preserved at the British Museum must have been made from the original matrix

---

[1] *Sheaf*, I, 53.
[2] Suggested by Mr F. Wormald of the British Museum.

which has been lost, perhaps during the Civil War. Dean Henry Bridgman (1660–82) had another matrix made from an imperfect impression on some old document and had his own initials added. The engraver no doubt did his best, but the seal he copied must have been a poor one and lacked the inscription which on the British Museum seal is FACTUM · ANNO · GRACIE · 15 · JULII · ANNO · HE ("Made in the year of grace 15 ... July in the ... year of Henry"). The supporters of the King are St Oswald and the Virgin Mary and the two kneeling figures in the foreground are two ecclesiastics, probably representing the Dean and Chapter, while T and D probably stand for Thomas (Clarke) Decanus.

THE FOUNDING OF THE KING'S SCHOOL

Most monasteries had a school attached to them and that St Werburgh's was no exception to the rule is shown by the fact that at the Dissolution John Byrcheley, "teacher of the children", received a pension of £6. That there were children in the Monastery is revealed in the evidence given by one John Brassie of Tiverton in 1575 in a lawsuit about the tithes of Hilbre. He deposed that his father was the Abbey bailiff for Tilstone Fernall and that he himself about 54 years ago (1531) "was one of the boys of his chambre to Abbot Birchenshawe".[1] It was therefore very natural that Henry VIII in founding the new cathedral and endowing it with monastic lands should lay down that the Dean and Chapter should maintain a school as the monks had done, and also send four scholars to the university, two to Oxford and two to Cambridge.

The Statutes of 1544 (cap. 26) lay down that the foundation scholars should be "poor friendless boys; they were not to be younger than nine (unless they were choristers) nor older than fifteen, and they must be able to read and write and understand just a little of the rudiments of Grammar". They were expected to learn to speak and write Latin in four years. ... "But if any boy shall appear remarkably dull and stupid and naturally averse to learning, we will that that boy after full trial be expelled by the Dean and sent elsewhere, lest like a drone he should devour the bees' honey."[2] School began with prayers at six o'clock in the morning and ended with prayers again at five o'clock in the evening. Whoever drew them up took care that the Royal

[1] *Sheaf*, 3rd Ser., I, 7.
[2] For the full text see Appendix.

Founder should not be forgotten, for the psalm (21) and the responses refer to the King.[1]

The Accounts show that the School must have begun with the founding of the Cathedral, for the boys were paid a quarter's exhibition at Christmas 1541. It consisted of a master, an usher and twenty-four scholars. The eight choristers attended the School but had a master of their own to teach them music, who was one of the petycanons. The Statutes laid down (cap. 25):

> For instructing them and inculcating in them as well good manners as also skill in singing we desire that one person should be elected by the Dean or (in his absence) the Vice-Dean, besides the six clergy above-mentioned [petycanons], who is of honest repute, of upright living, skilled in singing and playing the organ, who will apply himself diligently to teaching the boys, playing the organ at such time as he chooses (*suo tempore*) and to singing the divine offices.

This is not quite what we find in the Accounts of 1541, for the post was given to one of the petycanons and as the stipend was only £4 6s. 8d. this is quite intelligible. The difference is this, that whereas the Cathedral started with an organist and a Master of the Choristers, the Statutes combined the two offices into one. The headmaster of the School was paid £16 13s. 4d. p.a. and the usher £8. The value of the scholars' exhibition was £3 6s. 8d. Probationers were added to the choristers from time to time, called "demi-choristers", who received only £1 13s. 4d. Today all sixteen boys in the choir receive the same treatment, but only the first eight have the privilege of wearing a blue silk tassel to their "squares". Both Grammar School boys and choristers were boarded, if necessary, with one of the canons or petycanons to whom their exhibitions were paid, but more frequently the exhibition was paid direct to the scholars themselves, indicating that they were day boys.

Choristers. 3 *November* 1541

John Traver	Rafe Becket
Thomas Parker	Edward Morecroft
Matthew Wright	Richard Hough
Thomas of Prestbury	Thomas Wilcock

[1] Statutes, cap. 39. See Appendix.

The Grammar School

Schoolmaster: Mr Richard Wrench
Usher: Richard King
Scholars:

John Hulme	Rafe Morton
Edmund Hulme	Thomas Thornley
Robert Jackson	William Johnson
James Boothe	Thomas Rogerson
Thomas Newton	Richard Manering
Richard Broster	Alexander Elcock
William Ball	Robert Prestwich
John Shaw	William Ward
Thomas Manering	Richard Ward
John Traver	Christopher Coven
Robert Ap John	Henry Morecroft
William Bostock	Richard Kettle

It will be noticed that John Traver appears in both lists.

When the Statutes were published the system of boarding the boys with individual canons probably came to an end, for the Statutes established a common table and laid down elaborate rules for it. All the Cathedral officers, except the Dean and Chapter, were to feed together in the "common hall", which presumably means the refectory. The minor canons and the headmaster were to sit at the first table, the deacon, sub-deacon, lay clerks and the usher at the second, and the boys at the third. The servants had their meal after the others had finished.

The first exhibitioners at the University mentioned in the Accounts are as follows:

The vi daye of Decemb. to Mr. Paule Boswell the Kyngs skolare
student in dyvynytie for his q'rters exhibition to be due at
Christmas next   xxxiii s. iiij d.
To Sr. Thom's Francisse for his dim. yers exhibition   iii li. vi s.
[April 16 1542] to Mr. Typpyng for his exhibition   xxxiii s. iiii d.

Sir Thomas Francisse, whose title shows that he must have been in Holy Orders, was still drawing his exhibition in 1545, but the other three are new, Bradman and Roger and John Hulme. The last-named headed the list of the King's School in 1541.

It is not known where the School was situated. It can hardly have begun in the Refectory, if I am right in thinking that was the "common hall" where the school dined.

It appears from a document which has just come to light[1] that the School did not use the Refectory until the year 1571 and then only for a short period. This document contains the evidence given at a Visitation of the Cathedral by the Archbishop of York in 1578. The headmaster, Thomas Purvis by name, deposed as follows:

> To the ninth (article) he answereth, not only the church is ruinous but allso the schole where he teachethe, insomuch that stones diverse times dropping out of the walles have broken the schollers heades, whereof is no amendmente allthough ther have not wanted complaintes; and truely it cannot long stand unlesse it be presently looked into. But now in his fading yeares [he was forty years old] he feeleth more force of winter stormes there than he is able to abide, and likewise the children, which for the most part be sklenderly clad.

After this harrowing description of his present quarters, which may have accounted for him feeling "too old at forty", he goes on to say that the refectory or frater was formerly used as the School and is now standing empty and in danger of falling into ruin:

> Againe the fratry in some partes MINATUR RUINAM, which as the best and most aunccient of the city doe say, soone after the erection of this college by King Henry the eight of most noble memory was the schole and so appointed to be Anno 1571 about the xiith of September by the right reverend and honourable my lord of Yorke's grace his visitors, together with the consent of my L. bushop, and Doctor Pears then Deane of Chester, as it appeareth by such monumentes of ours as ther have beene suffred to remaine. To say the trueth a much fitter place to so good a purpose than that we have; allthough it have been spoyled since that day more and more. And to drive us quite out made it little better than a common privie, yet it self such as cost many hundreds the buildinge.

He then waxes eloquent about the bad state of his own house. It would seem then that the School did not begin its career in the refectory, but moved into it "soone after the erection of" the Cathedral and were officially settled there in 1571, but that it left it again for other premises before 1578, when the Refectory was left derelict. Its further wanderings are outside the scope of this chapter, but it may be briefly stated that it was at one time on the west side of Abbey Square between the two gateways; thence to the abandoned St Nicholas Church (now the Music Hall Cinema); which had become the Common Hall in 1545[2]; then to St Oswald's Church which was in the south transept

---

[1] By the courtesy of the Rev. Dr J. S. Purvis, archivist at York Diocesan Registry.
[2] *Notitia Cestriensis*, VIII, 112.

of the Cathedral, where it is mentioned in the Churchwarden's accounts for the years 1612–14, and at last it returned to the Refectory, where it remained until 1876.[1]

THE CATHEDRAL 1541

As soon as the letters patent were signed the newly-constituted Dean and Chapter were able to set to work literally to put their house in order. There was evidently much work to be done. It is not likely that the monks would have spent much in repairs after they knew that their days were numbered, and a year and a half had elapsed since they had vacated the buildings.

From 7 November to 24 December 1541, Thomas Wysall, mason, did three days' work and Richard Haselwell, mason, did nine days' work at 5d. a day. In the same period William Geste, bricklayer, worked for four days. All three men had a labourer to assist them who received 3d. a day. Also two glaziers named Daubye, father and son, did five days' work, receiving the same rate of pay as the masons and bricklayers, and in addition we read:

Nov. 7, to the said Henrye for mendyng wyndowes in the churche & in the Dean' logying	III s.	VIII d.
Nov. 19, to Henrye Daubye for mendyng the glasse wyndowes in the Churche II dayes & di. at v d. the daye		XII d.ob.

The Petycanons' lodgings were evidently a priority job. The chimney had to be rebuilt and both mason and bricklayer worked six days at it, supplying 500 bricks at 4s. 4d. a thousand. A new door to their dining-room was also necessary and Edmund Gee provided four boards for it for 10d. Meanwhile the carpenters were busy repairing the roof:

Nov. 19, to Laurence Massye for IIII dayes & di. wt. the peticanons———le daye	II s.	VI d.
The same daye to John Ashton carpentare IIII dayes & di. wi. the peticanons	II s.	VI d.
The same daye to Laurence Massye for di. c latts boght by hym for the peticanons		v d.
(Ditto) for spykyng nayles boght by him		IIII d.
(Ditto) for small nayles		II d.

[1] Today the Dean and Chapter no longer support twenty-four "poor friendless boys", but discharge their obligation by paying £297 annually to the King's School instead.

The Smiths also played their part, albeit a small one:

Nov. 13, to Sprag the smythe for a loke & a keye to the dor that goethe into the clauster	vi d.
Nov. 19, to Willy'm Hu'tyngton smythe for a crampe of yron for a dore cheke & for shapenyng the masons tools	iiii d.
Nov. 25, to Rog'r Sprag smyth for the loks & keyes for the petye canons	ii s. vii d.

In the same month the horse pond was scoured

Nov. 13, for castyng & makyng cleane the ponde in the courte	vii s. —

A pencil note inserted in the Accounts states: "This was a large pond in the Abbey Square close to the great gate, in which the Abbot and his numerous guests watered their horses." In 1505 there was an inquest held on the body of Roger Ledsham, "Keeper of the Great Gate of the Abbey of St. Werburgh, lately drowned in a certain pit called 'Horse-pole'. It was filled up and levelled in 1584."[1]

In December attention seems to have been concentrated on the church. Henry Daubey and Son had already spent two and a half days each upon the windows, and on 2 December paid 1s. 2d. for $3\frac{1}{2}$ lb. of "sother" (solder) "for to mende the wyndowes in the churche". Evidently they were in a pretty bad condition. However, by the end of the year the fabric of the church had probably been put in order—the xx d. paid to "the Tylare" on 4 January was no doubt a normal item in the winter when heavy rain or snow found out the weak places in the roof—and the Dean and Chapter were able to turn their attention to the furniture and fittings. From their expenditure we are able to glean something of the nature of the services which took place in the new cathedral during the last six years of Henry's reign, and we get the impression that they were identical with those of the old monastic days. It is true that a chain was procured for the English Bible which we discovered hidden away in the Dean's spare room:

Nov. 19, to Elys Byrche for a cheane for the byble in the church	ii d.
Nov. 25, (to Roger Sprag, smythe) for a plate & staple for the byble in the churche	i d.

Also on 3 December the two carpenters were paid 5s. for "makyng a pue to stand in the Chapell of Sainte Peter".[2] But as one swallow does not make a summer, so one Bible and one "pue" do not make a

---

[1] See *Sheaf*, O.S., ii, 180.
[2] Nothing is known of this chapel apart from this entry.

Reformation, and the Old Learning, as it was called, went on as before as the following extracts show:

Dec. 5, to a goldsmyth for polishing of II payre censors in the churche		VIII d.
Dec. 14, to John Harteswall Carver for makyng an angell for the sacrament	II s.	IV d.

This would be the carved figure of an angel to surmount the pyx containing the Reserved Sacrament which hung above the altar.

Jan. 2, to Henrye Banks for oyle wax candels & other necessarys for the churche	XII s.	XI d.
Mar. 10, for XXVII yards di. of lynen to make albes for the churche	XIII s.	XI d.

There is unfortunately a gap in the Accounts here and we have to jump to 1544, by which time only two of the original chapter are left, Wall and Bucksey. Such heavy mortality suggests an outbreak of plague, though none is recorded in the City annals for these years.

We may presume that by this time the Cathedral was in working order and that any repairs which are recorded are the result of ordinary wear and tear. For example the silver censers were giving trouble:

(Jan. 31, 1545). Itm for mendinge the rynge of the sylver senc'	II d.
(May 21). Itm for rynge to the sylver sence'	V d.
Itm for mending the shayne of the sylver sencer	III d.

I wonder if this was one of the pair of silver censers which the Dean and Chapter were reported by Edward VI's Commissioners (in 1553) to have sold in 1548 to enable them to repair their houses.[1]

Other items of interest are:

Itm for Russhes to the churche per an'	III s.	IV d.
Itm to the ryngers one all soles nyght		XII d.
Itm for repayryng of the broken albes		VI d.
Itm for lace & gyrdelle to albe and amyse		XI d.
Itm to a brotherer for vi days	IV s.	VIII d.
Itm for VI yards of canvase to the same		XX d.
Item for rybbands & threde		X d.
Itm for (blank) yardes of fryngs		XII d.
Itm for lynynge to the coverynge of the lect'rne[2]		VII d.
Itm for a frynge to the coverynge of the deske		XI d.

---

[1] Morris, op. cit., 152.

[2] *Rites of Durham*, Surtees Soc., CVII, 14. A lectern in the choir "where the monks did sing their Legends at Mattins and other times".

A certain amount of money was spent on repairing service books, which of course would all be in manuscript.

> Itm for Hymner to the quyre   vɪɪɪ d.
> Itm to Robert Bower for correctying the olde boke of the quere ɪɪ s.   ɪ d.
> Item to the same for a pressioner and an hymn'   ɪɪ s. vɪɪɪ d.

A processioner was a "book containing directions for the various processions, with the words and music of the antiphons etc. then chanted, together with certain offices connected with processions".[1]

> Itm for w'tynge the legente of J'hons' & Mary and for p'che-
> ment to the same   xɪɪ d.

This refers to the writing out upon a new piece of parchment of a Breviary lesson connected with St John and St Mary. The First Lesson for St John's Day refers to the scene at the Cross where both St John and St Mary are mentioned. Probably this was a replacement.[2]

> Itm to Raff Bent for a prycksonge boke   xxvɪ s. vɪɪ d.

This seems to have been a very expensive item. Mention has been made of an altar dedicated to St Peter. There was also one dedicated to St John.

> Itm for vɪɪɪ yards of lynon & clothe for an albe to Saynt John's
> altar   v s. vɪɪɪ d.

Each altar had its own vestments which were kept in a locker or aumbry alongside it.[3]

Wafers for the Mass were of two kinds. The large wafer used by the celebrant was called "singing bread" and cost 6d. a thousand. Altogether 3,500 of these were bought on three different occasions during the year, which gives us some idea of the number of Masses which must have been said at the Cathedral on the eve of the Reformation. The smaller wafers for the congregation were called "houseling bread" and only 8½d. was spent on these in the same period, although 8s. 7d. was spent on "houseling wine."

Another very interesting entry is:

> Itm for ɪɪ paxes to O Lady alt' & Saynt John' alt'   vɪɪɪ d.

The Kiss of Peace, which was part of the ritual of the early liturgies, was discontinued in the thirteenth century and for it was substituted

---

[1] *Durham Account Rolls*, Glossary, vol. 3, No. 103.
[2] Inf. ex Prof. E. C. Ratcliff.
[3] *Rites of Durham*, p. 2.

the kissing of an object called a pax which was passed round to be kissed by all in turn. It was commonly made of wood or metal or ivory and often had the representation of the Crucifixion on it. At Durham the cover of the Gospel book was used for this purpose.[1]

The services in Holy Week were very elaborate in character. Then, as now, the Gospel for the day contained the story of the Passion, beginning on Palm Sunday with St Matthew's account followed by St Mark's and St Luke's on the Monday, Tuesday, and Wednesday. The clerks who sang it were called "Passioners" and were recompensed with some form of drink. In the procession on Palm Sunday the Sacrament was carried under a canopy and a boy dressed up as a prophet chanted certain texts. All this is referred to in the following entries:

Itm upon palme Sonday to the passioners in wyne	viii d.
Itm for iij days following	xii d.
Itm to iiij men which cariad the canaby	iiij d.
Itm for a payre of gloves to the p'phet on palme Sonday & for	
his breakfast	iii d.
for his breakfast	iii d.
Itm for iiij staves to the canaby	v d.

On Maundy Thursday the commemoration of the Last Supper took the form of a supper for which special dainties were bought:

Itm for iij pounds of almonds ad mandat capith	xii d.
Itm for iij pounds of reasons	vi d.
Itm for iij galans of bragot [mulled or spiced ale]	xii d.
Itm for iij dozens of spysed cake	xviii d.
Itm in wyne & ale	iii s. ii d.

In the margin is written "*In cena dom* [*domini*]", which was the liturgical description of Maundy Thursday. Cakes and ale remind us of Sir Toby Belch's rebuke to the Puritan steward, "Thinkest thou that because thou art virtuous, there shall be no more cakes and ale?" but we are a little surprised to find them figuring in the middle of Holy Week.

Another event on Maundy Thursday was the consecrating of oil and cream by the bishop:

Itm for iii pewt' potts oyle & creme w'th a spone	iii s.
Item for holly oyle & creme	iiii d.

The pewter pots are the ampullas for the oil of the sick, the oil of the catechumens, and the cream or chrism for baptisms. The pots were

---

[1] Ibid., 9 and note on p. 200.

commonly of pewter, and the spoon was to mix the chrism with before it was consecrated.

At Easter the paschall was erected. This was a movable candlestick used only at this season in which the great Easter candle was placed and lighted with new fire from a flint.[1] So just before Palm Sunday we find this entry:

> Itm for mendynge the pascall case to Ric. Pedle   xII d.

This was probably in 1544 and there are no further entries connected with the worship of the church until after the death of Henry VIII, which occurred on 28 January 1547. This is referred to in the Accounts:

> Itm for syngynge to the king's dirige   xII d.

The Chapter over which the new Dean had to preside was constituted as follows:

William Cliffe, D.D., Dean	1547
William Wall, D.D.	1541
Nicholas Bucksey	1541
Peter Mainwaring	1544
George Cotes, D.D.	1544
John Gibbs	1544
John Lepyngton	1544

Peter Mainwaring was made a canon of the collegiate church of St John the Evangelist, Chester, on 22 May 1543, and moved to the Cathedral on 1 February 1944. But he seems to have retained his canonry at St John's, for he is included in the list of canons there in the survey made in 1548 after the college was dissolved. He died in 1550 at the age of eighty.[2]

George Cotes was elected a Fellow of Balliol College, Oxford, in 1523 and in 1526 a Fellow of Magdalen. He was at first a strong supporter of the Old Learning and was denounced to Cromwell by Bishop Latimer in 1535 as "wilfully witty, Dunsly learned, Moorly affected, bold not a little, zealous more than enough; if you could monish him, charm him, and so reform him, etc., or else I pray you, inhibit him my Diocese".[3] This seems to mean that he was a disciple of Duns Scotus and had followed the example of Sir Thomas More in not subscribing to the King's supremacy of the Church. But he was not prepared to die for his principles as More had done, and evidently

---

[1] Ibid., 201.   [2] Ormerod, I, 314.
[3] Strype, *Eccles. Memorials*, I, ch. 39, quoted in *C.A.J.*, *N.S.*, xviii, 83.

Cromwell succeeded in monishing, charming, and reforming him to such good purpose that in 1539 he was appointed Master of his old College, Balliol, much to the disgust of the Visitor, the Bishop of Lincoln, who wrote to Cromwell's secretary:

> Remember the matter of Baglive College. If Cootes should obtain it I reckon the College undone. The man is so wilful and factious that there would soon be few in that house but of his countrey [Yorkshire], and some of those now there should have little quiet.[1]

In reply Cromwell asks the Bishop to accept Cotes, reminding him that he can be expelled "if he transgresses the ordinances".[2]

John Gibbs is said to have resigned in 1554, and it is thought that he is one of the few who failed to survive the transition from the régime of Edward VI to that of Queen Mary.

John Lepyngton also disappears in that year and is said by Dr Cowper to have been deprived. If this be so, and his evidence is not always correct, these are the only two who failed to keep their posts through all the changes of the Reformation.

In January 1548, the Dean and Chapter were very busy building a "hovell" in the precincts:

> Itm to labor'es and weme' [women] for clensyng ye new wark
> & cariyng awey the hyll of romell w'thin our pr'synke   vɪɪ s.   ɪɪ d.

One would suppose that the women did the cleaning and the labourers carried away the rubbish. But no.

> Itm to ii weme' for carrying out of romell fro' the library &
> the stere for a day & a halfe   vi d.

Women, it seems, were paid 2d. a day.

DEAN WILLIAM CLIFFE 1547–1558

William Cliffe, D.D., succeeded Dean Henry Mann, who was consecrated Bishop of Sodor and Man on 14 February 1546. He relinquished his pension but was allowed to retain his Deanery and the two benefices of which he was rector, St Mary-on-the-Hill in Chester and Finningley in Nottinghamshire. However, he did not avail himself of this permission for long, for he resigned St Mary's in 1546 and the Deanery in 1547. In 1529 Cliffe was Archdeacon of London, and in 1533 Archdeacon of Cleveland. The following year he was made Treasurer of York Minster and Rector of Waverton.[3] In 1537 he was

---

[1] *L. & P.*, xɪv, pt. 2, No. 477.   [2] Ibid., No. 543 (ii).   [3] Ormerod, ɪɪ, 789.

a member of the Committee which drew up the *Institution of a Christian Man*, commonly known as the *Bishop's Book*, an official exposition of the Christian Faith. Ten years later on the accession of Edward VI Cliffe was induced to surrender the treasurership of York with all its possessions into the King's hands, and four days later he was appointed Dean of Chester. It is difficult not to see some connection between these two events, and it is generally supposed that his promotion to Chester was a reward for his surrender at York. The fact that he conformed to the Protestantism of Edward VI and the Papalism of Queen Mary shows that he was not of the stuff that martyrs are made of, though in this he was like most of his brethren, but he is chiefly remembered for the way in which he was bullied into surrendering the Cathedral lands into the hands of Sir Richard Cotton (see below, p. 24).

Before this happened, however, the new Dean was successful in recovering for the Cathedral an annual grant of £19 10s. od. which the Crown had been accustomed to pay to St Werburgh's Abbey and which had not been paid since the founding of the Cathedral. But what with lawyer's fees and a visit to London it cost the Dean and Chapter £22 in expenses. It is recorded in a document dated 26 November 1545, being a decree of the Court of Augmentations, which states that the Dean and Chapter having certified that the Abbey used to receive "by the hands of the receiver of the Chamberlain of Chester £19 10s. od. which sum has not been paid from the time of the erection of the said Cathedral until now; the Court therefore decree that the said Dean and Chapter shall receive the above sum with arrears".[1] The sequel to this can be read in the Accounts for the year 1547:

Itm to Vaudre for his fee paying the castle mone   x s.
Itm the quietans off ye receide ye on part in hys boke & ye other
delyvryde us   xii d.

The way this money was made up is not without interest:

		£	s.	d.
1.	Ancient alms payable annually to the Abbot on the Feast of S. Martin for providing a lamp in the Chapel of the Blessed Mary of Hideburgheye		10	0
2.	The tithes of the fishery of Dee Bridge		5	0	0
3.	Recompenses for certain tithes at Frodsham relinquished by the Abbot of S. Werburgh to the Abbot of Vale Royal at the request of Edward I		4	0	0
4.	The tithes of the City of Chester		10	0	0
		£19	10	0

[1] *Sheaf*, 3rd Ser., VII, 43.

It is unfortunate that the Accounts for the reign of Edward VI are incomplete except for the years 1551 and 1552, so that we have not a full record of the changes which were made in the services of the Cathedral and have to be content with a hint here and there of what was going on.

[Dec. 6, 1550]

Paid to Richard Hasilwell and his servant and for iiii berers [bearers] of stones from the alters for iii days and half after v d. the day   v s. vii d. ob.

And to the mason Hasilwell and his servant for vii days at the alters and about the wall between Doctor Coots and Doctor Wall and in the caleyard for hym self viii d. the day and his servant v d. a day   vi s. vi d.

[Dec. 13]

Paid to Turner for making the table in the quere for v days   ii s.   ix d.

Itm for a spare [spar?] to the table   vi d.

Itm to Hasilwell the mason helping the laborers to ley the greate alter stone   iii d.

Itm for thride to the vestre and mending the vestments   iii d.

[Christmas Eve]

Itm to the glaseor for mending the wyndow afor the table in the p'ish church and for his glass   xxi d.

[March 19, 1551]

Itm for russhes against Aester   iiij d.

Itm for wyne to the Communion in mavmesey x quarts in secke xv quarts in claret xxij quarts   xiiij s. viii d.

Itm for a quart to put in the wyne the ould quart remaynyng for sowder   xx d.

[April 5, 1551]

Item for singing at Easter   viii d.

Item for rosyn and chaulke   i d.

Itm for Mr. Turner the precher for his dyner   iiij s.

[After S. John Baptist's Day, 1551]

In primis for iiij lodes of woodde to the bonefire   xvi s.

Itm for fagotts   xii d.

Itm for the fire in the playe tyme   xvi d.

[July 9, 1551]

Payd to ii wemen for clenning the dortir and for mending the way under Mr. Gybbes house   xvi d.

[After Michaelmas]

Itm layd dune for the peticanons table for 11 monethes   v li.

There is one entry in 1551 which is of great historical interest. It will have been noticed that Richard Hasilwall's wages in the last extract were 8d. a day and his servant's 5d. a day. In 1541 a mason was paid 5d. and his servant 3d. (p. 13). This rapid rise in wages (and still more in prices) was a well-known phenomenon of this decade and was due in part to the depreciation of the coinage by Henry VIII and his son.

Silver coins issued in 1551 contained only one-seventh of the silver they had contained twenty-five years before and the weight of copper coins had also been lowered.[1] In 1551 a halt was called to this spend-thrift policy and a reform begun which was completed by Elizabeth. On 9 July 1551, a Royal Proclamation announced that henceforth a shilling would be worth only 9d. and a groat 3d. On 17 August the value of the shilling was lowered still further to 6d. and the groat to 2d.[2] The practical effect of these proclamations on the Cathedral revenues is shown in the following entries under 9 July 1551:

> Itm lost in the abbating or demynishing of the money nono die
> Julij the some of 163 li. 5 s. after the loss of v s. in the pound or
> the fourth part   XL li. XVI s. III d.
> [August 17]
>   Itm lost in the seconde change of money   XLIX li.
>   Itm more lost in twopenses, pens and halpens wheren the half
>   was abbatede   IIII s. IX d.

The Accounts end in 1551 and when they begin again in 1555 Queen Mary is in the middle of her reign. The rest of the story of Edward VI's reign as it affected the Cathedral is soon told. At the beginning of 1552 the Second Prayer Book was authorized by Parliament. It contained no Ornaments Rubric and consequently all the ornaments and vestments with which the churches were filled became redundant and were confiscated by the Crown. A Royal Commission for this purpose visited Chester on 20 May 1553, and made an inventory of the spoils. The best of the vestments were sent to the King's Wardrobe and the remainder sold for £5 11s. 3d. The list of what was left in the Cathedral gives some idea of what the Reformation meant in terms of worship.

> 2 chalices and patens.
> 3 table cloths.
> 2 long towels
> 1 "pillo" for the Communion table made of an old tunicle.
> A carpet for the Dean's stall.
> A covering for the pulpit.
> A covering for the Communion table, one side of crimson velvet and the
>   other green satin and white ——.
> 3 carpet cushions for the choir.
> A pair of organs.

---

[1] A. D. Innes, *England under the Tudors*, 180.
[2] Stow's *Chronicles*, 9 July 1551.

3 bells in the steeple by the choir and a clock.
2 great bells in the new steeple.
—— coffers or chests.

It was also reported that the Dean and Chapter had sold a great bell "which hanged in the new steple there, whiche bell was taken downe and solde by the Dean and Chapter of the same Cathedrall Churche the 4th of May, 4 Edward VI (1551) for the somme of xxxiii li. and the said somme is aledged by them to be paid unto the Ministers of the said church for there stypend". This is probably the bell now in Conway Church, which bears the following inscription:

> Ave fidelis domina Werburga Sanctissima
> Felix in Choro Virginum
> Ora pro nobis (ad) Dominum
> Joh'nes Byrchynshaw Abbas Cestre.

They had also sold a cross and two silver censers on 31 January 1548 for £3 and used the money for the "reparacon of their houses".[1]

Further light is thrown on the sale of the bell by a note contributed by Thomas Hughes to the *Cheshire Sheaf* in 1879 (I, 152) which is as follows:

> In the Treasurer's Accounts for 1550-1 is the following:
> Recevyd off Mr. Will'm Aldersaie and Sethe Rosomgreve off the citie of Chestur, for a Belle weghying xviij hundrerthe pounde, everie hundrerthe pownde at xxxvij s. the ij daie off Maie 1551, the sume of xxxiiij li; for the odde iiij s. the saide Mr. Aldersaie and Rosomgreve wolde not paie   xxxiiij li.
> Rec'd off Mr. Deane 3 May, the above xxxiiij li. p' me Will' Wall.

This has every sign of being an authentic extract from the Accounts, but it is not to be found there now.

There can be little doubt that the depreciation of the currency with the consequent rise in prices and wages was the reason why the Dean and Chapter had to resort to this method of raising money. In fact at Westminster, where the same thing happened, this is definitely given as the reason:

> In 1550 it was resolved to sell certain of the remaining articles of plate in order to pay the costs of alterations in the quire and elsewhere. A further sale of a similar character was ordered in the same year on the ground that the depreciation in the value of money had resulted in the fact that the treasurer had not enough in hand to pay the wages of the officers of the church.[2]

---

[1] Morris, 150 ff.   [2] Westlake, op. cit., I, 217.

We who live in a time of rising prices can sympathize with the Dean and Chapter in their predicament.

THE RAPE OF THE CATHEDRAL LAND

It may have been this report of the Commissioners that first suggested to Sir Richard Cotton a way in which he might enrich himself at the expense of the Dean and Chapter. It is an amazing story and throws a lurid light on the unscrupulous and greedy "lords of the nobility" who supported the Tudor Despotism for their own ends. Sir Richard had seen his elder brother acquire Combermere Abbey at the Dissolution and no doubt was on the lookout to enrich himself in the same way.

In 1552-3 the Dean of Chester, William Cliffe, and two Prebendaries "were imprisoned in the Fleet, by procurement of Sir Richard Cotton, comptroller of the King's household and under intimidation granted to him most of their lands in return for a fixed annual payment of £603 17s. 0d., although the rents of the property amounted to over £700". Such is the account given by Ormerod,[1] based on the Harleian MSS. in the British Museum.

It is now possible to supplement this account with some details from the Acts of the Privy Council which were not available when Ormerod wrote.

Cotton's appointment as Comptroller on 4 September 1552, carried with it a seat in the Privy Council and this gave him his chance. The minutes of that body record that at a meeting held on 8 November 1552 the following business *inter alia* was transacted:

> Letters to the Deanes of Chester and Peterborough to repayre hither and bring with them ij of theyr Chapter to aunswer to the taking downe of leade, according to the minute. A lettre to [blank] to repayre to Chestre to examin and trie out [sic] what leade, iron or other things have byn within these two yeres taken downe from the Cathedrall Churche there, who were the doers thereof, and to whose use the same was converted, and to certify hither what they shall have tried out. A lyke lettre to [blank] to repayre to Peterborough for the lyke purpose.[2]

And at a meeting on 14 February 1552-3, Sir Richard again being present, it was recorded:

> The Dean and two Cannons of Chester committed this day to the Flete for takinge downe the leade of theyr churche and other disordred doinges.[3]

---

[1] I, 254.   [2] *Acts of the Privy Council*, 163.   [3] Ibid., 218.

On 6 March of the same year:

A letter to the Warden of the Flete to set the Dean of Chester, being dangerously syk of the gowte, at his lybertie; commaunding hym to gyve his attendance on the Lordes of the Counsell to aunswer to that is layd to his charge.[1]

This looks as though the Dean had been kept in prison for twenty days without a trial. His two companions remained in the Fleet for another ten days, making a month in all.

On 16 March 1552–3: "The Prebendaries of Chester made theyr apparaunce this day." There is no further mention of them, so that presumably they were released, and nothing more is recorded about the Dean of Peterborough.

Shortly after this, i.e. before the death of Edward VI on 21 June 1553, the Dean of Chester granted the bulk of the Cathedral property to Sir Richard Cotton on the terms already stated.

Such are the facts, and putting two and two together it is natural to assume that Sir Richard was the informer against the Dean and that it was he who brought him before the Council, and that there was an obvious connection between the Dean's release from prison and his alienation of the Cathedral lands. But was the Dean guilty and if so, how did Cotton obtain his evidence? A paper in the Public Record Office, undated but almost certainly of the reign of Edward VI, throws some light on this question.[2] It is a charge brought against the Dean and Chapter by two of their own officials, Ralph Langley and William Glasier, reporting them to the Chancellor of the Court of Augmentation (Sir Richard Sackville). They say "that sundry of the said prebendaries have taken and receyed into their hands and custody gret substance of goodes, ornamentes, jewells, proffetes and revenue of the premises ... and converted the same unto their only privat uses ... and from tyme to tyme do denye to make any accomptes thereof before your beseechers". They have also let for their own profit "a gret part of the howses, byldynges and gardens of the sed churche being within the precynct of the same". William Glasier is described in a book of leases, now in the Cathedral Chapter House, as clerk to the Chapter in 1550 and in 1547 his name occurs in the Accounts:

Payed to Wyllya' Glasier the younger for owre sute in
ye lease agaynst hockenhull.   XXIII s. x d.

Langley seems to have been his junior and in the same year we find

Item to Rauffe Langley for laboryng for a com'ission   VI s.

[1] *Acts of the Privy Council*, 230.
[2] I am indebted to Miss Heather Peek for this paper.

It is very doubtful whether the Chapter knew what was being said behind their backs, for on Easter Eve 1551 they granted Glasier a yearly fee of £4 for life "for his diligence and labour endeavouring to gett such debts, arrears, and rents as are behind". William Glasier senior lived at Backford, two miles from Chester, and was Mayor of Chester in 1551. They were a family who were reputed to have done well for themselves out of the Dissolution of the Monasteries.

The above report may not have been the one on which Sir Richard Cotton acted, but it indicates the source from which his information came and suggests that there were some grounds for his accusation. Furthermore, the Council took no action until they had a report from their own agent who had been sent from London to investigate. On the other hand, this zeal on the part of the Council for the preservation of lead on church roofs is a little unconvincing when they themselves were busy stripping it off the roofs of abbeys all over the country.

The whole incident is an interesting illustration of the power of the Privy Council under the Tudors. As dispensers of the Royal prerogative they could take cognizance of any case, great or small; they were above the law of the land, and there was no appeal from their decisions. No wonder Cranmer when he was drawing up the Litany in 1544 thought fit to include a petition for "the Lords of the Council and all the nobility".

The conclusion of the story belongs to the reign of Elizabeth and will be told at a later date.

APPENDIX

CATHEDRAL STATUTES

No. 26. Of Grammar School Boys and Their Teachers

(Translation.) In order that piety and sound learning may for ever flourish in our Church and in their own time bear fruit to the glory of God and to the benefit and adorning of the Commonwealth ... we decree that by the election of the Dean, or (in his absence) the Vice-Dean and Chapter, there may be for ever in our Church of Chester twenty-four poor and friendless boys to be maintained out of the income of our Church, of good capacity (so far as is possible) and capable of learning; and we do not wish these to be admitted before they can read and write and understand just a little of the first rudiments of grammar, that is, in the judgement of the Dean and the Headmaster; and we will that these boys be maintained at the expense of the Church until they have attained to a moderate knowledge of Latin Grammar and have learned to speak and write Latin, for which purpose they will be given four years, or if the Dean and Headmaster think fit, up to a maximum of five years. But we will that none, unless he is a chorister of our Church of Chester, be chosen as a poor pupil of our Church under the age of nine years or above that of fifteen. But if any of the boys shall appear remarkably dull and stupid or naturally averse to learning, we will that the boy after full trial be expelled by the Dean and sent somewhere else, lest like a drone he should devour the bees' honey. And we lay it on the conscience of the teachers that to the utmost of their ability they apply themselves diligently to their work, whereby all the boys may make progress and become proficient in their studies. And that they may not permit any boy who is conspicuously lazy to remain too long uselessly among the rest, they shall report at once the name of that boy to the Dean, so that after his removal one more suitable may be chosen by the Dean, or (in his absence) the Vice-Dean and Chapter, to take his place.

We ordain moreover that one be chosen by the Dean, or (in his absence) the Vice-Dean and Chapter, learned in Latin and Greek, of good reputation and virtuous life, skilled in teaching, who may perfect in virtue and equip with sound learning these twenty-four boys of our Church as well as any others who come to our School to learn grammar. Let this man be the first in our School and be Headmaster and principal Teacher. Again, through the Dean, or (in his absence) the Vice-Dean and Chapter, we will that another man be chosen, of good reputation and virtuous life, and learned in Latin, skilled in teaching, who under the Headmaster will teach the boys the first rudiments, that is to say, of grammar and will therefore be called the Usher (Hypodidasculus) or Second Master.

But we will that these schoolmasters shall diligently and faithfully observe and follow the rules and order of teaching which the Dean and Chapter have considered should be prescribed. But if they are found lazy or negligent or unfitted for teachers, after the third warning by the Dean and Chapter let them be moved and dismissed from office. And they will promise with an oath that they will faithfully fulfil all the duties relating to their office.

The King's School Prayers

The following is a translation of that part of cap. 39 of the Cathedral Statutes which deals with morning prayers at the King's School:

At 6 a.m. the Usher entering the school shall say with all the scholars by alternate verses the psalm, The King shall rejoice in Thy strength, O Lord, etc.

Lord, have mercy upon us. Christ, have mercy upon us. Lord, have mercy upon us.

Our Father, which art in heaven etc.

O Lord show Thy mercy upon us etc.

O Lord, save the King etc.

Be unto him, O Lord, a tower of strength from the face etc.

Let the enemy prevail nothing etc.

O Lord, hear us etc.

We beseech Thee, Almighty God etc.

Prevent us, O Lord, in all our doings etc.

The choice of the psalm (21) and of the responses show that the School prayers were intended to be for the benefit of the royal founder rather than for the benefit of the School; evidently the King expected to receive in prayer value for the money he had spent. The boys were to be his bedesmen. For the psalm deals mainly with the King and contains such verses as "Thou shalt give him everlasting felicity and make him glad with the joy of thy countenance. And why? because the king putteth his trust in the Lord, and in the mercy of the most Highest he shall not miscarry" and much more to the same effect. The responses are even more revealing. They are all to be found in the Prayer Book, but could not have been taken from there, for the statutes were published in 1544 and the Prayer Book not until 1548. The compilers of these prayers took them from the Sarum Liturgy. The third one, "Be unto him a tower of strength", comes from the Visitation of the Sick and refers there to the sick person, but its position here immediately after "O Lord, save the king", makes it refer to Henry VIII. They can be found in our own Visitation of the Sick, where of course they are used properly.

Of the two prayers which follow, the first seems to have been the collect for the Fifth Sunday in Lent, but Cranmer slightly altered the original (which we have here) in his translation for the Prayer Book. Where he writes, "We beseech Thee, Almighty God, mercifully to look upon Thy *people*", the Sarum Rite had *family* which is much more appropriate to a school, and it goes on, "That by Thy great goodness they may be governed in body, and by Thy protection may be guarded in *mind*", which Cranmer has altered to *soul*.

The second prayer is also from the Sarum Rite and may be found in our Prayer Book among the Post-Communion prayers.

2

UNDER MARY AND ELIZABETH I

1553–1603

MARY 1553–1558

AT the accession of Mary Tudor to the throne of England on 19
July 1553, the composition of the Dean and Chapter of Chester
Cathedral was as follows, the names being arranged in order of
seniority:

William Cliffe, D.D., LL.D., Dean	1547
William Wall, D.D., Subdean	1541
Nicholas Bucksey, M.A.	1541
George Cotes, D.D.	1544
John Gibbs	1544
John Lepyngton	1544
John Whitby	1550

John Whitby, like his predecessor Peter Mainwaring whose stall he
filled, had also been a Canon of St John's, in virtue of which he
received a pension of £3, and that is all that is known of him.

As was expected, the new Queen undid all the changes made by
Edward VI and brought the Church back to the position it occupied
in the reign of Henry VIII before his quarrel with the Pope. What
would the members of the Chapter do? On the one hand they might
be expected to welcome this return to the *status quo ante,* for they were
all what might be called pre-Reformation in origin. The Dean had
been Archdeacon of London as long ago as 1529, Cotes had been
elected Fellow of Balliol in 1523, Wall was an ex-friar, Bucksey an
ex-monk of St Werburgh's, and Whitby an ex-canon of St John's,
Chester. On the other hand they had all accepted the reforms of Edward VI. What actually happened was that, as we have seen, only two
of them resigned or were deprived, John Gibbs and John Lepyngton,
while George Cotes was promoted to be Bishop of Chester in place

of Bishop Bird. The latter was quite prepared to carry on through the new reign if he had been allowed, but unfortunately for him he had incautiously availed himself of the permission given by Edward VI to the clergy to marry, and although he promptly repudiated his wife and tried hard to induce the Queen to allow him to retain his see it was of no avail and he had to resign. He retired to Great Dunmow in Essex, where he died in 1558. The three vacancies in the Chapter were naturally filled by the Queen with people of her way of thinking; they were John Wimsley or Wilmslow, Edward Gregory, and Thomas Runcorn, all appointed on the same day, 2 April 1554. None of them held office for very long. Wimsley and Runcorn both died in 1556 and Gregory in 1559.

John Wimsley, LL.D., alias Savage, was the natural son of the Rev. George Savage, rector of Davenham and half-brother to Edmund Bonner, Bishop of London.[1] He was educated in Broadgates Hall, Oxford. In 1541 Bishop Bonner made him a Prebendary of St Paul's, and in October 1553 added the Archdeaconry of London. However, he was not sufficiently active in restoring papal government to please the Queen, and he had to resign, but received instead the Archdeaconry of Middlesex and a stall in Chester Cathedral, both Crown appointments. He died in 1556.

Thomas Runcorn, M.A., was educated at Oxford, where he took his B.A. in 1518 and his M.A. in 1521. He was made Vicar of Bowdon in 1523 and Rector of Llanrhaider, Co. Denbigh, in 1540. A few years before his death he began to accumulate benefices; in 1554 a stall in Chester Cathedral with the rectory of Bebington and the vicarage of Weaverham, and the following year a stall in Lincoln Cathedral, and Ormerod says he was also Archdeacon of Bangor.[2] But alas for the vanity of human wishes, for in 1556 he died. From his will we learn that Edward Gregory was his great friend and that he left him the advowson of his archdeaconry. His will also reveals that his stables contained ten horses, five geldings, four nags, and "my young trotting horse".[3]

Edward Gregory. Nothing is known of him except that he was a Prebendary in 1554 and died suddenly in 1559.

George Cotes, the new Bishop of Chester, only lived to enjoy his new office for one year, for he died in December 1555. It is unfortunate for his reputation that during that year he should have been called upon to pronounce judgement on George Marsh for heresy and condemn him to be burnt at the stake. But Cotes could not very well help him-

---

[1] Ormerod, II, 235.   [2] Ibid., 270.   [3] *Sheaf*, 3rd Ser., XVIII, 53.

self. Marsh was a Lancashire man, born in 1520 but not ordained till
1552. He was rather violently Protestant, as may be seen by the words
in which he described the Bishop of Chester's visit to Lancaster while
he (Marsh) was in prison there. "The Bishop," he said, "being at Lancaster, there set up and confirmed all blasphemous idolatry; as holy
water casting, procession gadding, mattins mumbling, children
confirming, mass hearing, idols up-setting, with such heathenish rites
forbidden by God." This sort of language brought him to the notice
of the Privy Council, and Lord Derby in his newly-invented office of
Lord Lieutenant was told to look after this dangerous man. This
explains how it was that Cotes on his elevation to the episcopate
found Marsh in prison and had no option but to proceed against him.
Towards the end of 1554 Marsh was brought from his prison at Lancaster to Chester, where he was confined in the precincts of the palace
for about four months. Here he was argued with by the Bishop and
many others, including Wrench, the headmaster of the King's School,
and Archdeacon Bucksey. At last, probably in March 1555, he was
brought to trial in the Consistory Court, which was then held in
the Lady Chapel of the Cathedral, in the presence of the Bishop, the
Mayor, Dr Wall, the Chancellor, and many others. Marsh refused to
deny the articles which were read out to him, pointing out that "all
you now present did acknowledge the same in the time of the late
King Edward VI", which of course was perfectly true and must have
been very embarrassing for his judges. Here Foxe must be allowed to
tell the story in his own inimitable way. Though he was not present
himself he must obviously have owed his information to an eyewitness.

> The bishop took a writing out of his bosom, and began to
> read the sentence of condemnation; but when he had proceeded half
> through it, the chancellor [Wimsley] interrupted him, and said, "Good my
> lord, stay, stay; for if you read any further it will be too late to call it again."
> The bishop accordingly stopped, when his popish priests, and many other
> of the ignorant people, called upon Mr. Marsh, with many earnest words,
> to recant; and amongst others, one Pulleyn, a shoemaker, said to him,
> "For shame, man! remember thyself, and recant." They bade him kneel
> down and pray, as they would pray for him; so they kneeled down, and he
> desired them to pray for him; and he would pray for them.

Still Marsh refused to recant and so:

> the bishop then put his spectacles on, and read forward about five or six
> lines, when the chancellor, with flattering words and smiling countenance,
> again called to the bishop and said, "Yet, good my lord, once again stay;
> for if that word be spoken, all be past; no relenting will serve;" and the

bishop, (pulling off his spectacles) said, "I would stay if it would be." "How sayest thou," said he, "wilt thou recant?"

But Marsh remained obdurate and "the bishop then read out his sentence to the end, and afterwards said unto him, 'Now I will no more pray for thee than I will for a dog.'" Marsh met his death bravely at Boughton on the outskirts of the City, 24 April 1555, on the spot now marked by an obelisk.

Although Cotes was Bishop only for one year he was very energetic. He not only held an Ordination in the Cathedral at which twelve priests were ordained—the first ordination since 1547—but he also conducted a Visitation of his Diocese which reveals that the return to the Old Religion was at first generally welcomed.

The Chancellor, George Wimsley, who tried to save Marsh, must have had rather a guilty conscience, and his history well illustrates the seamy side of the Reformation. He was, as has been said, brother to Prebendary Wimsley and their father was Rector of Davenham, Bishop Bonner of London being their half-brother. In the days when they were born the wives of priests were not legally recognized and therefore both the Wimsleys were reckoned illegitimate, though this does not seem to have been a barrier to their ordination. George was made Chancellor of the new Diocese by Bishop Bird in 1541, which office together with that of Diocesan Registrar he held until his death. Although he was a priest he married and had four sons, the youngest an "innocent", and also two illegitimate sons. He was Rector of Tattenhall and died there in February 1560-61, after making a long and garrulous will which shows that during his lifetime he had made the most of his worldly opportunities. He had obtained the advowsons of Waverton, West Kirby, and Astbury, the last-named being worth a clear hundred marks a year, and also the advowson of the Archdeaconry of Chester, worth £50 a year. This was held at the time he made his will by Prebendary Percival who paid him an annuity of 20 marks for it. Further, he had the lease of the parsonage of Tattenhall, let to his brother Thomas for £9 10s. a year, and the lease of the parsonage of Castleton in Derbyshire. The benefice of Tattenhall was to be filled at the next vacancy by "my base sone Thomas" if he became a priest.[1] Wimsley died in the odour of sanctity and in communion with Rome, although he had conformed to the changes of Edward VI's reign and had condemned George Marsh to be burnt alive for not doing so.

[1] Piccope, 115.

The only accounts which have survived in this reign range from Christmas 1555 to Christmas 1556 and we have therefore no record of the way in which the old services were restored in the Cathedral, but we are able to glean a few extracts which throw light on what was going on in the Cathedral during the above-mentioned year.

Candlemas, for example, was observed in the old-time way:

> 1555 XIII pounde of wax agaynste Candlemas to the Churche XII s.   VIII d.
> The trysell [trestle?] for the pasche at Candlemas   v s.   IIII d.

Henry VIII's death was still remembered:

> the XXII of January at the Kynge dyrge for Rynggyng &
> to the bellman and to poore folke   III s.   III d.

There is, however, some discrepancy here, for he died on 28 January. The old ceremonies in Holy Week were still kept up:

> First to Thomas Barnes [Minor Canon] for a pottell of
> Malvesey and a pare of gloves for the prophet upon palme
> Sunday   XIII d.
> For bred wyne and ale for the Maundy as apperith hyn
> bill   II s.   X d.

There are three purchases of rushes during the year—"for the quier II sacks" at Easter, the second and third being at Whitsuntide and Midsummer at 10d. a time. Other interesting items are:

> for a penteyd clothe to Jesus altar wth a brother of velvet
> and sylke frynge   XII s.
> for a thousand of houselynge bred   X s.
> for wax to seale my Lords election   IIII d.

This refers to the election of Cuthbert Scott, D.D., by the Chapter to be the new Bishop in place of George Cotes deceased.

> for a paxe to the Ladye Altar   VIII d.
> for getting stones out of the horse pole   I d.
> for ringing at the assumcion of our Ladye and the
> dedication of a day   XVI d.
> for II censers to the churche   XIII s.

Cuthbert Scott, the new Bishop of Chester, was Vice-Chancellor of Cambridge in 1554 and 1555 and was an ardent supporter of the Papacy. He was Bishop for four years only, but during that time he conducted two Visitations of his Diocese and held nine ordinations. There must have been a dearth of clergy of his persuasion and much leeway had to be made up. In 1557 he ordained 17 priests and in

1558 no fewer than 68, 35 of whom, however, belonged to other dioceses.[1]

The Visitations do not concern the Cathedral except so far as they affected St Oswald's, of which it is recorded in 1557:

> The Church wants repair, the churchyard is defiled by animals and cattle. The curate has not access to the Holy Eucharist at night time, nor has he suitable dwelling house. The Churchwardens appeared and state that the duty of repairing the Church lies with the Dean and Chapter; that Thomas Green rents the churchyard, and that the keys of the Church are in the hands of the Clerks of the Cathedral Church. Ordered to communicate with the Dean and Chapter on the matter. Against Geoffrey Langley—carried off part of the tabernacle in spite of the Churchwardens. Excommunicated.[2]

Evidently the use of the South Transept as a church was not a very convenient arrangement, but it is interesting to know that in spite of it being used as a parish church the Dean and Chapter were still responsible for its upkeep.

It was in the reign of Queen Mary that a change was made in the appointment of the prebendaries of the Cathedral which still has effect today. At the founding of the cathedral the right to appoint was vested in the Crown; in 1557 or 1558 the Queen granted it to the Bishop of the Diocese. This was done to compensate him for the loss of the Rectory of Workington in Cumberland, which, after having been given to him by Henry VIII as part of the endowment of his See, was found to have been already given to someone else. The Rectories of St Bees and Cartmell were the other part of the compensation.[3]

On 17 November 1558, Mary's disastrous reign came to an end and on 7 December Dean Cliffe also died.

ELIZABETH I 1558-1603

Elizabeth came to the throne on 17 November 1558, and was proclaimed in the Cathedral on the twenty-fifth at a cost of 13s. 4d. That there would be religious changes under the new Queen no one could doubt, but what those changes would be and how far they would go no one had any idea. Two changes were, however, certain; the burnings for heresy would cease and the Papal supremacy in England would again be abolished.

---

[1] *Sheaf*, IV, 90.   [2] Ibid., 3rd Ser., I, 32.
[3] *Notitia Cestriensis*, p. 3. Ormerod, I, 97.

For the time being all went on at the Cathedral as before. The prophet had his gloves as usual on Palm Sunday and 2s. 8d. was spent on the Maundy Thursday feast. But only the day before (22 March) Parliament had passed the Act of Supremacy in spite of a vigorous speech against it by Bishop Scott. The Act of Uniformity was also opposed by Scott, but passed on 8 May and came into force on 24 June.[1] By it the Prayer Book of 1552, with a few specific alterations, was restored. In August Royal Commissioners were sent round the northern dioceses to see that the Acts were enforced and they carried with them Elizabeth's Injunctions. These were in the main a repetition of those issued by Edward VI and included those ordering that holy tables should be substituted for stone altars and that all shrines should be destroyed. If St Werburgh's shrine had not already suffered it could hardly fail to escape this second order. The Commissioners reached Chester Diocese at the end of September 1559. They sat at Northwich on 20 October, but there the chief Commissioners fled for fear of the plague, appointing local laymen as their deputies. These sat in Tarvin church on 24 October and in the Cathedral on the 26th. They noted in a memorandum in Latin that the "see was vacant long; that the Deanery had lain void two years, and there were but two resident prebendaries; and that the establishment was in such beggarly state that they could neither help the poor nor pay the ministers of the church their salaries".[2] This is manifestly inaccurate. Bishop Scott, after his vigorous opposition in the House of Lords, was deprived of his office on 26 June 1559, and imprisoned in the Fleet, so that the See could not have been vacant more than a few months at the most. Likewise the Deanery could hardly have lain void two years, for Dean Cliffe did not die until December 1558, though of course it is possible that he might have resigned two years before his death. As regards payments of salaries the Accounts show that salaries were paid to all the usual officials up to Michaelmas, after which the records are missing.

DEAN RICHARD WALKER 1558-1567

One of Elizabeth's first duties, then, must have been to appoint a new Dean to the vacancy in Chester. Her choice fell upon Richard Walker, the son of an artisan, who was born and educated at Lichfield and went from there to Jesus College, Cambridge. He was subsequently

[1] Both speeches are printed by Strype, *Annals*, I, pt. II, 408 and 438.
[2] R. W. Dixon, *History of the Church of England*, v, 154.

appointed Headmaster of Lichfield Grammar School and on his ordination in 1540 was made Rector of West Kirby. In 1542 he became Dean of the Collegiate Church of St John Baptist, Chester. On the dissolution of that College in 1547 Walker received a pension of £14 5s. a year and became Archdeacon of Stafford, this in addition to his Rectory of West Kirby which he still held. Having successfully survived the changes made by Henry VIII, Edward VI, and Mary, he could not have been a man of very strong convictions, in which he was not peculiar. In 1563 he initiated proceedings against the Cotton family to try to recover for the Cathedral the lands which had been filched from it. He died, however, in September 1567, before a decision could be reached.[1]

It will be well to look at the Chapter as it was in 1560, when the transition from the Marian system to the Elizabethan settlement was over:

Richard Walker, D.D., Dean	1559
William Wall, D.D.	1541
Nicholas Bucksey, M.A.	1541
Robert Percival, B.D.	1556
Thomas Wilson, B.D.	1557
William Collingwood	1557
Robert Hebblethwaite, M.A.	1560
Edward Hawford, B.D.	1560

There have been considerable changes, even more than this list discloses, for John Wimsley, Thomas Runcorn, and Edward Gregory have come and gone since the last list was made. (See p. 30.)

Edward Gregory is said by Ormerod[2] to have been deprived by Elizabeth, probably because he disappears in 1559, shortly before the Commissioners arrived in Chester. This is a very good instance of the danger of guessing when writing history. The Accounts show that he died suddenly, so suddenly that the clerk had written down his name in the list of prebendaries to receive his quarterly stipend at Michaelmas, but there is no sum of money entered against his name in the right-hand margin, while in the left-hand margin there is written in so small a hand that it is not noticeable at first, *non quod obiit*. The clerk was not a man to waste words.

Robert Percival, B.D., took his B.A. at Cambridge in 1543–4, his M.A. in 1547, and his B.D. in 1553–4. He was Rector of Toft, Cambs., 1554–6 and was made Archdeacon of Chester in the former year, an

---

[1] *Sheaf*, 3rd Ser., II, 54.   [2] Vol. I, 271.

office he held until 1559. He came to the Cathedral in 1556 and remained there till the beginning of 1563.

Thomas Wilson's career is not recorded by either Foster or Venn. Cowper fills the gap by stating that he was a B.D., and "having great preferments he quitted this prebend, having held it for about nine years", i.e. in 1566.

William Collingwood, who was also Rector of Christleton, died in 1560, according to the following entry in the Accounts:

> "Towards the payment of Mr. Collingwood's dette of such money as was dewe unto hym before his death that is to saye from Mydsomer a.d. 1560 untyll within one monthe of Michaelmas next after."

Robert Hebblethwaite, M.A., the spelling of whose name gave the clerk a perpetual headache, to judge by the different attempts he made at it, was a Cambridge man, who took his B.A. in 1537–8 and his M.A. in 1541, and was elected Fellow of St John's College in 1558–9. He was a schoolmaster all his life, first at the Chantry School, and then at the Grammar School at Sedbergh until 1585. There seems some doubt whether he is the Robert Hebblethwaite who was made Prebendary of Chester in 1561, for Venn uses the word "perhaps", but it would be surprising if there were two men of those names living and in Orders at identically the same time.

Edward Hawford, D.D., took his B.A. from Jesus College, Cambridge, in 1542–3, but took all his other degrees from Christ's College, of which he was Master in 1559–82. He was Prebendary of Chester from 1561 to 1582. In addition he was Rector of Glemsford, Suffolk, 1553–74; of Clipston, Northants, 1554; and Kegworth, Leicestershire, 1560. He was chiefly responsible for drawing up the Cambridge University statutes in 1570 and altogether he must have been one of the most learned prebendaries that the Cathedral ever possessed, though it is unlikely that Chester saw much of him. "Not once in ten years," said a disgruntled colleague.

It will be seen from the above that the Elizabethan Settlement made *no change* in the Cathedral Chapter. The four men appointed by Queen Mary, Gregory, Percival, Collingwood, and Wilson, who might have been expected to have had conscientious objections, all stayed on. It is true that the names of Percival, Collingwood, and Wilson appear in the list of deprived clergymen drawn up by Nicholas Sanders in 1571, but the Accounts show that he was wrong. They all died in harness. Either the Cathedral clergy of that day were a very time-serving lot, or else the changes made by Elizabeth did not seem

to them to be as important and far-reaching as we think them now to
have been.

The Accounts during Elizabeth's reign are fragmentary, for they
cover only the years 1559, 1561–3, 1567, 1572, 1574, 1578–9, 1583–5,
1588, 1597. On 17 September 1561, we get for the first time a summary
statement of account which is interesting in view of the Commissioners'
Report on the poverty of the Dean and Chapter.

> And so there is receaved [after payment of salaries] more than is laid forth
> the some of xxxii li. vi s. viii d. ob the wyche some . . . was deyveryd
> [delivered] unto Sir John Mayre [Minor Canon] deputy to the tresurare
> aforesaide to the use of the churche and chapter before namyd.

There is one item which occurs here for the first time, but which in
future is an annual entry:

> ffor iii nyghtes watchinge in Christmas   xii d.

In later years there is also a payment of 8d. for hire of harness. This
refers to the custom of employing extra watchmen on the nights of
Christmas Eve, Christmas Day and St Stephen's Day. It is supposed
to have begun in the time of the Welsh wars, owing to the inconvenient
habit of the enemy choosing those nights for making a raid on the
City. Sixteen houses were charged with the responsibility of supplying
each a watchman in virtue of the terms of their tenure. In 1542 the
Dean and Chapter owned two such houses (called Gable Rents) in
Watergate Street, but now apparently they had only one and they
hired a man to do the watching at 4d. a night. If they still had two
houses they must have paid their men only 2d. a night which seems
too small a payment even for those days.[1]

Another annual item is the Midsummer bonfire, which, says the
author of British Calendar Customs[2] is "of great antiquity and has
close associations with the rites and beliefs of Druidical times". Here
in Chester it evidently formed part of the Midsummer Show, of which
a full account is given by Morris.[3] What is remarkable is the expense
to which the Dean and Chapter went. In 1547 it cost 8s. 10d. In 1551
it was almost double—16s. In this year (1562) they spent 13s. 9d. and
in 1567 £1 4s. 6d. The details in 1562 are as follows.

> For carienge of iiiior loades woode to the bonefire   x s.   viii d.
> for a loade faggottes to the same   ii s.   i d.
> For makinge the same   xii d.

[1] Morris, 234. Ormerod, 1, 382.   [2] British Calendar Customs, iii, 6.
[3] Morris, 323–332.

In 1567 there are two additional items.

> To browen for makinge of the bonfyre   III d.
> For gorsses on Midsumer even to the bonfyre   VI d.

The Bishop appears in the Accounts from time to time. Bishop Scott, as we have seen, was deprived of his See on 26 June 1559, and after being imprisoned in the Fleet managed to escape to Flanders. The See was left vacant for nearly two years, and at last on 4 May 1561, the Queen appointed William Downham, Canon of Westminster, who had been her chaplain before she came to the throne. Downham was an easy-going man and was continually getting into trouble with the authorities for not exercising discipline in his diocese. In 1568 the Queen wrote him a personal letter on the subject, as we shall see later; in 1570 the Privy Council reported him to the Archbishop of Canterbury and in 1574 he was written to again. It was therefore quite in keeping with his character to buy off the Archbishop of York's Visitation of his diocese by letting him have the fees. Bishop Pilkington of Durham alluded to this in a letter he wrote to Archbishop Parker in 1564 full of grumblings about his brother bishops.

> The Bishop of Man [he wrote] liveth here at ease, and as merry as Pope Joan. The Bishop of Chester hath compounded with my Lord of York for his visitation, and gathereth up the money by his servants; but never a word spoken of any visitation or reformation. And that, he saith, he doth of friendship, because he will not trouble the country, nor put them to charge in calling them together.[1]

The Accounts, however, show that the Bishop did hold a Visitation in the autumn of 1561:

> Payed the first daye of my L. Visitation for a dynner to
> him   XXXI s. XI d.

and the following year he duly collected the Archbishop's fees for him:

> payed the XVIIth of February to my L. Bishopp for p'cura-
> cones due at my L. Yorke's visitation   III li.

In December 1562 the Bishop was given another dinner, but not such an expensive one:

> Spent upon my lorde busshope at his going up to parla-
> mente to hys farewelle   V s.   II d.

Parliament was prorogued on 10 April 1563, and the Bishop was welcomed home again:

> For ryngyng at my lord busshopes comynge home   VIII d.

[1] Strype, *Parker*, Bk. II, ch. 26.

4

Now follow a few extracts which throw a little light on the Cathedral in the first decade of Elizabeth's reign:

> 1561 payed to my L. Busshopes man for a table of command-
> ments   xiiii d.

Elizabeth ordered the Ten Commandments to be set up at the east end of the chancel in a letter to the Ecclesiastical Commissioners dated 22 January 1561. This entry in the Accounts was made in the autumn of that year. The letter states that the Commandments were not only for edification but also "to give some comely ornament and demonstration that the same is a place of religion and prayer".[1] To such a pitch of bareness had our churches been reduced by this time.

> 1562 payed to Mr. Willm. Glaseor for his wages and fees for
> one hole yeare and a halfe endit at Midsom' 1562   xxxvii li.   x s.

Glasier, who as Clerk to the Chapter took upon himself to report them to the Court of Augmentation, was now seneschal or steward of the Cathedral, holding a position similar to that held by Lord Derby in the Abbey. His duties could not have been very onerous and the post seems to have been a lucrative one.

> 1563 January For anyrne [an iron] for the church to smyte
> fyrere   vi d.

We are so accustomed to matches that we forget what a trouble it must have been to "smite fire" without them.

In 1563 there was evidently some trouble over the subsidy. The clergy at this date still retained the right to tax themselves in Convocation, but in the reign of Mary the amount of their subsidy was fixed for them at £20,000, so that the privilege did not mean very much. The representative of the Dean and Chapter in Convocation was Prebendary Hebblethwaite.

To Sir Rondull Barnes [Minor Canon] rydyng in the churche cause to Lytchefelde	xi s.	vi d.
(April) To a messenger to the northe country to Master hebletwhat	vi s.	viii d.
(June) To Mr. hebletwahat for his expenses to Yourcke	vi s.	viii d.
To a messenger to luchfealde with letters concernyng the subsedye	ii s.	viii d.
(July 20) To John Shawe for his cost to london to make answer to my lords graunt Mr. [sic.] for tenth & subseidie	xxvi s.	xiii d.
For his horshyre		viii d.

---

[1] Proctor and Frere, *A New History of the Book of Common Prayer*, 109.

It seems to have been the custom to reward the man who brought the first tithe salmon. Salmon fishing in those days and until quite recently did not open at Chester until May 1.

1563 In reward for a teathe sameunde   viii d.
1567 Pay'd the first day of May to him that brought a tithe
     samon   viii d.

We get very little information about the conduct of the services within the church beyond the usual entries for bread and wine and candles and besoms and rushes and ringing. Now and then money was spent on the choir:

1561 To Sir John Mayre [minor canon] for one communyon
     boke and one psalter bought at the commandmente of
     Mr. Wall being subdeane   [no entry]
1563 For prickynge of dyvers strange songs to the quyre   ii s.
1572 For viii singinge bookes for the quere   x s.

These would be for the eight choristers.

1563 For reparying of the coupes in the church in buckerram
     and rybban   vii s.   viii d.
1575 ii pounde candles for the lanterne in the churche and for
     the clerke to shutte the doores   viii d.

Perhaps this is the lantern which now hangs over the font and which was "found crushed into a shapeless mass of tin, and restored under the guidance of Sir A. Blomfield".[1]

Repairs were continually being made to the buildings and sometimes we can get an indication of how the buildings were being used. There was, for example, a Choir School, probably for instruction in singing only, as the choristers were included in the list of King's School scholars.[2]

1562 For repering of the Queresters schole   [no entry]
1576 A lok and kaye for the dore of the singing schole   vi d.
1578 For two double spars bought by Richard Done to stay
     the roof of the Choristers schole   xvi d.
1585 April 21. To Edward Dawby for xxi ffoote of new
     glasse for the windows in the songe schoole at 7d. the
     ffoote   xv s.   ii d.
     Paid to hym for mendynge the ould glasse in the same
     schoole   iii d.

[1] E. Barber, 34.
[2] In Randle Holme's plan the south-west porch of the Cathedral is labelled Singing School Porch.

The minor canons seem to have lived together and they kept a common table, taking it in turns to act as "steward menstrual" or mess president each month.

1563 To Sir Roger Houghton stuward menstruall   XLV s.   IIII d.

This sum did not vary from month to month, and it would seem, therefore, that the six canons' food cost no more than 3d. a head per diem.

January. For reparying the pety Canones house	V s.
Aug. 19, to a wryghte a wycke for workynge on the Ruffe upon the pety cannons house	V s.
Oct. 22. for soder to repear the ledes over the pety cannons chamber	XVIII d.
1576 To the same Dalbye for mendinge the windows at the pety canons house called the Misericord	XVI d.
1585 Pd. to hym [Edward Dawby] for mending 3 windows in the misericorde called the P. Canons Dining hall	VII d.

The Misericorde was a room provided out of "pity" where the monks might eat meat, which they were not allowed to do in the refectory.

The lay clerks, or conducts as they were called, also appear to have lived together.

1563 For a locke and a kaye and two hynges with other necessary reparatyons to the chanters house   II s.

Extensive repairs were done to the Cathedral barn in 1567.

June 27, to a carpenter for putting up a tree in the mynster barne	x d.
More to a laborer to helpe get up the same	VI d.
To Thomas Johnston for a tree to undersett the minster Barne	VI d.
July 2, to Skinner for Roddes for the Barne of the Minster	III d.
July 11, for a lode of claye to the Minster barne	VI d.
For carienge water to the same and carienge claye and other necessaries to the laborors	III d.
To danet for daubinge	VI d.

The "tree" was probably a triangular framework or principal which was put together on the ground and then hoisted into position. In this connection may be mentioned timber "tryes" which may have been the curved timbers still sometimes seen in half-timbered buildings, called "crucks".[1]

[1] Fred. H. Crossley, *Timber Building in England*, p. 112.

1563   To Robert Skinner & a wryght with hyme to Hunting-
      don to make devysys of the tymber tryes   xiii d.
      For lx tryes   vii li.
      For caryage and knotting of the same   iiii li. iiii s. iiii d.

On the Cathedral itself very little money appears to have been spent
in the years for which the Accounts have survived. In 1562 gutters
were laid at a cost of £1 0s. 2d. and the clock was repainted. The
glazier and his man were at work for 12 days (16s.) and again (November) for 3 days (3s.). In 1567 there is a reference to a new aisle in the
church which is difficult to understand and must mean a newly restored
aisle.

      Inprimis iiii li. and a halfe and syx owences of sowder
      spent by Robert Skinner upon the newe yle in the
      church   ii s.   iii d.

The Whitsun Plays 1567.

      Paid for a brod clothe against the Witsun pleas   vi s.   viii d.
      For a barell of bere to gene[1] to the pleares to make them
      to drinke   vi s.
      For packe thread at Witsun to hange up the clothe   ii d.
      On Witsun even for russhes for the quire   xvi d.

In 1573 a barrel of "byre" was provided for the players costing 8s.
and a cloth was provided for "the mansyon over the gate" (6s.) and
cords for it (1s. 4d). It looks as though the front of the Abbey was
draped for this occasion.

There is one item in 1562 which is a complete puzzle and the context
in which it appears does not throw any light upon it.

      For a cast of lyans   vi d.

A cast of hawks meant "a set or couple of hawks", but we cannot
suppose that the Dean and Chapter kept a couple of lions!

DEAN JOHN PIERS 1567-72

There were several changes in the Chapter during the first decade
of Elizabeth's reign. The old veteran and ex-monk Nicholas Bucksey
died in 1567 and was succeeded by Dr Piers who held office for less
than a year and then on the death of Dean Walker was made Dean, 4
October 1567. His place on the Chapter was taken by John Nutter,
another Dean-to-be. Thomas Wilson disappears in 1566 and is succeeded by Thomas Dunne, who appears in the Accounts as Treasurer

---

[1] *Gene* is said to be a Cheshire dialect word meaning "to give".

in the following year. Robert Percival, appointed by Queen Mary in 1556, was followed by John Hardyman, D.D., who was appointed in June 1563. Anthony Wood in his *Fasti Oxonienses*[1] writes of him:

> I find a supplicate made in the behalf of one John Hardyman, a doctor of divinity of Cambridge, that he might be incorporated in the said degree, but whether he really was so I know not. He ran with the mutable times of Henry VIII, Edward VI, and Queen Mary, and being in shew a zealous Protestant in the beginning of Queen Elizabeth's reign was by her made the first canon in the second stall in the Collegiate Church of Westminster in the year 1560. At which time being well known among the puritanical party (who began to show themselves betimes) he was made their instrument to break down the altars and to deface the ancient utensils and ornaments of the church of Westminster. For which, upon complaints, he was deprived by the Queen's Commissioners for Causes Ecclesiastical, an. 1567.

Dr Cowper copied this, but carelessly left out the word "Westminster", so that it appeared that it was in Chester Cathedral that he did the damage. Ormerod of course followed him.[2] Hardyman was probably too busy at Westminster ever to come to Chester, but it is a fact that he left Chester in the same year as he left Westminster and it may have been at the wish of the Queen. All we know for certain is that in that year Thomas Herle took his place. The complete list of Dean and Chapter in 1567 is, then, as follows:

John Piers, D.D., Dean	1567
William Wall, D.D., Subdean	1541
Robert Hebblethwaite, M.A.	1560
Edward Hawford, B.D.	1561
Thomas Dunne, D.D.	1566
John Nutter, B.D.	1567
Thomas Herle, B.D.	1567

The new Dean, Dr Piers, was very much an Oxford man, as he was born at South Hinksey, a village near Oxford, was educated at Magdalen College School and became a Fellow of that College in 1546. After his ordination he held the country living of Quainton near Aylesbury from 1559 to 1566, returning to Oxford in time to preach before the Queen on her visit to that University. His text was: "And kings shall be thy nursing fathers, and their queens thy nursing mothers" (Isaiah, 49.23). Whether it was the result of this sermon or not we do not know, but rapid promotion followed. Early in 1567 he was

---

[1] Wood, 3rd ed., P. Bliss, 1815, p.110.   [2] Ormerod, I, 170.

made Prebendary of Chester Cathedral, as we have seen, and in October of the same year he was made Dean. In 1570 he added to his office the post of Master of Balliol College, which he held for one year, relinquishing it to become Dean of Christ Church and in the same or following year Dean of Salisbury. For a time, therefore, he held by royal licence three Deaneries together and it is not likely that Chester saw very much of him.[1]

Thomas Dunne was Vicar of Ilford, Essex. He died in 1575.

John Nutter, B.D., was educated at Manchester Grammar School, where he may have overlapped with his future bishop, for Chaderton was also educated at that school. Nutter went from there to B.N.C. Oxford, in 1556. He took his B.D. in 1575. He was curate of Eccles in 1563 and was made Prebendary of Chester in 1566. He was also Vicar of Bebbington and Rector of Sefton, Lancs., where he made his home. In 1577 he acquired the Rectory of Aughton, Lancs.

Thomas Herle, B.D., was a Cambridge man, taking his M.A. there in 1558 and his B.D. in 1561. Love of money seems to have been his undoing. In his early days he was described by Archbishop Parker as "a grave priestly man" and was marked out by him as a possible Bishop of Bangor at the next vacancy. Patronized by the Archbishop and a Chaplain to the Queen, it is not surprising that he received one benefice after another in quick succession. When he was given a prebendal stall in Chester Cathedral in 1567 in succession to John Hardyman he was already Prebendary of Worcester (1558), Rector of Bromsgrove and Warden of the Collegiate Church of Manchester (1559). He resided in Manchester and managed to alienate the revenues of the College to his own advantage. "When he came to that great Benefice", says a contemporary account, "he sould all the Lands and Tithes and all other commodities belonginge [thereto], a few only except, and the House itself to the Earle of Derby (in whose hands it now is), and granted long leases of most or all of the tithes, Colledge lands and other spiritual livings to one Killigrewe, and Killigrewe granted them to the Queene, and she to them that are now possessed of them, to the utter overthrow of that rich colledge, so that he left nothing to the mentenance of such a post as in times past had been kept." By 1575 he had made himself so unpopular that he was deprived by the Queen, who no doubt was glad of an opportunity to dissociate herself publicly from the man whom she had aided and abetted in his malpractices, not without benefit to herself of course. Herle was given a pension of £20 a year for life, and when in 1580 Bishop Chaderton

---

[1] *Sheaf*, 3rd Ser., III, 1.

objected to this, Sir Francis Walshingham asked him to let "Herle, he
old Warden, enjoy his pension. I can see soe little hope that he will
doe good anie where, that for the benefit of the Church generallie I
think it less hurt that he enjoy the pension from that Colledge, than by
easing that house thereof to place him in such a *Benefit* [benefice ?] as
he is utterly unable to instruct." So Herle continued to enjoy his
pension of £20 until his death in 1587, and also continued to hold his
prebend at Chester (worth £20 a year also) and his prebend at
Worcester and his rectory at Bromsgrove (another £20). The Bishop's
protest seems quite justifiable, but it was not entirely altruistic, for he
himself had been made Warden of Manchester in 1579 and therefore
Herle's pension was virtually coming out of his (the Bishop's)
pocket.[1]

From the Dean and Chapter we pass to the Bishop. We left him
being welcomed home from Parliament with the ringing of the
Cathedral bells in 1562. On 21 February 1568, the peace of this good
man was rudely disturbed by what can only be described as a "rasp-
berry" from the Queen. At this time the Papists were beginning to
cause her considerable anxiety, especially in the north of England and
particularly in Lancashire where many of the ancient families still
clung to the old Religion. Out of 8,512 recusants in England at this
time it was reported that 2,442 resided in the Diocese of Chester, which
of course included Lancashire at this time.[2] In her letter the Queen
says how disappointed she was in the Bishop:

> Expecting in you that diligence and carefulness for the containing of our
> subjects in the uniformity of religion, and in the service of God, according
> to the laws of the realm, as now upon the credible reports of disorders and
> contempts to the contrary in your diocese, and especially in the County of
> Lancaster, we find great lack in you, being sorry to have our former
> expectation in this sort deceived.

She then compares him unfavourably with Lord Derby, who has been

> very careful and faithful for our service. Now therefore [she goes on] we
> will and charge you further to have other regard to your office; and
> especially to foresee that all churches and cures be provided of honest men,
> as well learned curates as ye can cause to be provided; using therein the
> ordinances and censures of the Church to the remedy of the defaults, and
> suffer not for lack of your personal visitation, by repairing into the
> remotest parts and especially into Lancashire, that obstinate persons having

[1] Strype, *Parker*, Bk. III, ch. 5.
[2] Morris, *Chester*, in Diocesan Histories Series, 136.

been most justly deprived, be not secretly maintained, to pervert our good subjects within any part of your diocese; as we understand they have now of long time been. . . .

It is not surprising that such a letter should have galvanized the Bishop into activity and sent him trundling northward in his coach as soon as the summer arrived. On 1 November 1568, safely back from the wilds, he wrote to Cecil to say he

> had the last summer visited his whole diocese, which was of length six score miles, and had found the people very tractable; and nowhere more than in the furthest parts bordering upon Scotland; where, as he said, he had the most gentle entertainment of the worshipful to his great comfort. That his journey was very painful by reason of the extreme heat; and that if he had not received great courtesy of the gentlemen, he must have left most of his horses by the way; such drought was never seen in those parts.

If "parts bordering upon Scotland" may seem rather an exaggeration it must be remembered that in those days the Chester Diocese included Grasmere and Keswick, the boundary being the River Derwent.

Thus did this modern Balaam bless those whom he was sent to curse. But he does not seem to have realized how exasperating his conduct must have appeared to the Queen, for he took this occasion to ask a favour of her. He had for the last seven years been allowed to hold two livings in plurality in order to augment his income. The period for which they were granted to him was now coming to an end and he writes to Cecil to ask him to get the Queen to grant him the livings for life,

> and that in so doing, he should be able to maintain the like port that he had hitherto done; otherwise, he should of necessity be constrained to abate his household, which he would be very loath to do. He added, that he had of the bishopric nothing but bare rent, and much of it illy paid; and that it was the least revenue that any man of his calling had in the realm. That he had paid yearly out of the same, as he was able to make a perfect account, above 500 marks, so that there were not much more than 500 marks for him to maintain himself and his poor family. That he kept every day to the number of forty persons, young and old, besides comers and goers; which could not be maintained with any smaller portion. That he was no purchaser of lands; that he bestowed all in housekeeping; and that he was glad to make even at the year's end; and yet, he thanked God, that he was out of debt. This he wrote from his house at Chester.[1]

---

[1] Strype, *Annals*, I, pt. II, 250 ff.

We have seen Bishop Downham abroad in his Diocese; we are now to have a glimpse of him at home in the bosom of his family. The occasion is the appointment of a prebendary to fill the place of William Wall, Sub-Dean, the last survivor of the original foundation, who died in 1573. So much has happened since his appointment that it is hard to realize that he was once Warden of the Grey Friars in Chester. He was buried under the west window of the Cathedral which used to bear this inscription:

SUB HAC FENESTRA JACET WILLIELMUS WALL, NUP' HUJUS ECCLESIAE PREBENDARIUS AC OLIM MINORITA, FILIUS WILLIELMI WALL PAUPERIS HEREMITE QUI POST MORTEM UXORIS SUAE SOLITUDINEM MONTIS MULICARNI SE CON-TULIT IBIDEM SOLITARIA' VITAM DUCENS ORATIONE JEJUNIO ET CONTEMPLATIONE.[1]

Under this window lies William Wall, late Prebendary of this Church and formerly a Minorite, son of William Wall a poor hermit who after the death of his wife betook himself to the solitude of Mount Mulicarnus, leading there a solitary life in prayer, fasting and meditation.

We are lucky to possess a detailed account of the way in which Wall's successor was appointed. It has been left to us by the rejected candidate, the Reverend Thomas Purvis, Headmaster of the King's School, and is contained in his reply to one of the questions asked in the Archbishop of York's Visitation in 1578.[2] His reply is so condensed and assumes so much knowledge of what has gone before that I print an expanded version of it.

On 21 February 1573, Thomas Purvis was presented to the vacant prebendal stall by the Dean, Dr Piers. The Bishop had the right of appointment, but in 1568 he had granted the next prebend that should be vacant to five trustees among whom were the Dean, Sir William Davenport and Sir George Calveley.[3] It would seem that on this occasion the Dean had acted on his own initiative without the consent of the others. Armed with the necessary documents Purvis waited upon the Bishop to get his appointment confirmed. It must have been with some trepidation that he did so, for at the last "Metropoliticall" Visitation in 1571 he had dared to find fault with his Lordship. However, Bishop Downham was not the man to bear malice, and "after sharp expostulation" he consented to admit him. "You

---

[1] Harl. MS. 2151, f. 43, quoted in *Sheaf*, 3rd Ser., XVIII, 91, and Ormerod, I, 298, n.

[2] York Dio. Registry, Cause Papers, File R. VII, G. 1883.

[3] *Notitia Cestriensis*, 4.

shall have it," he said. "Registrar, make out his institution." At this Mrs Downham intervened. Starting up from her stool, she exclaimed, "If I were a man he should not have it", and much more to the same effect. "But my Lord answered, 'Why, woman, the writings are in order. It must be so. Cotgreave (turning to the Registrar) make out his institution. Mr Purvis, leave your writings with me that he may make it out.'" The schoolmaster thanked him and departed joyfully. Soon after he had gone the Chancellor came in and Mrs Downham enlisted him on her side. He studied the "writings" Purvis had left behind and gave it as his opinion that the appointment was irregular because only one of the five trustees had made the appointment. But—illogically as it seems—he went on to say that "if any of the other feoffees would present some other clerk" Purvis might be excluded. Sir George Calveley, who lived at Lea Hall near Aldford, was sent for "with convenient speed" and for the next four days poor Purvis was denied access to the Bishop. Then his Lordship informed him that he had sent a messenger to Dr Piers, who was probably at one of his other Deaneries, "to know his mind concerning the advowson", and that he would be back in ten days' time. "*Interim* nothing shall be done prejudicial unto you." But about the tenth day Sir George Calveley arrived with his nominee, Edward Bulkeley, who was forthwith admitted to the vacant stall. The Bishop, however, being a kindly man, suggested that Purvis ought to be compensated for his disappointment, but, said he, "Marry, what it shall be we may not say before he (Bulkeley) is inducted, for fear lest we commit simony." Purvis protested that no action ought to be taken until his appeal had been heard. He "required a caveat *ne quisquam admitteretur pendente lite*", but the Bishop answered brusquely, "After he is installed, take what caveat you will; before, you shall have none, I promise you." Purvis appealed to the Archbishop of York who refused to hear him and so he was forced to accept whatever compensation was offered him, after the induction. This amounted to £20 in two payments from Mr Bulkeley and a promise from the Bishop that he "would give me another advowson and place me here prebendary at midsummer or Michaelmas next at the farthest". When this did not materialize, "I followed mine appeal both at York and at London to my further undoing, *ut Hesiod*." The schoolmaster was fond of using Latin tags and the allusion here is to the poet Hesiod who was involved in a dispute with his brother about his patrimony and lost his case.

The whole story is worthy of the pen of a Trollope; the kindly but weak Bishop with his masterful wife and the worldly-minded and persistent pedagogue with whom one can have little sympathy. The Dean seems to have raised no objection to his nominee being replaced, and this is perhaps explained by the fact that he resigned the Deanery on 28 February of that year (1573), retaining only the Deaneries of Salisbury and Christ Church. Promotion continued to come his way, for two years later he was made Bishop of Rochester (15 April 1576) and in less than two years more was translated to Salisbury where he was already Dean. For a time he held both these offices together. In 1589 he became Archbishop of York, and a long Latin epitaph in a corner of All Saints chapel in the Minster there records his life's history. In spite of his pluralism he was very highly regarded by his contemporaries for his generosity, kindliness, and Christian meekness.[1]

DEAN LONGWORTH 1573-79

Dr Richard Longworth, who succeeded Dr Piers as Dean of Chester, was a Lancashire man, born at Bolton. He went to Cambridge in 1549 and had a successful career, ending up with a D.D. in 1567. He was a Fellow of Queen's College, 1553-7, and Fellow and Master of St John's, 1564-9. Ordained deacon in London in 1560-1, he became Prebendary of Durham 1567-72, and of Worcester, 1568-79. He was made Dean of Chester in 1573, resigning his prebend in Durham but keeping that of Worcester. He was also Rector of Cuckfield, Sussex. He was evidently not popular at St John's. The following indictment of him is contained in a petition presented to Cecil in 1565 by the Fellows of St John's and recorded by Strype.[2]

> He had snatched at his promotion [it was said] by violating the statutes; and he was corrupt and partial in his management. He took private rewards for the letting of leases; he took the College coal for his own firing; he appointed a bad and unlearned Bursar who defrauded the College of nine loads of coal. He had for his chief favourite a young man named Fulk, whom he made Fellow without the consent of the [other] fellows, a preacher of the College without a license to preach, and head lecturer contrary to the order appointed in the statutes. . . . As Longworth was said never to study and to discharge his own share of preaching so negligently as to disgust others, the power of Fulk's oratory was the greater over him.

In the autumn of 1569 the Bishop of Ely visited the College and expelled the Master for his Puritan tendencies. In these circumstances it is a little surprising that the Queen should have appointed him as her chaplain, and in 1573 made him Dean of Chester. Not that it

[1] *Sheaf*, 3rd Ser., III, 4.   [2] Dixon, v, 69 and 207.

mattered much to Chester, for the new Dean spent most of his time in London in attendance on the Queen. However, his house at Chester was put in order.

1573 For III loade of clay and III lode of Roddes to Mr.
Dean's house   II s.   VIII d.
Paid for spykes   II d.
Paid for two thraves of barley straw   IIII d.
Paid to tow laborers IX dayes uppon Mr. Deane's house
after VI d. a daye   IIII s.   VI d.

Evidently the part of the Deanery which they were repairing had a thatched roof, and was composed of wattle and daub. In one way the Dean's presence in London would benefit the Chapter, for it was just at this time that the long-drawn-out litigation about the Cathedral lands was coming to a head and it would be convenient for the Dean to be on the spot. This was probably the business that took Prebendary Lane to London in 1579.

Allowde to Mr. Lane for his journey to London about
business of the house   VIII li.

It was an expensive journey to London in those days and as the Dean tried to keep control of the Cathedral by letter, which involved the employment of a special messenger on each occasion, it must have cost the Cathedral a pretty penny. His commands were not always received with good grace, as for example when the Treasurer wrote in his book:

Bestowed upon one Sharples a singing man upon special
letters from Mr. Deane contrary to our statutes and
without the consent of the Chapter   VI li. XIII s. IV d.

In 1576 further repairs to the Dean's house were carried out:

For timber to make clamstaves for the backe court of
his house with roddes to winde the same   XVIII d.
Workman for one day in daubinge the same with
beverage   VII d.

This reads oddly, but of course the beverage was the food and drink allowed the workman as part of his wages. "Clamstaves" is an unusual word which I have found only in two other places in the Accounts. They were the upright staves round which the hazel "rods" were wound or woven to make wattle.[1]

[1] I am indebted to Mr D. G. McIntosh of Heswall for this information. He refers to Randle Holme's *Academy of Armoury*, III, 14, (1688), in which is mentioned "dawbing of radling walls with clamstaves and rods". He says also that the word is still used in rural parts of Lancashire amongst old-time builders.

Repairs to the Cathedral do not seem to have been any more extensive in the 'seventies than they were in the 'sixties, so far as one can tell
from the Accounts which have survived. In 1572 10 feet of glass were
bought to mend a window in the choir (7s.) and another 20 feet later
on (13s. 4d.) and in 1573 glass and workmanship to the parish church
(St Oswald's) cost £12. This last entry reveals two things, one that
the Dean and Chapter were responsible for keeping St Oswald's in
repair, and two, that they had been very lax in doing so, for the
windows must have been in a very bad state to require £12 spending
on them all at once.[1] A "hanglock" (padlock) bought for the south
door completes the expenditure for the year. In 1575 some of the old
lead was taken off one of the roofs of the church and sold and new lead
put in its place. It could not have been a very extensive operation as it
took only three workmen three days at a shilling a day—or else they
worked more quickly in those days. 148 lb. of old lead was sold at 13s.
the 100 lb. and 510 lb. of new lead was bought at 15s. In 1576 the
leads between the "parish church and the south Ile of the quere"
received attention.

To John Kingley carpenter & his man for one day and a halfe workinge of the same Church	II s.	I d.
To John plimmer and his man for one day worke in layinge the same lead	II s.	
For caryinge up clay to the same worker		II d.
To dawlbye the glasior for workinge two dayes and halfe with his boye with hym glasinge the south Ile of the quere in the house sense	II s.	IIII d.

There is no doubt that this is what the clerk wrote, but what he
meant by "house sense" is a puzzle.

There is an interesting mention in this year of the parclose screens
which in those days filled the arches in the choir east of the stalls:

To Thos. hulme the smythe for a kaye to the chapter house doore with other two kayes and mendinge the lock and also pikes of iron for the part closes of the Iles of either side of the quere	XXII d.

What these pikes of iron were for is disclosed by another entry two
years later.

For making xx[tie] barres of iron and setting the same upon the parte closes of either side the Quier for boies climbing over with nailes to the same	XVI d.

[1] Or was it the removal of stained glass?

Evidently the Elizabethan schoolboys used to clamber up the panelling and wriggle through the open part above it, and the pikes alone were not enough to stop them; they had to be reinforced with iron bars put in to strengthen the stanchions and fill up the openings. These screens remained in position until 1845 when they were swept away in the Anson restoration, but not before Charles Brandon had made a drawing of six tracery heads for his *Analysis of Gothic*. Five of these may be identified among the twelve heads which today adorn the backs of the stalls on either side the western piers of the tower.[1]

An interesting case of deodand occurs in 1575.

> To Edwarde Powter and Robt. Allarde for thayre
> expenses & paynes in seeking of the deodant mare   v s.
> To Richd. Predam for that he layde out & spent in
> seeking the same mare alowed to hym by Mr. Subdeane
> & Mr. Lane   vi s.   viii d.

The law, which was not abolished until 1846, prescribed that any animate or inanimate thing which caused the death of a human being was forfeit to the King. Originally it was handed by him to his almoner to be devoted to pious uses, hence its name, *deo dand*, that which should be given to God, but in course of time it became an ordinary source of revenue and as such was probably among the rights and privileges granted by the Crown to St Werburgh's Abbey and thence to the Dean and Chapter. We may suppose that this elusive mare had in some way caused the death of her rider and had not unnaturally been hidden by the owner until the search had died down.

Most of our information about the buildings in this period come from mention of locks and keys, which are remarkably numerous.

> 1573 For . . . mendyng of the iii locks of the tresury dore   ii s.
> 1575 Unto Thos. Holme the smith for mending lockes boltes
>   & hinges of the great gates behind Johnsons house with
>   the 3 posterne dores within the court [Abbey Square]
>   with great neales and also for one new lock and key and
>   mending the dore betwext the Court & the cloyster   ii s.   viii d.
> 1576 Aug. 7, payd to Thomas Holme smith for a locke & a
>   keay for the posterne dore by Mr. Deanes house with
>   stables and hinges for the same   xx d.

[1] These drawings are reproduced by Mr F. H. Crossley, F.S.A., in *L. & C. Hist. Soc.*, xcvii (1945), 66. The taste of those days is exemplified by the following extract from J. Hicklin's *History of Chester Cathedral*, 1846: "Between the eastern part of the Choir and the aisles there existed the remains of rather common-looking oak screens, which were so greatly damaged as to be past the power of restoring."

1578 For a lock & kay for the frater doore with great neales
    setting on the same   XVI d.

This last entry must be read in the light of the schoolmaster's evidence at the Visitation in the summer of this year when he said that the Frater was "little better than a common privie".[1] Evidently he had stung the authorities into action.

After so much about locks and keys it is a relief to come to the human touch in the following:

1575 Layd oute for Robert Cooke for his aparill and other
    wages by the desire of Mr. Nutter subdeane & Mr. Lane xxv s.   III d.
    To Rodger sonne the kitchin boy by the advice of Mr.
    Lane towarde byinge his clothes   II s.   III d.
    Unto Henry Man at is going to service   V s.

Robert Cooke appears for the first time at the bottom of the list of the King's School scholars on the page immediately before this last entry and does not appear again.

In November 1577, Bishop Downham died and was buried in the choir of the Cathedral. William Webb, writing in *Vale Royal*, has preserved his epitaph which, he says, was "upon a plate of brass":

> Gulielmi Downham ter sex qui claruit annos
> Praesul, in hoc tumulo flebile corpus inest.
> Bis triginta et sex vixit, vixisset et ultra,
> Multorum possunt si valuisse preces;
> Insignis peitate Pater, solamen amicis,
> Pauperibus stricta non fuit ille manu.
>
>   1577, Decemb. 3tio.

"In this tomb is the much lamented body of William Downham, who ruled with distinction as bishop for eighteen [*sic*] years. He lived sixty-six years and would have lived longer if the prayers of many could have prevailed. He was a father distinguished for his piety; a solace to his friends, and to the poor his hand was never closed."

Prebendary Lane, the only one on the spot at the time of the Bishop's death, dispatched a messenger to the Dean in London at a cost of 16s. to report the event. He need not have been in a hurry, for once again the thrifty Queen kept the See vacant for two years, the revenues going of course to the Crown.

An extract from King's *Vale Royal* should find a place in this section, recording a long-forgotten quarrel with the City: "1573. This year the Corn-market place, that was made when Mr Webster was mayor, was

---

[1] See p. 12.

removed to the other side of the street, under the Bishop's house. For which cause the dean and chapter have begun their suit in the exchequer, claiming the ground whereon the house standeth to be theirs". The exchequer was the County Exchequer Court at the Castle. The ground in question would be the broad pavement in Northgate against the King's School. The matter was settled in 1575 thus:

> 1575. Henry Hardware (mayor) caused the Corn-market-house, which Mr. Dutton had builded near the bishop's palace, to be removed into the Northgate ditch. . . . Whereupon the contention ceased, which the dean and chapter had begun.[1]

During the vacancy of the See the Archbishop of York took the opportunity of holding a Visitation which took place in the summer of 1578. It proved to be an expensive business.

To the paritor that brought the admonicion for the Archbishop's visitation		II s.
For ringinge the greate bells at the recevinge of them into the churche		XXII d.
Paid for procuracions due at the Visitation	XLVII s.	XI d.
For an acquittance of the same		XII d.
For their dinner with wine to the same	XXX s.	
To the Register for his fees	XIII s.	IIII d.
To the apparitor for his fees	IIII s.	
To the Visitors for their visitation	IIII li.	

Before the Visitation a questionnaire was circulated to all the Cathedral staff down to and including the "under Sextons", and the answers give us a detailed account of the Cathedral at this time.[2]

The questions are not given but can be easily deduced from the answers. No. 1 dealt with the residences of the Dean and Chapter. John Nutter, Subdean, did not mince matters but went straight to the point:

> To the first article he aunsereth that neyther the deane nor yet any one of the canons of the said churche are in the same resident attending their severall offices and functyons in all thinges according to the statutes of the same; and further saith that to his knowledge the said deane has not in person been present at all above twise sithence his entrance there (in 1573) Mr. Dr. Hawforde once in tenne yeres past, Mr. Herle scarce once in thre yeres, Mr. Bulkeley and Mr. Hyde once by yere. So that in trothe the

---

[1] Ormerod, I, 236 and Morris, 298.
[2] This document I owe to the kindness of Dr J. S. Purvis, D.D., Diocesan Archivist at York. See p. 48.

greatest burden or rather almost all if not all indede is contynually pressed upon Mr. Lane and this respondent, whereat they no little greve and thereof wishe to be eased.

Sir Roger Houghton, minor canon of long standing, added the information that the Dean was absent "because that he ys resydent and daylie attendant upon the Quenes majestie, Mr. John Nutter subdeane commyth to the sayd Church verey often when occasyon fallyth, and preachyth godly and syncerely at his comying, Mr. John Lane ys for the most part resydent the whole year." The reason for Mr Hawford's absence was that he was Master of Christ's College, Cambridge, while Mr Hyde "contynuyth in the unyversyty of Oxford".

No. V dealt with matters religious. The only one who had any fault to find here was Thomas Purvis, the Schoolmaster, who "marvelleth much at that nowe dwelling here allmost XIII yeares he cannot remember that ever he saw Deane or Prebandaryes once minister or receive the Communion". He suggests that the reason may be that wafer bread is still used "although the print of the wafer yrnes be smoothed of late".[1]

No. VI. Sir Roger Houghton reported that "too clarke vycars or conductis [minor canons] are wantynge, the one is in prison and can nott do hys dewty, the other dyede of late"—certainly two good reasons for non-attendance. Also "ther wantyth a deacon which should reade the Gospell dealye ... and also Mr. Wm. Jewett, a laye man, hath the place of a petty canon and cometh seldom to the sayd church and doth but lyttyll servyce for the same".

In the absence of the Gospeller the Petycanons took it in turns to fill his place, as we read in the Accounts.

> Allowed unto the peticanons for reading the Gospell
> vicibus alternis by the speciall commandmente of Mr.
> Deane as appeareth by his letters   XXVI s. VIII d.

No. IX concerned the fabric of the Cathedral. The Subdean admitted that it was "in some ruyne and decaye namelye for want of leade glasse and slayte"; but said they had spent on it all the money they had to spare after all salaries had been paid "and the excessive charges of our suytes from tyme to tyme borne" (as for example the

---

[1] Edward VI's Injunctions (1549) had ordered that the bread should uniformly be "unleavened and round as it was afore, but without all manner of print, and something larger and thicker than it was". This was repeated by Elizabeth in her Injunctions.

action against the City mentioned above and the litigation with the Cotton family over the Cathedral lands which was going on at this time in London. See below, p. 72). Sir Roger Houghton said that "certeyn buyldynges belongynge unto the sayd Church were pulled downe in the tyme of King Edwarde the syxt by the Deane and prebendaryes that then wear".

Sir John Mayer, the doyen of the Petycanons, and formerly a monk of St Werburgh's, added that "Mr. Doctor Hawford hys howse ys in ruyne throwe the default of Mr. Parvys scholemayster who hath the same howse in occupynge". Mr Purvis thought otherwise.

> Doctor Howford's house [he wrote] asketh much reparacions which I have upheld this XII yeares with my great charges, although others have the commodity [use] of his calliarde [kale yard] and some parte of it alsoe, and the said honourable visitors anno predicto decrede that it should be from time to time repayred but not at my coste, which [who] have not one day of it assurance, or any hold else to lay my head; which seemeth but evill provision for painfull teachers that communly in other towns and colleges be allowed ther houses and gardens etc.

The "honourable visitors" must refer to a previous Visitation, perhaps the one in which he censured his Bishop. Purvis's grievance makes him a little obscure, but it is evident that he thinks the Headmaster of the King's School should have a house provided for him and not be forced to live in one in which he had no security of tenure and where he was not even allowed the use of the kitchen garden.

No. XI inquired how the Statutes were observed. The Subdean admitted that there were "many things in and about the said churche done and commytted contrary to the statutes thereof", and many things omitted which "wold growe in infinitum if curiouslye he should sifte the querke of every particular statute; so wold the same become a labor moste vayne unles due reformacion mighte thereupon followe". This could only be effected "by calling the deane and canons home", or by dismissing or punishing them for their absence "which thing is at all times rather to be wished for than at any time hoped for".

Sir Roger Houghton did not presume to criticize his superiors, but found fault with "the clarkes of the Churche" [sextons] who "sett boyes to serve in ther places" with the result that the ringing for services was unpunctual. "Also the fame goythe throwe the Cytty that the Scholemayster and the ussher do nott their dewtyes in the scole in bryngeynge up the youth of the Countre accordynge to the trust reposed in them."

Sir John Mayer complained that many rich men's sons were given the exhibitions which were intended for the poor.

Mr Purvis added that he wishes a gate could be made and locked every night "about the Northgate on the wall. . . . For it is thought that this sanctuary in the absence of the reverend men which ought to be resident here, is sometimes most shamefully abused; namely the Cloisters and such other voyde places as may yeld darkness."

There is still a doorway on the Wall leading into Abbey Green, which is probably the one referred to here.

This Visitation does not disclose a very satisfactory state of affairs, with the clergy absent, the buildings in a state of disrepair and a general slackness in the performance of the services.

It so happens that we can supplement the picture with another and this one from a hostile source. It is to be found in an anonymous report to Cecil written from internal evidence between 1575 and 1580 and endorsed "a prive state of the Coledg of Chester" and in another hand "the state of Dean and Prebendaries of Chester".[1] In it the virtuous Nutter does not appear in quite such a good light. The report is as follows:

> Yf it please your honour to call for the thesourar's booke of receipts and paymentes your honour shall see xx li. allowed to Mr. Lane and yearely payd hym for reading of the Divinitie Lecture, which payment is no parcell of the proposicion. By the same booke your honour shall perceive that [over and above] all wages payde there remayneth aboutes xxxvii li., which appeareth uppon their accompt to remayne that was receyved by the thesourar. This they make a dividemt amongst them.
>
> If your lordship examine their recepts and proposicion then it commeth to [o] short for, in the same, c. li. yearely ought to be bestowed uppon reparacions of the churche which is in great dekay and the glasse thereof [is] carryed to their pryvate benefices, as somme by Nutter into Lancasshyre to Sefton, and so by others as is sayd. Also x li. for mending of hey wayes and to the pore. So that your lordship accompting this way shall never trye it out but only by that former degre.
>
> The prebendes also sett their howses for rent, as Nutter setteth his howse to one Doctor Cannon a phisicion and straunger and when he commeth to the cyttie lighteth and lyeth in an inn. Bulkeley setteth his to one Darby a phisition. Hyde setteth his to one Wettenhall a lawyer. Hawford; in his howse is the scholemaster Parvis, and he absent. Erle hath sold his prebend to one Wright, the late bisshoppes sonn in lawe, but neither of bouthe commeth there. Lane most there, but at ii s. vi d. the weeke when he is there with the petty cannons. The deane absent by cause he is the queen's chaplyn and no howse kept by any of them the more pytty.

Still further evidence of the state of the Cathedral at this time is afforded by the Bishop's triennial Visitation on 26 June 1583, but before we come to examine it we must say a word about the Bishop himself and the Chapter whom he visited, for many changes have taken place in it since we last saw it in 1567.

William Chaderton, D.D., was consecrated Bishop of Chester on 8 November 1579. Educated at Manchester Grammar School he went to Cambridge, and subsequently became Fellow of Christ's College and then President of Queens' College (1568) and Lady Margaret's Professor of Divinity (1569). He was also chaplain to the Queen who gave him a Canonry at Westminster in 1576, and—what was equally important—he was also chaplain to the Earl of Leicester. He was very energetic in trying to suppress the recusants of Lancashire and resided most of his time at Manchester so as to be on the spot. He is perhaps best remembered for his lugubrious views on marriage, for he is reported to have said (in a wedding sermon, of all places!) that "the choice of a wife was full of hazard, not unlike as if one in a barrel full of serpents, should grope for one fish. If (said he) he 'scape harm of the snakes and light on a fish, he may be thought fortunate. Yet let him not boast, for perhaps it may prove but an eel." In spite of this, he himself after consulting his patron ventured in 1569 to plunge his hand into the matrimonial barrel, though what sort of a fish he brought out history does not relate. We only know her name, Katherine, the daughter of John Rewell of London.[1]

THOMAS MODESLEY 1580–89

The year 1579 saw a new Dean appointed to Chester as well as a new Bishop, for Dean Longworth died in the spring of that year and his successor, Robert Dorset, D.D., was installed by proxy on 10 September. Possibly it was illness that prevented him from appearing in person, for he died in May of the following year and was buried at his rectory of Ewelme, Co. Oxon. He was succeeded by Thomas Modesley, B.D., who was presented 12 August 1580.[2]

His chapter was constituted as follows:

Thomas Modesley, D.D., Dean	1580
John Nutter, B.D., Subdean	1567
Thomas Herle, B.D.	1567
Edward Bulkeley, D.D.	1574

[1] Morris, *Chester* in Diocesan Histories Series, 135, quoting Strype.
[2] Ormerod, I, 266. n.

Thomas Hide   1574–75
Robert Rogers, D.D.   1580
David Yale, LL.D.   1582

Of the new Dean practically nothing is known and the same is true
of Thomas Hide, except that he died in 1596.

Edward Bulkeley, D.D. We have seen the hurried way in which
Bulkeley was appointed to his prebend. He was a native of Woore in
Staffordshire and went to St John's College, Cambridge in 1555,
graduating in 1559–60. He was made a Fellow of his college in 1560
and Rector of Odell, Beds., in 1572. He then became a prebendary of
three cathedrals in quick succession. Chester in 1574, Westminster in
1583, and Lichfield in 1594. He was also Vicar of St Mary's, Shrewsbury, 1578–82. He is supposed to have resigned from Chester in 1594
on being made Prebendary of Lichfield. He died in 1620 and must
have been about eighty.

Robert Rogers, D.D., was a student of Christ Church, Oxford, where
he took his B.A. and M.A. in the same year, 1551. In 1574 he supplicated
for his D.D. as a B.D. of ten years' standing. He was Rector of Gaws-
worth in 1665 and a Prebendary of Chester Cathedral in 1580. He died
in 1595. This is the famous Archdeacon Rogers, the pioneer of Chester
historians, whose "Collection of Ancient Times relating to Chester"
is printed in Ormerod and is our chief source of information about the
Whitsun Plays. He is also thought to have begun the Annals of Chester
which Aldersey continued.

David Yale, LL.D., went to Cambridge in 1555, where he was a sizar
at Queens' College, but apparently did not take his degree of B.A. until
1563–4. He was elected a Fellow of his college in 1565. His benefices
were Llandegla, Co. Denbigh, 1564; High Offley, Staffs., 1572–3;
Prebendary of St Asaph, 1578, of Chester Cathedral, 1582–1608; and
he was Chancellor of the Diocese of Chester, 1587–1608. He is said to
have died in 1613 and is buried in the Cathedral.

We now come to the Visitation report of 1583 of which the
following is an abstract[1]:

> Robert Rogers said he was the only one who had remained upon his
> Prebend according to the Statutes. Himself, Mr. Nutter and Mr. Hide had
> kept residence; but Mr. Dean, Mr. Herle, Mr. Bulkeley and Mr. Yale had
> not done so. The fabric of the Cathedral, especially the Choir, was in decay;
> but the Dean and Prebends had allowed upwards of £200 for repairs, half
> of which had been expended, and they had arranged that £100 a year

[1] *Chetham Soc.*, N.S., v, 79, n.

should be so appropriated, besides eight windows in the new work of the Cathedral furnished by the same. The Clergy were negligent in attending services; Mr Dean sometimes attended in apparel [i.e. robed] and so did Mr. Nutter, Mr. Hide and himself; but Mr. Herle, Mr. Bulkeley and Mr. Yale did not. Nutter and Hide administered and received with Rogers the Blessed Communion, but none of the rest had done so. It was also stated that if the Queen's Injunctions required *four* services of the Canons in a year they were preached; if not *per se, per alios*. The Dean had kept worshipful house in Chester, and Nutter, Hide and Rogers also, but none of the rest had satisfied the order. The mansion houses of the Prebendaries were in good repair, and the Cathedral was being repaired. The Petti-canons had the New Testament both in Latin and English, and conferred daily. Chapters were not kept as frequently as the Statute appointed.

The mention of "the eight new windows in the new work of the Cathedral" is interesting. It cannot really have been new work and must refer to a restoration. The only part of the building where eight windows are to be found together is in the South Transept, where there are four on each side. The Accounts confirm that work was going on "at the west end of the church", which might mean St Oswald's Church (July 1584).

1584 July. To Hugh Skinner for xii barell bordes to make
barres for ii of the newe windows   viii d.
Paid to Hugh Skinner for lyme which went to the newe
windows in the church   iii d.
Paid to Hugh Skinner for a lode of sand   viii d.
Paid to Hugh Skinner for xxviii barell boardes to make
barres for iiii of the newe windowes   xvi d.
Payd to Edward Dawbye for glasing of iiii wyndowes
in the west end of the churche   xv li. iiii s.

There are many other interesting items in the Accounts during the 'eighties. For instance, there are three mentions of the visits of the Players:

1583 May 14. Payd unto Mr. Rogers which he gave to the
Earle of Essex players when they woulde have played
in Mr. Dean's house   ii s.
1589 To the Q. players by the appointment of Mr. Deane &
the Chapter   xx s.
1590 Dec. 5 to the Queene Maj. players   xx s.   x d.

In 1572 an Act had been passed against "Vagabonds and Common Players unless belonging to any Baron of the Realm or Towardes any other Person of greater Degree". Travelling companies of players had, therefore, to protect themselves by seeking the patronage and using the name of some nobleman or even of the Queen herself. In 1583 the Dean (Modesley) seems to have been absent and Archdeacon Rogers had to compensate the players for their disappointment. It is interesting to notice that they had expected to play inside the Deanery. If any one wishes to picture young William Shakespeare among the Queen's Players the dates permit him to do so, for nothing is known of his movements from the time he went to London in 1585 until 1592.

Another interesting series of entries refers to the visit of the Earl of Leicester, Chamberlain of the County Palatine, on 3 June 1583, accompanied by the Earls of Derby and Essex. The City Annals record that:

> they were met and attended by most of the gentlemen in this Shire, with their whole train, and as it was thought, they were in the whole 1500 horse, they were received at the High-cross by the Mayor and his brethren and the whole council of the city. They lodged at the Bishop's palace, dined by the mayor the fourth of June, and presented with a gilt cup, and forty angels therein.[1]

The Dean and Chapter made their own preparations for this great event:

> Paid to Mr. Doctor Bulkeley for his chardges in goinge
> to Shrewsbury to the Earle of Leicester for the house use   v s.   ii d.
> Paid to Hugh Skinner for the cariage of the filth before
> the gate to fill the hole in the Court viii lodes ii d.
> the lode   xvi d.
> Paid to Mr. Deane towards his chardges at my L. of
> Leicester cominge hither   iiii li.
> Paid to iiii prebendaries, Mr. Subdeane, Mr. Bulkeley,
> Mr. Hide, Mr. Rogers for the same purpose   viii li.
> [The absentees were Messrs. Herle and Yale.]
> Paid to Edward Griffith for boughes, rishes and other
> thinges according to a bill allowed by the Deane and
> Chapter at what time the Earle of Leicester came hither xviii s.   ii d.
> Paid to Alexander Button for ringers, rishes, etc. at the
> beinge here of the Earle of Leicester   ix s.   iiii d.

This lavish expenditure was not a sign of Leicester's popularity but of his power. He was hardly likely to be popular with a Dean and Chapter whom he had helped to rob (see below, p. 74) but nevertheless they had to keep on good terms with him and so no expense was spared on the occasion of his visit.

The "hole in the court" was almost certainly the horse pool in the

---

[1] Ormerod, I, 236.

Square.[1] The mention of it in close connection with Lord Leicester's visit suggests that this was the reason for it being filled up. What surprises us is that there should have been eight loads of "filth" lying handy outside the Abbey gateway.

As in previous years, the supplying of locks and keys leads to the mention of buildings we might not otherwise have heard of:

> 1584 Paid for a keye and mendinge the locke of the slaughter
> house dore   III d.
> Paid for one staple and settinge on the bolt of the
> calliard [kale yard] dore   II d.

The minster barn was always giving trouble:

> 1584 Dec. 18, to 2 laboringe men for caryinge Tymber laths
> & slates from the tethe barne unto the store house beinge
> fallen downe at one tyme   VI d.
> 1585 Reparacons on the teithe barne at the appointment of
> Mr. Deane for Ao. 1585   XXXII s.   XI d.

Other building items are as follows:

> 1585 January. pd. to the sayd Robt. Lech (barber) for payn-
> ting & gyldinge the R. armes over the Mynster gates XXIII s.   IV d.
> Pd. likewise to John Tydder almsman for the reparing
> of his chamber within the Mynster alowed unto hym by
> the Chapter   VI s.   VIII d.
> April 15, pd. for a load of claye to Mr. Rogers to stoppe
> rotten holes in the lyme house and other places   VI d.
> July 28, pd. at the appointment of Mr. Subdeane for
> caryinge of water out of the Cloysters and the Church
> after the great Rayne   III d.

This was a storm of rain and hail on 24 July which lasted from noon till midnight and was thought worthy of a place in the City Annals.

> Sept. 8, pd. unto Thomas bath wryght for puttinge up
> a beam in the new south syde Ile at the speciall
> appoyntment of Mr. Deane and Subdeane   VII s.

As before, this must mean the newly-restored south aisle.

From 1583 onwards we get mention of repairs to the King's School which according to the Headmaster's evidence in 1578 was "within the minster of Chester" and was ruinous, "insomuch that stones, diverse times dropping out of the walles, have broken the schollers' heades, whereof is no amendment, though ther have not wanted complaintes".[1]

1583 Paid to Hugh Skinner for lyme to the schole and to . . .
the church   III d.

1585 Feb. 27, for clente naylls and single spickes to mende the
floor in the free schole   IIII d.
Pd. to Laurence pott one of the R schollers allowed
unto hym by the Chapter at the last audit for his paynes
in teachinge the schollers after the death of the usher
untill another usher was by them provided   XIII s.   IV d.

1589 To Mr. Starkey [schoolmaster] by the appointment of
Mr. Deane to by a dictionary for the schoole   XX s.
Pd. for the cariage of Cowpers dictionary from Cam-
bridge   IX d.

Thomas Cooper's dictionary was the enlargement of Eliot's Latin dictionary which he issued in 1548; it was known as "Cooper's Dictionary" in 1565. Cooper was Bishop of Winchester 1584-94.[2]

The next Accounts which have survived begin in December 1588, too late for any reference to the defeat of the Armada in that year. The only change in the Chapter is that Roger Parker has taken the place of Thomas Herle. Work on the Cathedral and precincts continued.

1588 For XII dosen of Tyles wh. Jo. Done bought for the
Church floore at xd. the dozen   X s.
Bought 9 dosen of tyles more for the Churche floore   VI s.   VIII d.

1589 March 15, to grasse & his man V dayes hewinge stones
& makeinge the stones to passe thorowe the Dorter   IX s.   VII d.
To grasse and his man VI dayes makinge up the wall at
the ende of the Common privies & the new particion
in the Cloisters   X s.
Layd out by Banester the Carpenter for a spar & a post
for the Raile up the staiers   XVII d.
To III men workenge IIII days in makinge cleane the
particon betweene Doctor Bulkleys house and the walls   VIII s.
For a tree to make II stayes or propps for a Roofe in the
dorter redy to fall   X s.
To II laborers for II dayes in makeng cleane the Common
privey house   II s.   VIII d.
For II bourds & nayles to make the p'ticon betweene the
II churches [i.e. Cathedral and S. Oswald's]   II s.   VIII d.
To a smythe for IIII lockes viz. II for the dorter dores &
II for the dores wh. passe to the Cleystere   II s.   VIII d.

[1] See p. 12.

[2] I am indebted to Mr J. Fergusson Irvine for this information.

Here we get a little information about the use that was being made of the old monastic buildings. The dorter was being repaired and so was presumably in use. The late Mr Hugh Dutton, in a paper he wrote for the King's School Year Book in 1913, said that "the cells above the roof of the cloisters were known since the Dissolution of the Abbey as 'the singing-men's chambers' ", so perhaps the six lay clerks, if unmarried, slept there. Mr Bulkeley's house was evidently on the green where the monks' infirmary used to stand, part of which (the misericord), was still used by the minor canons, and was near the City Wall. The wooden partition between the two churches must have been in existence long before this, and the two boards would be for repairs.

DEAN NUTTER 1589-1603

In 1589 Dean Modesley died, leaving no memorial behind him. It is strange that nothing is known about him and one would like to think that it is because he stayed at his post and did his work instead of holding two or three offices in plurality. The evidence of Archdeacon Rogers given at the last Visitation has a bearing upon this point; the Dean, he said, had not kept residence, and yet he had kept a "worshipful house in Chester", which means that he exercised hospitality, and sometimes attended the Cathedral services. Though this may seem to damn him with faint praise it is better than the record of his predecessors.

The new Dean was John Nutter, Subdean, who was presented to the vacancy on 4 July 1589. There is an echo of his installation in the Accounts:

> To Stevensone the Joiner for makinge & findinge Tym-
> ber for the frame over Mr. Dean his stall agaynst his
> installacon xx d.

Sir Peter Leycester, writing a century later (1671) says of him: "He was a man of great wealth; Queen Elizabeth termed him 'a golden ass'. He died suddenly as he was at supper at Sefton, anno Domini 1603, where he was buried."[1] That Nutter was wealthy there is ample evidence to show, but there is no reason to suppose that he was a fool and I hazard the suggestion that the Queen, who was well versed in the classics, was thinking of the "Golden Ass" of Apuleius when she

[1] *Historical Antiquities*, 169, quoted in Ormerod, I, 266.

gave Nutter this nick-name. The evidence for his wealth is found partly in documents which show that he was not above doing a little money-lending on occasions and partly in the account of the search for his treasure immediately after his death. This was found hidden under the floor of the upper closet in Sefton Rectory and was taken into safe custody by a neighbour, Sir Richard Molineux, with the consent of the nephew of the deceased, who had assisted his uncle to hide it. There were twelve or thirteen leather or linen bags, three or four of them being made out of chrisoms, "quite half of them large enough to contain £100 in silver". They actually contained gold as well as silver, but "were not above half full". So said the witnesses before a Commission held to inquire into the subject.[1]

When Nutter took office he presided over a Chapter which had had only two changes since Dean Modesley was appointed, but by 1596 it had almost entirely changed.

John Nutter, D.D., Dean	1567
David Yale, LL.D.	1582
Roger Parker, D.D.	1587
Peter Sharpe, B.D.	1588
George Downham, M.A.	1594
John Meyre, M.A.	1596
Nathaniel Dodd, M.A.	1596

Roger Parker, D.D., a Yorkshire man from Browsholme, took his B.A. from Queen's College, Cambridge, in 1578 and became Prebendary of Chester from 1587 to 1604. He was also Fellow of the Collegiate Church of Manchester until his death. In 1597 he was made a Prebendary of Lincoln and also Precentor, and held these posts until 1613 when he was elected Dean. He died in 1629, aged seventy-one, and was buried in the Cathedral there.

Peter Sharpe, B.D., was made Rector of Heswall in 1583 and left it for Dodleston in 1596, where he died in 1616.[2]

John Meyre, M.A., was almost certainly one of the Meyres of Mere, near Knutsford. He went to St John's College, Cambridge, in 1565, becoming a Fellow of it in 1572. In 1585 he succeeded Robert Hebblethwaite as Master of Sedbergh Grammar School, a post which he held until his death in 1623. He was made a Prebendary of Chester in 1596, but, says Dr Cowper, "was afterwards presented to the Rectory of Winwick in Lancashire, upon which he quitted his prebend" in 1620.

George Downham, M.A., does not figure in either Foster or Venn, but

[1] *Sheaf*, 3rd Ser., XVIII, 38.   [2] See also p. 85.

Dr Cowper, quoting Anthony à Wood's *Athenae*, writes: "The son of William Downham, Bishop of Chester, he was educated at Christ's College, Cambridge, of which he was elected a Fellow about 1585, and was remarkable for philosophy. He came into this, the third, stall in 1594 and was afterwards made Bishop of Londonderry in Ireland, where he died April 17, 1634."[1]

We turn now to the Accounts to see what they can tell us of the Cathedral during the rule of the "Golden Ass".

In 1589 there was a good deal of work done in the Sprise, also called the Pyce in 1548 and now known as the Cloister Garth.[2]

to III poore fellowes for makeinge cleane the sprise		XIIII d.
Charge layd out for makeynge the walles rounde aboute the garden	XL s.	
1590 March 20 pd. to hym [Hugh Stockton] for a lock & key & some neyles to the sprise dore		XII d.
March 24, for 2 keyes for the sprise dore the one for Mr. Deane & the other for Mr. Subdeane		VIII d.
Sept. 2, to William Walsh for IJ loades of lyme for the sprice wales		XVIII d.
Sept. 4, to Mr. Walsh for one C of brickes to mende the wyndoes aboute the sprice		X d.
pd. to hym for 1 dayes labor for the same worke & mendinge a hole in the dorter—12d. and one man to helpe him—10d. & a boy—6d. & for a mayde to carry sande, water & bricks—5d.	II s.	IX d.

Quite a family party in fact. But fancy mending the cloister windows with bricks!

The Dean seems to have introduced a new custom with regard to sermons preached in the churches dependent on the Cathedral and served by curates. This is the first mention of it, but it occurs frequently after this.

1590 To Mr. Deane for 2 sermons by hym made this quarter the one at Shotwick & the other at Brombroe	XIII s.	IV d.

The following miscellaneous information is interesting:

1590 For a new verge and a fine kase thereunto	III li. VIII s.	VII d.
1591 For mending the ould verge	XXIX s.	I d.

[1] For Nathaniel Dodd, see p. 86.
[2] Ormerod (I. 257), says that it "has latterly (i.e. *c.* 1819) been called the Preese". No one knows the meaning of this name, which has not been found elsewhere. Cf. *Sheaf*, 3rd Ser., XIX, 66.

This verge did not survive the Civil War; the present one dates from the Restoration.

1591 (Autumn) Bestowed upon the earle of essex his musitions	II s.	
For wyne & sugar	II s.	
To the Quenes players	XL s.	
1592 The xxth of July unto G. Becke and Jo. mellon for 2 dayes a pece removeinge the tymber of the barne & caryinge the slates & tymber of the Waters-leaders stable into the store house[1]	II s.	
The vith of September to Wm. Welch Jo. Welch and 3 laborers for caryinge into the Chapter house the Roufe of G. bell house & other leade & tymber blowen downe by tempestuous weather	III s.	

In 1592 the Chancellor held a Visitation of the Diocese and had some criticism to make of the Dean and Chapter's neglect of Bromborough chancel, which as rector they were bound to keep in repair. His report ran: "Against the Dean and Chapter. The chancel verie ruinous insomuch they are not able to saie service and there books and Registers bee spoiled and they require reformation." The Chancellor must have had his tongue in his cheek, for he was Dr Yale and as one of the Chapter was partly responsible for the condition of the chancel.

In the autumn of 1597 the Audit Chamber was renovated:

paid for 2 yards brode clothe popinge greene coulor for a carpett to the Audyte Chamber at x s. the yard	xx s.	
for 3 cushins	vi s.	
for 3 skinnes of Redd lether to lyne them with	vi s.	ii d.
for vii pound flockes to stuffe them at 6d. the pound	iii s.	vi d.
for xv yards of whyted flaxe for 2 doss. napkins allowing to every napkin 1 yard halfe quarter xiii d. the yard & for 4 yards more of the same to make a square table cloth being in all 19 yardes at xiii d. the yard	xx s.	vii d.
for iii yards of cloth at xii d. the yard for another table cloth	iiii s.	
for makinge the sayd table cloths & napkins & for washing thereof	ii s.	
1 yard & a quarter to make a cupboard cloth		xviii d.
to the wright for co'passing a doore topp in the Audite Chamber		vi d.
for ii joyned doores in the Audite Chamber	viii s.	

[1] Morris (p. 281), says: "The citizens generally were supplied with unfiltered water from the Dee by the Water-leaders or Drawers of Water, who formed a numerous body, and as late as 1587 considered themselves of importance enough to petition for a charter of incorporation." They seem to have rented a stable in the Minster barn.

for masons worke & fastening the doors   IIII d.
for a square table and pannell board   v s.
for 2 payre of hynges 14d, for catch & latch & with
nailes 3d.   II s.
for pinne dust for the Audite   II d.

There are several interesting words here which call for explanation.

Popinge greene coulor. It has been suggested that this is really "popin-jay green", popinjay being a local name for the green woodpecker.

Pannell board. If this was a board divided into panels or columns and if it was connected with the counting of money, as its presence in the audit chamber suggests, it points to the use of the same method of accounting as was in use in the Exchequer at Westminster in the reign of Henry II. For the exchequer was a four-sided board measuring 10 feet by 8 feet with a raised edge round it, and covered with a black cloth ruled into seven columns with white lines a foot apart. These columns were divided into squares like a chess board and each column was for a different sum of money, £10,000, £1,000, £100, £20, £1, 1s., 1d. When the sheriff paid the taxes of his shire, counters were placed in the respective columns to denote the money which he handed over. If there were any deductions due to him counters would be removed from the board and the final total could be read off at a glance.[1] I suggest that the panel board of the Dean and Chapter placed on its square table with its square table-cloth of four yards of whited flax was a kind of exchequer. It would be about the same size and I believe we have here evidence that the ancient system of computing with counters was still in use in Chester at the end of the sixteenth century.

Pinne dust. The O.E.D. defines pin dust as dust formed from the filings in the manufacture of pins, the first mention of it being in 1552. Why was it provided in the audit chamber? There could only have been one reason—it must have been used as pounce, which is "a fine powder as pulverized sandarac, or cuttle-shell, used to prevent the ink from spreading in writing over an erasure or on unsized paper, and also to prepare the surface of parchment to receive writing", but the O.E.D. does not mention the use of pin dust in this connection.

In December 1596, we have a very curious entry:

to Edward porter for bringing home of the stockes
wheron he was sett at Mr. Subdeane's appoyntment   IIII d.

We gather from this that the Dean and Chapter kept a pair of stocks

[1] *Dialogus de Scaccario*, O.U.P. ed. 1902, 38–40.

in the cathedral precincts and had the power of putting people into them. This was done abroad—the High Cross where the pillory stood was the usual place—and the porter was paid fourpence by order of the Subdean for bringing the stocks home again. They must therefore have been on wheels.[1]

In 1596 the great gates or doors to Abbey Square were remade and the detailed statement is bound up with the Accounts. If space permitted, it would be worth printing in full. They cost £13 10s. 8d. and included 4 planks 22 feet long, 3 12-foot spars, 2 more spars one of 12 feet and the other of 10 feet, a plank 20 feet 2 inches, and a half-inch board 8 feet long. "Rooses" is a strange term used here. There were 382 of them, and some were extracted from the old doors. It is suggested that they were the large-headed nails or studs with which these old doors were covered.

On 22 November Prebendary Sharpe went to Hilbre with two companions and drank two quarts of wine with their supper and three pints with their breakfast. "Horse meat" cost 3s. 4d. It is a strange commentary on the times in which we live that what suggested provender for horses to the Elizabethan suggests food for human beings to us.

It is evident that a good deal of litigation was going on at this time:

1592 Jan. 18 for a pottell of muskedyne & cakes bestowed by
      Mr. Deane & Mr. Subdeane upon Mr. Warburton his
      cominge from London   II s.   II d.
      March 2, pd. to Mr. Warburton his man in regard of
      there paynes presenting the sute   X s.
1596 Dec. 17, for a pottle of wyne sack & claret when we
      came from the Exchequer on wh. day our matter past
      by Mr. Subdeans appoyntment   XVIII d.

This would be the County Exchequer Court sitting at the Castle. Citizens were not supposed to prosecute one another in it and in 1562 one was disenfranchised for doing so.[2] But the people the Dean and Chapter were prosecuting were not citizens, for

1597 April 21, To Mr. Tho. Case the chardges he layd out for
    the Deane & Chapter in three severall sutes in the
    Exchequer namely Mr. Rowlands, Mr. Tattens the
    vickaw of Eastham and Mr. Hocnell (Hockenhull)   IIII li. XIII s. VIII d.

A pottle was two quarts—not an excessive amount for three or four clerics to celebrate with. Thomas Case was the Chapter

[1] Cf. Morris, 193.   [2] Ibid., 198.

Clerk. He was also attorney in the Court of Exchequer, and died 23 July 1634.[1]

Another law suit is referred to in this same year:

> Nov. 22, To John Tyrer wh. he layd out for the house
> in the sute between them & Sir Rowland Standly   XXXII s. x d.

John Tyrer was one of the Lay Clerks of the Cathedral and he must have been a very versatile man, for in addition to his music and his knowledge of the law he seems to have added engineering. In 1601 he undertook to convey water from the Dee to any part of the City and to any houses, and for this purpose was allowed to build a lofty octagonal tower on the Bridge Gate. Two water wheels supplied the power.[2]

In 1595 Bishop Chaderton was translated to Lincoln. His successor was Hugh Bellot, D.D., of whom the City Annals record under the same year: "Hugh Bellet, D.D., was installed bishop of Chester the first of November, who lived but seven months after, was buried at Rixham [Wrexham] and his funeral solemnised at Chester the twenty-second of June."[3]

Nearly two years seem to have elapsed before another Bishop was appointed, and then we read in the Annals: "1597. The 16th of May, Doctor Vaughan, bishop of Bangor, was made bishop of Chester. About the tenth of November Doctor Vaughan was installed bishop." This is confirmed by the Accounts:

> May 16, to Shawman for fetching the Mayor to the
> Election of the Bishop   VIII s.

But though the Mayor seems to have attended the Chapter meeting, for it was the Chapter who had to elect him, the Dean did not, and the *conge d'élire* had to be sent to him at Sefton. The spelling of it was a sore trial to the writer of the Accounts, but he did his best.

> To a poore man for carieng the Conqidislier & Letters
> Missives to Sephton   II s.   IV d.

The last page in the Accounts for the year 1597 is headed "Pauperibus" from which two extracts may be made:

> Given to William Hearne a very good singing man
> staying for wynd to Ireland at the request of all the
> Quier   V s.

A pleasing gesture. Contrary winds must have been very expensive

---

[1] Tait, *Chartulary of Chester Abbey* (Chetham Soc., 79), 62.
[2] Morris, 103, 287.   [3] Ormerod, I, 237

sometimes to travellers en-route for Ireland and Hearne was not to be the last musician to be delayed in Chester by that cause.

> To an Hungarian who collected through England for
> Ransome of certayne Christians taken by the Turke   v s.

Which reminds us that in Elizabeth's reign the Turks were in possession of the greater part of Hungary.

Two further and final extracts from the Annals will take us down to the end of the century:

> 1597 "The long west roof of the minster was covered with lead, and much of the timberwork repaired."
> 1600 "The flagging of the long west ile in the Minster was this year begun by Dean Nutter."

A few years before it was said to be lying unpaved like a barn floor (see below, p. 80).

The Accounts show that it was not finished until the end of the following year and that the versatile Lay Clerk, John Tyrer, was put in charge of the work. To a man who at that time was engaged in supplying the City with water the paving of the Cathedral nave would have seemed child's play.

> 1601 Dec. 5 payd to John Tyrer allowed unto him by the Dean & Chapter for his travayle & paynes taken on & about the Reparacons of the Church   IIII li.
> Dec. 12 to III labourers for making cleane the long paved Ile and getting away all the earth at x d. a day   II s.   VI d.

THE RAPE OF THE CATHEDRAL LANDS

The strange story of how Sir Richard Cotton forced Dean Cliffe and two Prebendaries to grant him most of the Cathedral lands in return for a fixed annual payment of £603 17s. 1od. has already been told. We have now to follow the struggle of the Dean and Chapter to get them back, a struggle which went on throughout almost the whole reign of Elizabeth. Most of the documents in the case have been carefully copied out by Randle Holme and are preserved in two folio volumes in the British Museum.[1] Amongst them is Dean Longworth's petition to the Privy Council in 1578, which is taken as a basis for the following summary.[2]

Dean Cliffe died in 1558 and it was left to his successor, Dean Walker, to initiate proceedings for the recovery of the freehold. By this time the matter had been complicated by Sir Richard Cotton, who, know-

---

[1] Harl. MS. II, 2060 and 2071.   [2] Ibid., 2071, f. 137.

ing the weakness of his case, "after he had made and taken all the commodities of all the said lands and manors that he could", sold them[1] to certain Cheshire gentlemen, of whom Sir Thomas Venables, Sir Hugh Cholmeley, Sir Roland Stanley, Sir George Calveley, Thomas Leigh, Thomas Wilbraham and Henry Mainwaring were the chief, so that now the Dean and Chapter had practically the whole County ranged against them.

Dean Walker claimed that the freehold of the lands should be restored to the Cathedral on three grounds: (1) that the Dean and two Prebendaries had no power to act for the whole Chapter, (2) that the grant was made under compulsion, and (3) the rents assigned them were more than £100 less than the rents they had been receiving. However, Dean Walker died in 1567 before judgement was given, and the next Dean, Dr Piers, though he "did prosecute the said matter", resigned in 1573, so that it was left to Dean Longworth to carry on the struggle. It was in his time that a new and important factor emerged. In 1575 it was discovered that the word "Cestrie" had been omitted from the letters patent by which Henry VIII had founded the Cathedral, and it was counsel's opinion that the omission of this word made the whole document null and void, so that the Cathedral lands were *and always had been* the property of the Crown. This being so, it was impossible for the Dean to have granted to Sir Richard Cotton what was not his to grant. Here was a piece of good fortune which brought a ray of hope to the harassed Chapter. The omission of the word "Cestrie" was not, as is sometimes stated, the cause of Sir Richard Cotton's seizing the property; on the contrary, it constituted the one hope the Dean and Chapter had of getting it back. They therefore petitioned to surrender all their lands into the Queen's hands in the confident hope that she would give them back again with a proper title. But in those days it was advisable to have a friend at court, and so the Dean.

> opened the matter to the Rt. Hon. the Earl of Leicester. His Honour of the good zeal he beareth religion dealt with Her Majesty therein and found Her Majesty as ready to grant the said lands and manors unto the Church again as His Lordship was. . . . And Her Majesty further wills him to write to the Lord Chief Justice, Justice Manwood and Mr. Attorney General that they should set down their opinions what they thought in law was therein; and so according thereto Her Grace would proceed to the benefit of the Church.

That, at any rate, was how the Dean understood it.

[1] "For two years' purchase" says a marginal note in the MS.

The Judges very naturally replied, on 1 December 1576, that they would give their judgement if and when the case came before them in court, and to that end suggested that an action for intrusion on Crown lands should be brought on the Queen's behalf against the fee-farmers. They added that if, as it appeared, the Queen wished the Dean and Chapter to have their lands back, a new letters patent containing the missing word "put them in good security for the maintenance of thier house henceforth". But this was apparently not an alternative to the law suit but dependent upon it.[1]

In the meantime George Cotton, who had succeeded to the family estates on the death of his father in 1556, and other fee-farmers began to withhold their rents pending a decision of the case, and accordingly the Privy Council had to be moved to write a letter to Cotton saying:

> that where[as] he pretendeth to holde in fee farme all the landes and tenementes or the moste parte thereof, belonging to the Colledge of Chester of the foundacion of King Henrye the VIIIth, and have of long time paide yearlie to the Deane and Chapter thereof VI c li. and odde, and because their Lordships are informed that there is some suite depending in the Exchequier by informacion of intrusyon of the Queen's Majestie against Sir Hugh Cholmeley, Sir George Calveley and Richard Hurleston, under-tenantes of some parte of that landes, whereby the validity of his fee farme may come in question, and that he is minded to withholde as well the rente which is alreadye due to the said Deane and Chapiter, as also that which shall be due hereafter;

he is hereby required and commanded to pay what was due from him without prejudice to his title to the land. The other fee-farmers were dealt with in a letter to the Earl of Leicester, as Chamberlain of Chester, informing him of what had been written to George Cotton and requiring him to tell "all the fee-farmers and occupiers" the same.[2]

That this order proved effective is shown by the Cathedral Receipts for 1577 which reveal that George Cotton paid in full for that year.

The advice of the Judges was taken and the case was heard in London. "The law was effectually followed for the defence of Her Majesty's right and inheritance at the great costs and charges of the said Dean to his impoverishment", and it looked as though victory for the Cathedral was certain when the fee-farmers, seeing that they were bound to lose, managed to get the case withdrawn from the Exchequer and heard by the Privy Council, by the simple expedient of bribing the Earl of Leicester with six years rent of the lands which were in

---

[1] The letter of the judges is printed in Ormerod, I, 255, n.
[2] *Acts of the Privy Council,* 1575–1577, 308.

dispute. Another four years passed before the Privy Council Commission issued their award on 19 December 1580,[1] both parties having
surrendered their rights to the Queen in October 1579. The award was
in the fee-farmers' favour in so far as they were allowed to keep the
lands they had obtained from Sir Richard Cotton, but the rent charges
payable to the Dean and Chapter were raised from £603 18s. 10d.
to £802 1s. 2d. The rest of the property which had not been alien-
ated to Sir Richard was re-granted to the Dean and Chapter with
a valid title. It consisted of the benefices of St Oswald and Shotwick,
the tithes of thirty-two parishes or districts, the advowson of nine
parishes and the rent of £19 10s. issuing from the Earldom of
Chester.[2]

For the time being the Dean and Chapter would appear to have
recovered their normal income, but the value of money was rapidly
falling and would continue to do so, and in consequence land was
increasing in value. What Dr Trevelyan has written of the chantry
and gild schools is equally true of the Cathedral—"Lands of great
potential value were taken from them, and they were compensated
with fixed stipends in a rapidly depreciating currency."[3] Hence the
poverty of the Cathedral during the next two centuries.

The expense of all this litigation must have been very great. At the
Visitation in 1578 Subdean Nutter had called attention to "the
excessive charges of our suytes", and at Christmas 1583 he had to
advance the money for the wages of the Cathedral staff out of his own
pocket. There were also travelling expenses to be considered and the
cost of lodging in London, for which 4s. 8d. a day was allowed. It is
unfortunate that the Accounts for 1580–82 are missing, but the
following extracts from other years will illustrate the above statements:

1583 April 25. pd. unto Mr. Deane and Subdeane by them
    disbursed in suits in London for and in behalfe of the
    house   XLVI li. IX s. VII d.
    December. paid to Mr. Deane for chardges at London
    about the affaires of the house   v li.
    paid to John Done for his pains in bringinge xxx li. wh.
    Mr. Subdeane lent to the house toward the payment of
    Christmas wages   II s.
1584 To Mr. Subdeane for his chardges to London about the
    house business from the 25th of June until the 20th of
    July inclusive, viz. 26 days at 4s. 8d. p. diem   III li. XVIII s. VIII d.

---

[1] Ormerod, I, 255.   [2] Called "Castle rent", for which see p. 20.
[3] *English Social History*, 114.

It was also apparently considered necessary to make legal agreements with each of the fee-farmers, which involved a good deal of travelling:

	the porters chardges in his journey for the house 2 daies for the sealinge of an obligacion by Mr. Leigh of Adlington and Mr. Manneringe of Chester	III s.	IIII d.
	for his horse the said dayes	II s.	
	to Mr. Cases man for a copie of Cottons lease and a bond of 900 pounds by the Dean and Chapter to him passed	VI s.	VIII d.
1585	pd. unto Mr. Tho. Case for his travell & payments & other charges disbursed by him in going unto Mr. Warburton and other fee-farmers about the sealing of the annuities	LIX s.	IIII d.
	April 7, to Mr. Rogers for the hyer of a horse for one daye goinge to Sir George Calveley for the sealinge of the Annuities		XII d.
	to the said Mr. Rogers for his passage overe in Eaton boate the same tyme		IIII d.

The ferry at Eaton was a possession of the Grosvenors, who inherited it from the Etons. Robert de Eton claimed it as long ago as the time of Edward III.[1] In 1771 a horseman could be ferried over for one penny, a footman for half as much,[2] so the charge for the Archdeacon seems excessive. Rogers must have gone through what is now Eaton Park. The ferry was then almost opposite the present Hall about a mile and a quarter above its present site. His destination was Lea Hall, now a farmhouse with traces of a moat round it near to and east of Aldford. This was the ancestral home of the Calveleys of Lea.[3]

Audit day now took on a new importance and special preparations were made for it:

1584	paid to Hugh Skinner for II lodes of turves for the audit time the 9 daye of October		VIII d.
	paid to Hugh Skinner for coales for the audit time	IV s.	VI d.
	paid to Mr. Thomas Flether draper for one yarde and halfe & halfe quarter of grene cloathe for the table in the audit house	V s.	V d.
	a quier of paper for the audit		IIII d.
	a joyned stole for the audit		XVI d.

[1] Morris, 500.   [2] *Sheaf*, I, 101.

[3] And not, as might have been expected, Calveley Hall, which is the next house to it, but in Handley Parish. This was probably not built until nearly a century later, when Dame Mary Calveley, widow of Sir Hugh Calveley, the last male heir, made her home there. If so, she must have moved the magnificent staircase from Lea Hall, for it is too big for its present position and has Sir Hugh's arms carved upon it. See *Sheaf*, 3rd Ser., XVII, 36 and XVIII, 32.

a chamber pot for the audit	II s.
for a pound of candles	IIII d.
for wyne, sugar, & cakes when the fee-farmers came to pay there money	II s. IX d.
for charges at our Audyt & Dynner	v li. XIII s. IIII d.
to the musicions the same day we had our Dynner	IIII s.

This long-drawn-out struggle is corroborated more or less in the Receivers Accounts, so far as they have survived, but they cover only parts of the years 1550, 1556, 1557, 1559, 1577, 1582, 1583–4. The only complete year is 1582. In 1550, before the Cottons appeared on the scene, payments were made by bailiffs, each for his own bailiwick, but the Accounts are not sufficiently complete to show what the total income for the year was. In 1556 Sir Richard Cotton died, leaving a son and heir, George, aged only eighteen. Next year, however, a payment of £422 13s. 5½d. is entered under Sir Richard's name. In 1559 the late Sir Richard is credited with £385 7s. 6d. and a note at the bottom of the page says that he still owes £218 11s. 4d., which would make the required sum of £603 18s. 10d. exactly. In 1577 George Cotton, influenced no doubt by the Privy Council's letter, makes his payment in full, albeit in seven instalments. In 1582 the fee-farmers pay for themselves. One naturally wonders why they had not done so before if they had actually *bought* their lands from Sir Richard, and it is note-worthy in this connection that the Privy Council described them as "undertenants".

"Concealed" Lands

It might be thought that the troubles of the Dean and Chapter were now over and that their income was assured to them, and certainly there is no hint in the Accounts that this was not so. And yet right down to the end of the century the Award was being contested. This further struggle cannot be understood without a knowledge of what was meant by "concealed" lands and here we come upon an amazing and little-known episode in Elizabeth's reign.

As a result of the Dissolution of the Monasteries in the reign of Henry VIII and of the Dissolution of the Chantries in the reign of his son a vast amount of land passed from the Church to the Crown and was leased or sold to laymen. But in certain cases, Chester being one, the lands were re-granted to the Church by letters patent from the Crown; owing to the inefficiency of the lawyers some of these letters patent were badly drafted and whenever this mistake was discovered it was held that the title deeds to the land were null and void, that the land had therefore always been the property of the Crown ever since the Dissolution, that the ecclesiastical owners had no right to it whatever and had in fact been "concealing" it from the Crown ever since they took possession of it, even though they had acted in perfectly good faith. Nowadays the matter would be put right by the issue of new title deeds, but it was not so in the spacious days of Queen Elizabeth. Incredible though it may appear, Elizabeth from time to time granted commissions to one or other of her courtiers authorizing them to search for these "concealed" lands, with the promise that she would lease to the discoverer all the lands he could find which had not a valid title, regardless of the fact that they were already leased to other tenants by the Church. The commission ordered the Lord Treasurer and the Chancellor to effect the necessary transaction, with the proviso that any dispute arising therefrom should be heard in the Exchequer Court and that any grants should be suspended until the case had been decided. The result was that during the reign of Elizabeth these "greedy cormorants", as one exasperated bishop termed them, might visit any ecclesiastical body and examine its title deeds in the hope of finding a flaw in them. They even had the power to empanel juries and take evidence on oath. It is hardly likely that they expected to be able to retain permanently the "concealed" lands which they discovered, but they rightly calculated that their owners would rather come to terms with them than undertake an expensive law suit. So they were prepared to sell their title for a consideration and the lawful owner of the land was often only too glad to buy it.

It is an amazing story. For example, the Bishop of Norwich joining the Master and Brethren of a Hospital in 1547 in surrendering its lands to the Crown, by an oversight surrendered all the lands of his bishopric. This was not discovered until 1585 when they were granted as "concealed" lands to Lord Wentworth.[1] The Dean and Chapter of Norwich were also in danger of losing all their lands, and to the same man, on the grounds that the Priory of Norwich at the Dissolution was transformed into the Dean and Chapter without having been first surrendered or dissolved; for the Priory (said the lawyers) could not have been transformed without the consent of the founder, who was one Herbert, Bishop of Norwich in the reign of William Rufus![2] What a lucrative time the lawyers must have had in the sixteenth century.

We are now in a position to understand the documents which Randle Holme so industriously copied out and which are preserved in the British Museum. It will be remembered that in 1575 the Dean

[1] Cal. State Papers, Dom. 1591–1594, p. 576.
[2] Strype, *Annals of Elizabeth*, Bk. I, XXVI.

discovered the flaw in the Cathedral title deeds which had the effect of making all the Cathedral land Crown property. It also made them technically "concealed" lands. This came to the ears of a man named Francis Hitchcock who joined with one Lancelot Bostock in turning it to his advantage. The man who actually got the commission from the Queen to search for these lands was Peter Grey, but it is evident that he was acting in collusion with the other two. On 10 September 1577, he

> had a bill assigned by Her Majesty for having in fee farm lands and tene-
> ments to the value of £200 p.a. The 16th day of the same month, 18
> Q.E., Hitchcock knowing the imperfection of K. Henry 8 grant aforesaid
> and also the subtilty of Sir Richard Cotton, did bargain and compound
> for the passing of the said lands in the first booke that should pass from
> her Majesty of concealed lands. Whereupon the said Peter Grey got a
> commission for Cheshire to find the said lands,

and it would not take him long to do so. "The Treasurer did give the bill," is written in the margin of the next document, and on 8 March 1577–8, Peter Grey was granted by the Queen a lease of Boughton, Ball's Farm, Upton, Wervin, the Long Meadow in Backford, Moston, Upton [sic], Salghton (Saighton), Tilstone Fernall, Tarvin. On the following day he conveyed all the above lands to Hitchcock and Bostock who, however, did not take possession in due form of law until 1583. Meanwhile the Dean, probably quite oblivious of what was going on, was fighting it out with the fee-farmers before the Privy Council with the result that that we already know and on 15 July 1580:

> Her Majesty granted again all the said lands to the fee-farmers and the
> rents to the Dean and Chapter, they not regarding or making any account
> of her Majesty's former grant of the same lands ... made two years before
> unto Peter Grey, dated March 8, 1577.[1]

It was now Hitchcock's business (Bostock had died soon after this) to exploit as fully as he could the situation he had contrived to bring about. He seems by this time to have been possessed of much more than lands to the value of £200 p.a. as specified above—in fact all the fee-farmers found their leases were in danger. As no doubt Hitchcock expected, many of them came to terms with him and bought up his title, and others were expected to do so.[2] Among them was no less a person than Sir Christopher Hatton, Lord Chancellor of England, who had years ago bought the lease of some Cathedral land from Sir

[1] Harl. MS. II, 2071, f. 146; 2760, f. 51.
[2] Ibid., 2071, f. 147, gives lists of those who have and have *not yet* purchased Hitchcock's title.

Richard Grosvenor. When Cotton seized the lands he sold those leased to Sir Christopher to Sir Hugh Cholmeley. Sir Christopher, in order to strengthen his claim against Sir Hugh, bought up Hitchcock's title through his agent, Thomas Knight. (The lands in question were the manors of Great and Little Sutton, Ince and Bromborough, and the parsonage of Ince.) Sir Christopher died in 1591, but the case was contested in the law courts after his death, which brings us to the following letter, important for the light it throws on the Cathedral in the 'nineties and upon the equivocal position of the Dean and Chapter at that time. There is no clue to the identity of the writer of the letter, or to the person to whom it was written, except that he is addressed as "your Honour"; he was evidently a party to the suit and a member of the Privy Council.

The writer, having outlined the previous history of the case, proposes that "your Honour", having received the lands from Hitchcock and Knight, "will proceed presently to the trial of the title by law", Hitchcock to pay the costs and "your Honour" to supply the necessary influence—"Your Honour to do your best that the cause may be favoured in right by Her Majesty and others—in obtaining the lands by the said title of Hitchcock." The loot when obtained was to be divided on a fifty-fifty basis between "your Honour" on the one side and Knight and Hitchcock on the other. "And the same lands so obtained by law the one moiety to be and remain to your Honour and your heirs for ever, and the other moiety to Mr. Knight and Hitchcock and their heirs for ever." Then follow his proposals about the Cathedral:

And if your Honour do recover these lands you may give the Cathedral Church of Chester the parsonage of Astbury, the parsonage of Bebington which is worth £500 yearly; then they have besides that £115 of the old rent yearly in tithes and tenements . . . within the City and liberties of Chester, which is a large and sufficient portion to repair (?) the Church and bear all other charges. And after the death of the Dean and six prebends let their pensions [stipends] die also. And then there may be a parson and a vicar [i.e. a curate] and 6 singing men in the place of the said Dean and Chapter, and so it will be a good parish church; for it is used no otherway at this time; it lieth unpaved like a barn floor, for nether the Dean nor the six prebends are there all the whole year except 20 days before Christmas to receive their rents and make division thereof among them, and so departeth every man away till the next year. If they deliver a sermon before they depart that is all their labour and charge and good they do in the City and whole shire. This may be required of those that are the fee farmers of the said lands.

An abstract of this letter is given in the catalogue in the British Museum and against it the compiler of the catalogue has written in the margin "Fowle instructions", which shows where his sympathies lay. If this suggestion did not find favour with his Honour the writer has another suggestion to make—that his Honour should take the fee farm of the lands to himself and his heirs and "assure the Dean and Chapter a sure and good estate in law of their old yearly rents", and give the fee-farmers leases of thirty-one years for the lands they hold.

> Thus doing [he writes] the Churchmen may think themselves much bound to your Honour for providing the security of their rents for their maintenance, which now they have no assurance of. So your Honour shall have the commanding of a great many tenants besides the friends of the freeholders and the perquisites of the courts.

We gather from this that the award of 1580 was in danger of being set aside and that the Dean and Chapter, having lost the freehold of their land, were not even sure of getting the rents.

What a light all this throws on a little known side of social history in the sixteenth century. Everything is dominated by the scramble for land, in which scramble the highest in the country were not ashamed to take part. Evidently land was expected to increase in value, as of course it did, and when we see the price the speculators were prepared to pay for it and the expensive law suits they were prepared to engage in in order to keep it, we realize what a blow it must have been to the Dean and Chapter to lose their freehold rights.

We are now in a position to see what effect the Reformation had on the everyday life of the people, and it would appear from the foregoing that this effect was not good. Nor is this to be wondered at when we consider the many religious changes the people had had thrust upon them by force and the natural drift of the really keen people to one of the two wings, Puritan and Papist, both of which were for political reasons suppressed by the Government. There is no doubt that religion was at a low ebb at the end of Elizabeth's reign. On the other hand we must realize that the most prominent weaknesses of the Church—pluralism, absenteeism, and simony—were not due to the Reformation but were an inheritance from the Middle Ages and were accepted as the normal thing in the sixteenth century. It is all too easy to fall into the mistake of judging past ages by present standards. It must also be remembered that historical records are more likely to preserve the vices rather than the virtues of a past age, for the latter are taken for granted and moreover are not "news". It is at least something that in these disturbed times the Cathedral services were carried on, the Cathedral itself kept in being, and there can be no doubt that in spite of the shortcomings of those in high places there were many simple nameless folk who continued to worship devoutly and to live sober and God-fearing lives.

3

UNDER JAMES I AND CHARLES I

1603–1649

JAMES I 1603–1625

BEFORE we enter upon the seventeenth century, a word must be said about the financial position of the Dean and Chapter at this period. The gross income of the monastery had been £1,080,[1] most of which passed to the Cathedral whose income in the second year of its existence was reckoned at £964 12s. 9d.[2] Then in 1553 came the seizure of the Cathedral lands by Sir Richard Cotton with a corresponding reduction of income by about £150. The Earl of Leicester's award of 1582 restored the £150 and we find that the income in the following year was £986 13s. 4d. It follows that from 1553 to 1582 it must have been about £836. Now out of this the Dean and Chapter were bound to pay about £30 to the chaplains who served their churches and £106 16s. 5d. to the Crown in tenths and firstfruits. Salaries and wages took £690, making a total of £826 16s. 5d. It is not surprising, therefore, to find hardly anything spent on the fabric of the Cathedral during this time, seldom more than £1 at a time. In fact Bishop Bridgeman in his Visitation hinted that the Dean and Chapter of those days robbed their church instead of repairing it. If the above calculations are correct we ought to find a marked change after 1582 and so we do. In 1584 there is a lump sum entered in the Accounts for repairs done during the first half of that year amounting to £94 13s. 0d., and in the next year Prebendary Rogers said at the Bishop's Visitation that they had allotted that year £200 for repairs and in future would spend £100 annually upon them.

A copy of the Leicester Award, dated 13 February 1582, is included in the Cowper MSS. and portions of it are worth quoting. The judges were Lord Burleigh (High Treasurer), the Earl of Leicester, Sir

---

[1] *C.A.J.* xxxvii, pt. I, p. 10.   [2] *Ledger*, p. 47.

Christopher Hatton (Vice-chamberlain), Sir Christopher Wray (Lord Chief Justice), and Sir Walter Mildmay (Chancellor of the Exchequer Court), and they laid down the following rules for the expenditure of the extra £150 which the Dean and Chapter were to receive under the Award:

We have thought it most meet and requisite [they write] upon humble suit and mutuall consent of Thomas Modesley and John Nutter, Batchelors in Divinity, Deane and Subdeane of the same Church, that the said revivall of £150 shall be yearly from henceforth imployed and distributed in manner and form following, viz.

	£	s.	d.
1. To a divinity lecturer reeding twise weekely for the space of ten weeks together in every quarter of the yeare	4	0	0
2. To the head Schoolmaster over and above his yearely allowance by the Statutes of the said cathedrall church limited and appointed	5	6	8
3. To the under Master or Usher above his like yearely allowance by the said statutes	2	6	8
4. To the Master of the Choristers and organist pricking from time to time all necessary song bookes for the use of the said cathedrall church	2	6	8

The rest of the said yearely revivall to witt £100 during the time and terme of [the next] five yeares ... shall be yearly used as followeth, viz.

1. Towards the reperacons of the ruinous and greatly decayed Church there and other edifices to the same belonging	24	0	0
2. Towards the repairing and furnishing of one large and stately roome called the fratree to be transformed into an Hall wherein the said Dean and chapter shall keep their commens together at the severall times of their two general chapters and their audit quolibet in anno	6	0	0
3. To the Master of the worke to be yearely chosen by the Deane or Subdeane and the chapter towardes his paines and charges therein to be sustained from the 1st of March to the 23rd of June singulos per annos	10	0	0
4. Towards the furnishing of their library with books of Divinity	4	0	0

And further wee think it requisite that ... after the expiration ... of the said five yeares the aforesaid some of a hundred pound shall be yearely divided and bestowed as followeth.

1. To the Deane according to his presence and residence according to the statutes of the said church	20	0	0
2. To the six Prebendaries according to their like presence and residence	4	0	0
3. To the Petty Canons dayly reeding the Gospell by course and keeping a table together	6	13	4

		£	s.	d.

4. To the six Conducts dayly reading the Epistle by course   8   0   0

5. Towards the charges or commens of the said Deane and chapter or each of them as shall yearely keepe their Generall Chapter the 23 day June and view that yeare's worke   6 13 4

6. [Ditto] the 25 of November and likewise their Audit then   10   0   0

We learn from the above that the Cathedral was in a bad state of repair, as might have been expected; that the refectory was still out of action; and that the Petty Canons still kept a common table, as indeed the Accounts show. (In 1602 it cost £23 8s. 0d. for the year.)

It does not appear that the Dean and Chapter paid the least attention to these rules, but paid the whole £150 into the common fund. When they did augment the salaries of the Cathedral staff, which they began to do in 1590, they did it by giving a bonus every year to everyone, including themselves, amounting to £47 in all.

DEAN WILLIAM BARLOW 1602–1605

James I ascended the throne on 24 March 1603. Dean Nutter, the doyen of the Chapter, died on 30 March 1602, and William Barlow was installed in his place 30 June of the same year. Cowper says that he descended from the ancient family of Barlowe of Barlowe near Manchester. He had been a Fellow of Trinity Hall, Cambridge, and came to Chester from being a Prebendary at Westminster. He stayed only three years, moving to the see of Rochester in 1605 and to Lincoln in 1608. But in those three years he took his part in making history, for he was a prominent member of the Hampton Court Conference, so much so that Archbishop Whitgift asked him to write an account of it which he did. It is entitled *The Summe and Substance of the Conference* and remains the chief authority on the subject. He was also selected to work on a new translation of the Bible, which has given us the Authorized Version.

His Chapter was constituted as follows:

William Barlow, D.D., Dean	1602
David Yale, LL.D.	1582
Peter Sharpe, D.D.	1588
John Meyre, M.A.	1596
Nathaniel Dodd, D.D.	1595
Roger Ravenscroft, M.A.	1599
Griffith Vaughan, M.A.	1604

Peter Sharpe, of St John's College, Cambridge, took his B.A. in 1579 and his M.A. in 1579, but for his B.D. he went to Brazenose College, Oxford, in 1590. He was Rector of Heswall in 1583 and installed

Prebendary of Chester Cathedral in 1588. He left Heswall to go to Dodleston in 1596. He also received the sinecure rectory of Pennant, Co. Montgomery, in 1595 and the benefice of Llanrwst, Co. Denbigh, in 1601.

Roger Ravenscroft, M.A., was born at Bretton in Flintshire, four miles from Chester. He went to New College, Oxford, and graduated in 1590. He was Vicar of Clent (Worcs.),[1] but resigned in 1598 and came to Chester Cathedral in the following year. In 1616 he succeeded Sharpe at Dodleston, about a mile from his old home. He died there in 1635 and was buried in the Cathedral.

Nathaniel Dodd was a Londoner, born in 1564, educated at Westminster School and Christ Church, Oxford, where he graduated in 1586. His benefices were Llanwenarth, Co. Monmouth in 1595, Newent, Co. Gloucester, in 1605 and Bennington, Co. Herts., in 1614.

Griffith Vaughan was one of the two Rectors of Malpas for the three years immediately preceding his appointment to a prebendal stall. Ormerod states that he was treasurer of Bangor and prebendary of St Paul's, and died in 1612 when he was succeeded by Patrick Young.

The Bishop at this time was Richard Vaughan, D.D. Dr Cowper says: "He was a person of a public spirit and very much promoted the repairs of his cathedrals; at Chester he restored all the west roof, and got the bells to be new cast and hung in the great tower." He was in Chester only from 1597 till 1604, when he was translated to London, and the only other mention we have of him is in connection with the plague. The bubonic plague was endemic at this time in England, and on this occasion the outbreak lasted from September 1603 to February 1606. The Annals have this account of it:

> The plague began generally through England and in this City in the house of one Glover, a musician in St. John's Lane, and so continuing increasing till there died 50 or 58 or thereabouts weekly a long time. There were cabins made in the quarry near the New Tower for poor infected people that were unable to maintain themselves. Also Bishop Vaughan caused public preaching two days in a week to move God's mercy and pity, but it increased so sore that he fled and many citizens more of the chiefest sort.[2]

The Bishop did not flee further than Aldford, and the Cathedral Accounts go on as usual, the only references to the plague being the following:

1605 for pitch and frankincense to perfume the Church and
      Quier at the burial of Mr. Ireland   II s.

[1] *Wm. Salt Soc.*, 1915, p. 64.   [2] *Sheaf*, 3rd Ser., IX, 32.

Given to the Maior of the Citty of Chester for and
towards the relief of the poor inflicted cabbaners by the
hands of Mr. Gamull, Ald.   1 s.

Bishop Vaughan was succeeded by another Welshman, George
Lloyd, who is chiefly remembered for the house in Watergate Street
which still bears his name although it was never the episcopal residence.
But Bishop Lloyd deserves to be remembered for another reason—for
being the only King's School boy to become Bishop of Chester. He
was at the King's School from June 1575 until he went up to Cambridge in 1579 and two of his brothers had already settled in Chester.
David was Mayor in 1593 and Edward carried on a mercer's business
in the City. George was Rector of Heswall from 1592 to 1599, when
he became Bishop of Man.[1]

THE SWORD INCIDENT

In 1607 the Bishop was called in to mediate in the controversy
which arose between the Cathedral and the Mayor over the mayoral
sword. The story is told at length in the Assembly book of the City
Council. On 13 January the Mayor came to the Cathedral in state
preceded as was usual by the mayoral sword carried point uppermost,
and as he was going towards the Bishop's Court Peter Sharpe "did put
down with his hand the sword carried before the said Mayor".
Sharpe's action was, of course, a protest against the claim to jurisdiction
over the Cathedral which the carrying of the sword upright might
imply. The City Fathers took the matter very seriously and complained
to the Lord Chancellor. Sharpe's defence was that "he only reverently
put his hand on the sword without either holding it or griping the
same, so that if the sword was bare, it was the gladinesse (?) of the
scaberd, not the violene of his hand that caused it. For he thrust it not
downe, but, touchinge it reverently, said only these words, 'I pray you
forebeare in this place'."[2] But worse was to follow. A little later the
man who had carried the sword died, and when his body was brought
to the Cathedral for burial on 2 February attended by the Mayor and
Corporation, Prebendary Ravenscroft actually "caused the west doors
of the Cathedral to be shut against them". This made some action by
the City inevitable. The case was heard by two judges of the Assize at
the Exchequer Court at the Castle in Chester, who gave judgement in
favour of the Mayor: "We do order that the said Mayor and citizens
and their successors at all times hereafter shall freely and quietly pass

[1] *Sheaf,* 3rd ser., II, 313 and *C.A.J.,* x, 86.
[2] Morris, p. 184, quoting Harl. MS., 2173, f. 11.

7

and repass through the said great west door into the said Church at the time of any funeral or attendance upon any dead corpse to be buried in the said Church." They further ordered that when the Mayor came to the Cathedral, having his sword carried before him, the Cathedral officials "shall permit and suffer the said Mayor and swordbearer quietly to carry the sword of the said City with the point up in the said church as heretofore hath been used and accustomed". So that all that the two prebendaries achieved by their ill-judged protest was to change what was formerly a custom into a legal right which is carefully observed to this day.

Such is the official account preserved in the Assembly Books, but it so happens that we can fill in some picturesque details from the newly rediscovered Cowper MSS. The account of this incident is contained in a buff-coloured note-book bound in leather and labelled "8 C.C.". After relating how Ravenscroft had the great west doors shut in the face of the funeral procession of "Mr. Nicholas Mercer, late sword-bearer", protesting that he did it "in defence of the Liberties of the Church", the account goes on:

> Upon which the Corps was sett down without the gate; But Mr. Mayor and his Brethren enter'd the Minister at the south door under the Singing-school [the south-west porch] and proceeded with the sword borne upright before them, to their usual Place in the Choir, but all the while the Corps was kept without the West door, which however was at length open'd and the Body brought in. This affair was warmly resented; But Dr. Lloyd, then Bishop (a Gentleman well respected by the City) interposed, and obliged the Offenders to ask pardon for what they had done, and the matter dropp'd.

The only reference to all this in the Accounts is:

> Given to Sir P. Lewkener Chief Justice his man for a
> copy of the order set downe by him and Sir T. Town-
> send his assistant   x s.

We turn now to the Accounts to see what light they throw on the short period of the two Deans, Barlow and Parry. No mention will be made of repairs to bells or organs, as the former has been dealt with by Mr J. W. Clarke, and the latter by Dr Bridge.[1]

The sixteenth century ended with "flagging of the long west ile in the Minster" begun in 1600 by Dean Nutter. One of the first surviving entries in the Accounts for 1601 records its completion

---

[1] In *Lancs. and Ches. Antiquarian Soc.*, LX, 89 and in *C.A.J.*, XIX, pt. II, 63 respectively.

and the fact that the lay clerk, John Tyrer, superintended the work:

> Dec. 5 payd to John Tyrer allowed unto him by the
> Dean and Chapter for his travayle and paynes taken on
> and about the reparacons of the church   IIII li.
> Dec. 12 to III laborers for making cleane the long paved
> Ile and getting away all the earth at x d. a day   II s.   VI d.

Repairs to the fabric:

> 1602 payd unto Sconce slater for mending over my lord
> Bishop's Chamber but yet upon our roof [i.e. the N.W.
> tower]   II s.
> for tyle to amend the Cloysters agaynst Mr. Dean came
> down   XVI d.
> 1605 Jan 12, to Wyan the mason for stone to make a window
> pillar [mullion] in the south side of the Quier 12d., for
> workmanship to 2 men for 2 days 14d. the day, 4s. 8d.
> in toto   V s.   VIII d.
> to the mason for setting up the pillar for 2 days   II s.   IIII d.
> to his man for one day and a half at 14d. the day   XXI d..
> March. payd unto Nicholas Garde glaseor for work
> done this winter both new and old   III li.   III s.   II d. ob.
> payd for mending and cleaning the sprice being broken
> down   VI s.   VIII d.

Repairs to furniture:

> 1602 to Holmes for disfiguring of Moyses face and making
> the place in same good order agayne   VI s.   VIII d

This is a very interesting entry. "Holmes" is evidently the famous Randle Holme (I). The only place in the church where one would expect to find a representation of Moses in 1602 would be on the board containing the Ten Commandments which Elizabeth had ordered to be set up. Can it be that Puritan feeling had grown so strong by this time that even this was an offence? It looks like it, and the Accounts show that by this time the Holy Communion was celebrated only on the four great festivals with two exceptions, 5 August, called "The King's Day" and (after 1605) 5 November.

> November, payd for II plates of iron and nailes for the
> feete of the pulpitt in medio Chori wh. was broken in
> two   VI d.
> payd for a little deske for Mr. Bateson his organ booke   VI d.

This was the celebrated Bateson, the most gifted of all the Chester Cathedral organists and one who is, in the words of Dr Bridge, "unanimously acknowledged to be one of the finest of our Elizabethan Madrigalists".

> 1604 Feb. 26 to the mason for taking down the font and paving the broken places wher was needfull at 14d. the day   III s.   VI d.
> 1605 payd for a great round hanging locke [padlock] for the greate dore on the south syde by the singing schole   xx d.

The Singing School was over the south-west porch in what is now the muniment room. It is interesting to know that there was a font in the Cathedral before Bishop Bridgeman presented his. This was not the case at Peterborough where Bridgeman also presented one, the first they ever had.

> 1601 payd the charges bestowed upon your Diett in time of the Auditt   VIII li. VI s. VI d.
> payd to the poore woman in the kitchen in tyme of the Auditt   xx d.

The Audit dinner, for which extra help was required in the kitchen, was an annual event and a very expensive one. In the following year the cost was cut down by half (£4 8s. 10d.) and the "poore kitchin wench" only got 1s., but in 1612 the dinner cost £12 12s. 6d. About £8 was the average. We must suppose that all the fee farmers who came to pay their rents were entertained and so the numbers would vary, for sometimes many of them were in arrears and therefore would not come.

> 1605 Feb. 1, payd unto Mr. Sharp for a fatt cow bestowed upon the mayor of the Citty by warrant of Mr. Sub-deane and the rest of the Chapter   III li. XIII s. IV d.
> 1607 payd for a fatt cow to give unto my L. Bush at his going for London   III li. XIII s. IV d.

What unusual presents to give, and it will be noticed that both cows cost exactly the same, which is also unusual.

> 1605 payd to John Welsh for the bonfyre the 24th of March   II s. VI d.
> Aug. 5, payd for the bonfyre made that day   II s. VI d.
> payd to the Ringers for ringing all that day in number xv, VIII d. a peece   x s. VIII d.

March the twenty-fourth was the King's Accession Day, but August the fifth commemorated an event in the life of James which took place before he was King of England and it is surprising to find his English subjects celebrating it each year with bells and bonfire. This event was his escape from the Gowrie conspiracy when Alexander

Ruthven, brother of the Earl of Gowrie, tried to murder him in 1600. In 1609 the St Oswald's Accounts have "Item the Vth of August, delyvery from Gowrye . . ."

In 1607 the Archbishop of York held a Visitation:

> payd to the B. of Yks. Receiver for procurations payd
> by us for certaine charges XLVII s. VII d.
> payd for barrel of duble brew and another of small to
> dine the B. of York his commissioners as afore XV. s.
> Given to Mr. Gamuls man that brought a samon to us
> to entertaine my L. of Yorks Commissioners VI d.

William Gamul, who was Mayor in 1601, lived at Crabwell Hall, Mollington. The Annals speak very highly of him. "He was but a young man but yet very wise and prudent in all his affairs. He got much love of the citizens. He kept a very worthy and plentiful house; the poor much relieved at his gates; he was born in the City."

DEAN THOMAS MALLORY 1607–1644

Thomas Mallory, D.D., was installed Dean of Chester Cathedral on 25 July 1607, and so began his long reign of thirty-seven years, for he did not die until 1644 at the age of seventy-eight. He was the sixth son of Sir William Mallory of Stewdley in Yorkshire and married Elizabeth, daughter of Bishop Vaughan, by whom he had eight (or ten) sons and four daughters. With a bishop for a father-in-law preferment in those days came easily. In 1601 he was given the living of Davenham, two years later he was made Archdeacon of Richmond, a sinecure worth £50, and in 1621 he left Davenham for Mobberly, having purchased the advowson himself in 1619. Thus began the connection of the Mallorys with Mobberly which still continues. Thenceforward he lived at Mobberly until he was turned out by Parliament in 1642 and forced to take refuge in his Deanery inside the walls of Chester. In spite of his preferments he appears to have been in debt, for which perhaps his large family will account. For in 1624 the York Convocation on his behalf recited the Act of 8 Henry VI which gave proctors freedom from arrest on their way to and from Convocation and stated that "Mr. Thomas Mallorie Dean of Chester is at this instant much molested with divers persons, or some one at the least, with troublesome suits of lawe so that he is thereby hindered for [sic] attending his Majesties service at Convocation now at York dependinge."[1]

[1] *Surtees Soc.* No. 113, 249.

It will be convenient to carry the next state of the story to the coming of Bishop Bridgeman in 1619—a period of twelve years. It was a time when the Puritan movement in the country was gathering strength, as witness the pulling down of crosses at Christleton, Tarvin, and Vicars Cross "by certain precise fellows who were more fanatical than wise".[1]

In the Cathedral considerable sums of money were spent on repairs to the fabric and on furniture, of which the following are examples. The stone tracery of the windows seems to have been in a very decayed state and the plumber and glazier were kept busy.

1607 July 14, To Stanney and his fellowes for work about the
Ile at the back of the quire   VII li. VIII s. IX d.
To George Salt plummer for worke done about the Ile
near the consistory [i.e. the north choir aisle]   LXVI s. II d.
1608 To Stanney for VI trees in Hatton wood [?Hatton
Heath]   IIII li.
To John Larg for carrying the 6 trees from Hatton
Wood   XLII s. VI d.
To the plummer for work about the parish church   VI li. X s. XI d.
1609 Payd to a smith for making one payre of hynges for the
door of the Bishopes sea [sic] being broken on the holy-
dayes   VIII d.
1610 June 8, payd to Ricd. Bradshaw mason for a springall
stone of a frett for the upper part of one of the north
windows at the higher end of the Quier being forlen
downe   IIII s.

"Frett" here probably means tracery, and "springall" the springing of the arch in the head of the window. In this same year £18 6s. 7d. was spent on glass and in the following year Thomas Runckhorne was paid £17 12s. 0d. for "flagginge in the Church".

1611 Dec. 10, payd to John Higgins joyner for makinge my
lord pew in the Quier   I s.

This would be a pew for his family, as the Bishop already had his throne.

1612 April 2, payd to a mason for setting up the square
stowne under the great tree   VII d.

This might mean either a mounting block in Abbey Square or a corbel stone under the end of a roof beam.

May 22, payd for makinge II new pillars of stowne in
in the large South window in the parish Churche ...
and for glazinge agayne of the same window as much as
was taken down   XII li.   X d.

[1] "An Original MS. List of the Mayors of Chester" in the Chester City Library.

1613 payd to Arratt Watt for taking downe the Roofe of the owld steeple [i.e. the present consistory court]	xx s.	iiii d.
payd for mending the 4 velvet cushions wh. lye in the Quier		x d. ob.
1614 payd to Tho. Eaton, Smith, for 6 li. iron for a curtain Rodde to stay up the vault over Mr. Deanes seate for workmanship and nailes	ii s.	i d.
1615 payd to Arratt Watt and his man for taking up the plankes under the Bells to vewe the crosse Arche and for nayles to the same	iii s.	iiii d.
to Richard Done for making cleane the Rood lofte and chuch after ye [sic] had covered the bell floore		iiii d.

It is evident from these two entries that the bells were rung from a floor placed below the groined ceiling of the crossing and this is confirmed by a statement in an anonymous History of Chester Cathedral, dated 1793, to the effect that there was at that time "a modern bell loft" under the stone-vaulted ceiling of the crossing.

payd for a Board 4 foote at 1½d the foote and for half spars of x foot long and for a peece to barre the inside of the Dore in the owld Seller for nayles and for workmanship of the same to kepe out strangers	iiii s.	iiii d.
to a mason for making new the stayres going down to the sprice for the wall being fallen all into the sprice	iiii s.	vi d.
1618 for mending the great gate towards the Cowlane in the Calliard	xii s.	viii d.

General:

1610 payd the last of April for Mr. Deans and Mr. Subdeans journey to London about the house busyness	xxxii li. iiii s.	v d.
Bestowed in wyne upon the gentlewoman wh. lent us for a fortnight 88 [li] to discharge the Kinges Majesty Receiver		xvi d.

This was in October and Audit day was on 25 November, but evidently the King's Receiver could not wait till then for his £106 16s. 5d. "The gentlewoman" may have been "the Lady Grenour" (? Grosvenor) who on 29 November 1641 was paid £5 8s. 0d. "for the interest of her lxviii li. this last year". That would be 8 per cent.

Bestowed in wyne upon the Kinges Majesty Receiver when we fetched out the gould and for cariage of the money to Wrixham and for Mr. Sharps man his dinner	iii s.	viii d.

In 1615 the Dean and Chapter had to borrow again, from a man this time:

Bestowed upon Mr. Drinkwater who lent us 50 li. to the Kinge Auditors in sacke	ii s.

Drinkwater was an ironmonger by trade and was mayor in 1624.[1]

> 1612 Nov. payd to Roger Davies for roddes and clay to mend
>   panes [?panels] of the owld kitchin   xviii d.
>   to widdow Davyes who dwelled in the owld kitchin   xx s.
> 1613 Payd for the new Bible with cariage from London   lxix s.

If this was the Authorized Version they were rather slow in obtaining it, for it was issued in 1611, but there was no reason why they should have obtained it at all, for in spite of its name it was never authorized and made its way by its own superlative merit.

> 1614 Dec., payd for ringing at my L. coming home from
>   London   xii d.

He had been to the "Addled" Parliament, which lasted only two months.

> 1618 For mending the Church Bible by Robt. Browne   ii s.
>   Bestowed upon sergeants and officers to find out things
>   lost from the church   v s.
>   To Edmund going to train a light horse   ii s.   vi d.

A light horse, which included a man to ride it, was the Cathedral's quota towards the militia. We shall hear a good deal more of it in the future.

The Merchant Aisle

The Merchant Aisle appears in the Accounts for the first time in 1607 and occurs again in 1610, 1612, and 1615, but not afterwards. The will of Nicholas Ince who was mayor in 1627 gives us the clue to its position, for it states that it was in St Oswald's church. There are only two aisles in that church (the south transept), and the following extract makes it clear which of the two aisles it was, for only the west aisle has a door to it:

> 1612 Payd to Jeonson Smithe for making a new hinge to one
>   of the long dors in the Marchante Ile and for spike nailes
>   the 2nd June   viii d.

In Randle Holme's plan, undated, it is labelled "trough ile". This is even more difficult to explain than Merchant aisle and I am going to hazard the suggestion that Holme meant to write "Through" aisle and that the "h" has been omitted. This would be perfectly intelligible, meaning the aisle with a door at each end of it, allowing a through passage in contrast to the other aisle which had no through

[1] *Sheaf*, xxx, 73.

passage. There must have been a door connecting St Oswald's church with the rest of the Cathedral and what more natural than it should have been at the end of the aisle by which the church was entered?

Bishop Lloyd died on 1 August 1615 at his Rectory of Thornton-le-Moors "at about the hour of eleven of the clock at night". A MS. volume of *Antiquities of Chester* says he "was interred that night in the quoir of Chester". The City Annals in *Vale Royal* say "he was privately buried in the choir of the cathedral; his funeral was performed the Sunday following", while the funeral sermon was preached by his chaplain, Mr Shute or Suit, in St Oswald's church on 6 August.

Burials at night were the fashion in those days, but this one seems to have been impossibly speedy. The Bishop's epitaph was inscribed on a plate affixed to an alabaster stone in the middle of the choir, which has long since disappeared. The following is a translation of the Latin which has been preserved by William Webb in King's *Vale Royal*:

> Untimely death has put an end to this heart of George Lloyd, whose memory Chester reveres. He was Welsh in nationality, educated at Cambridge, a doctor in theology, eminent among theologians, He was promoted to and graced [*praefuit et profuit*] the Bishopric of Sodor [and Man], ruling there for five years. Mother England recalled her child, and deemed him worthy of the bosom of the Bishopric of Chester, where, after the lapse of eleven harvests, not without tempests of troubles, in the 55th year of his age on 1 August, A.D. 1615 he died, mourned and rightly mourned.
>
> A stainless life, a griefless end.

Thomas Morton, D.D., who succeeded him, was consecrated at Lambeth 7 July 1616 "and after being recovered from a violent fever, he began his journey towards his see, and when he approached the confines of his Diocese he was met by all the principal gentlemen and clergy in that County, who conducted him to Chester".[1] He remained there only three years and then was translated to Lichfield. "He was a great scholar and writer against the Papists," says *The Antiquities of Chester*,[2] "but no great housekeeper and did not obtain the love of the clergy." And so enters Bishop Bridgeman.

BISHOP JOHN BRIDGEMAN, D.D 1619–1644

As this is the history of the Cathedral and not of the Diocese the Bishop is only mentioned where he comes in contact with the Cathedral, but Bishop Bridgeman's relations with the Dean and Chapter were exceptionally close and his life therefore merits a special attention. He

[1] Cowper MSS., 13 C.C., p. 41.   [2] Preserved at the Town Hall.

was a Devonian, born in Exeter, educated at Oxford and at Cambridge and elected a Fellow of Magdalene College at the latter university in 1598. He was ordained in 1601 by Dr Thomas Dove, Bishop of Peterborough, after whom he named one of his sons. He then proceeded, as the custom was, to collect a number of benefices, including prebends at Exeter and Peterborough Cathedrals. In 1605 he was made a chaplain to King James I and in the following year he married Elizabeth Helyer, the daughter of one of the Exeter Canons. In 1615 the King gave him the rectory of Wigan, which was one of the "plums" of the Northern Province, so that he was able to resign several of his other benefices. He was a favourite with the King and often preached before him, and so became friendly with another of his chaplains, William Laud, afterwards Archbishop of Canterbury. On 9 May 1619, he was consecrated Bishop of Chester, but continued to reside at Wigan and did not enter his cathedral city until 14 November 1620. His residences at the palace were few and brief; he complained that it was unhealthy.[1]

Before we go further we ought to have a look at the composition of the Chapter, for there have been many changes in the last ten years. In 1620 it was as follows:

Thomas Mallory, D.D., Dean	1607
Roger Ravenscroft, M.A.	1599
David Ellis, D.D., Subdean	1608
William Case, M.A.	1613
Robert Ashall, B.A.	1616
William Foster, D.D.	1618
George Snell, D.D.	1620

For the sake of completeness we must include Patrick Young and Thomas Dod, who both resigned before 1620.

Patrick Young (1613–18) was at the Cathedral for only five years, but was one of the ablest men who ever filled one of its stalls. He was exceptional if only because he was a Scot, graduating from St Andrews in 1603 and following his king southwards, in this case to Oxford, where he became chaplain of All Souls in 1605. He was employed at court as correspondent (in Latin) with foreign rulers and was librarian at St James's Palace successively to Prince Henry, James I, and Charles I. He was appointed to Chester in 1613 and resigned his stall in 1618. Three years later he was made Prebendary and Treasurer of St Paul's Cathedral and given the Rectory of Hayes, Middlesex, which he held until it was sequestrated in 1647.

[1] Bridgeman, p. 191 ff.

Thomas Dod, B.D., was a Cheshire man and no relation to the Nathaniel Dodd who preceded him, being the son of Peter Dod of Shocklach. He entered Jesus College, Cambridge, about 1592 as a sizar, and five years later was elected Fellow of his College, 1597–1603. In 1606 he obtained the Rectory of Eastwell, Lancs., which he resigned when he was made Prebendary of Chester, for with the prebend he was given the valuable living of Astbury and also the Archdeaconry of Richmond. In 1619 he exchanged his prebend in Chester for one in Lichfield Cathedral and was also made Chaplain to the King. He returned to Cheshire four years later as Rector of Malpas (Lower Mediety) and died and was buried there 1647–8.

David Ellis was a Welshman from Denbigh. Born in 1570, he went to St Mary's Hall, Oxford, at the early age of fifteen and took his B.A. three years later in 1588. He took his B.D. in 1600 and his D.D. (from Jesus College) in 1608, becoming Prebendary of Chester in the same year. He held various livings in Wales and in 1622 left Chester to become Canon of St Asaph.

William Case was the son of Thomas Case, Attorney in the Exchequer Court and Clerk to the Dean and Chapter. He went to Brazenose College, Oxford, in 1602 at the age of seventeen, took his B.A. in 1605 and his M.A. in 1612, and joined the Cathedral Chapter in the following year at the age of twenty-eight, which suggests parental influence, though of course it was the Bishop and not the Dean and Chapter that made the appointment. Unlike his colleagues he seems to have lived at Chester and been content with a small remuneration. He was Vicar of Over for two years (1613–15) and Rector of St Peter's, Chester for three (1624–7), after which he seems to have been satisfied with the vicarage of St Oswald's, which was not usually held by a prebendary. In 1611 he petitioned to be a freeman of the City on the ground that he had lately married the widow of a freeman. "The Assembly thereupon, in respect of the good affection they bore towards the petitioner's father," granted his request, a kindness that they must have bitterly repented of in later years, as we shall see.[1] He died in 1634 and there is a tablet to his memory in the South Choir aisle.

Robert Ashall was a sizar at Queens' College, Cambridge, in 1589–1590, took his B.A. in 1593, and was Rector of Swettenham from 1605 till his death in 1632.

William Foster was made Rector of Barrow in 1602 and the inscription which he had carved on the back of his pew still survives, though

[1] *Sheaf*, XVII, III.

it has been incorporated into the back of a later pew which is now in the tower:

> Stallvm Gvliel. Forster sacrae theologiae doctoris et hujus eccl'iae rectoris locatv 1604.

Foster went to St Catherine's College, Cambridge, in 1589, took his B.A. in 1593 and his D.D. in 1618, the year that he became a Prebendary of Chester. In 1625 he was Rector of Northenden and in 1634 was consecrated Bishop of Man, but died at Barrow the following February and was buried there.

George Snell went as a scholar to Caius, Cambridge, in 1600, but graduated at St John's. Later on in life he became a D.D. of St Andrews and also of Oxford. In 1618 he was made Archdeacon of Chester by Bishop Morton and in the following year he obtained the living of Wallasey where he built the south-west portion of the old rectory.[1] In 1621 Bishop Bridgeman, his brother-in-law, made him prebendary of the Cathedral, but he resigned his stall in 1632 in favour of William Bispham, who is said to have been his wife's kinsman, and was given the living of Waverton instead, which he held in plurality with Wallasey by a dispensation from the Archbishop. In the same year he was appointed Rural Dean of the Deaneries of Chester, Frodsham, Malpas, Middlewich, and Nantwich, an office which in those days was a place of profit and was usually leased by the Bishop for a considerable sum. Snell was still at Waverton when the Civil War broke out and he did his best to cling to his benefice, professing his "real affection" for Parliament. He seems to have protested too much, for the Committee for Compounding pronounced him "a delinquent, scandalous, and non-resident, pluralist, a time server and one that never showed his zealous affection to the better sort of people in all his time". Not content with sequestrating his livings, they took from him a third of his capital (£330) which consisted of land in Guilden Sutton and Hargrave, and he died in obscurity in the former village, 5 February 1655.[2] He was buried at St Mary's on the Hill, where his epitaph records that he was forced *"per injuriam temporis in communionem laicam"*.

Chester did not see much of its Bishop until 7 July 1623, when he came to carry out a Visitation of the Cathedral, the result of which is contained in the Injunctions he issued on 12 July. The Cathedral copy of these Injunctions is not in the Chapter Minute Book, but together with the Injunctions of Bishop Cartwright and Bishop Stratford is

---

[1] Bridgeman, p. 262.   [2] Walker, p. 94.

copied into a folio book of leases, which was discovered in Durham County in 1884 and has now been restored to the Cathedral.[1] The Bishop also had them copied into his Ledger, a bulky book stored with information about the Diocese and now in the Diocesan Registry, an invaluable source of information for this period.

From these Injunctions, based on the answers made by the Dean and Chapter to the questions put to them, we can learn a good deal about the state of the Cathedral at the end of the reign of James I.

No. 1 deals with residence. The Bishop orders that the year is to be divided into four quarters, beginning with Michaelmas. The Dean is to reside the first quarter, the two "ancientist" prebendaries the next quarter and so on. The penalty for non-residence was to be a fine of £20 for the Dean and £10 for the Prebendaries to be stopped out of their stipends by the Treasurer and divided equally amongst (1) "the poor prisoners in the Castle and Northgate and other poor of the City who might have had relief by their residence and hospitality if they had not been absent", (2) the other members of the Dean and Chapter "who do reside according to these Injunctions", and (3) "the Singing men who shall be found resident and diligent that year".

2. While in residence they must "diligently resort to Divine service in their surplice and hood . . ." and "shall likewise in the time of their residence have the government of the Quire; and where their authority comes short they shall inform the Bishop that he may censure the offenders by suspension or otherwise". Penalty £5 to be divided equally between the poor and the Petty Canons and Singing men. "And because great complaint hath been made of the negligence [of the Chapter] in preaching their courses in this Church, some of them never or very seldom preaching, and most or all of them leaving their courses either unprovided altogether or supplied by mean and insufficient men . . . from henceforth the Dean and the Archdeacon and every Prebendary shall in their own persons preach so oft as it comes in their course on pain of 40s. for each default", to be distributed among the prisoners and the poor "that those who do not carefully feed the souls of the people who would hear them may at leastwise necessarily feed the bodies of the persons who cannot come to hear them".

3. The Petty Canons and Choir are to be fined 2d. each time they are absent (except for six weeks holiday every year). "And every one of them who shall come tardy after the Confession is said or go out before the end of divine service shall forfeit 1d. for every such default." On the Festivals of Christmas, Easter and Whitsunday the Dean shall

[1] *Sheaf*, III, pp. 199, 204.

sing or say divine service in the choir "unless the Bishop himself shall please to do it in his own person (as in the best ordered churches of this land the Bishops have used to do)".

4. The Organist, young Mr Thomas Jones, comes in for very heavy censure, though too much should not have been expected of such a mere boy. He was appointed organist in 1614, having been senior chorister in 1610, and it would not be surprising if he were found incapable of controlling the boys, some of whom may have been "on the desk" with him. However, the Bishop came down heavily upon him. "And because the defect of the organist," he wrote, "or his neglect in tutoring the choristers hath unsufferably impeached and impaired the service of God and almost utterly spoiled the children— he is therefore (besides the censure now to be laid upon him) admonished to present reformation", with the threat that he will be dismissed if there is no improvement before Michaelmas. As he continued to be organist until 1637 we may conclude that the necessary reformation was forthcoming.

5. In the King's School the Subdean and Prebendary in residence shall examine the scholars four times a year and report any they find "indocible" so "that they may be removed and others placed in their rooms". Rich men's sons are not to be made King's scholars and the Dean and Chapter are warned against taking bribes.

6. Bedesmen must "come daily into the church unto divine service, but shall forfeit for every day's absence 4d.".

7. "Because the use and service of Cook, Cater, Butler, Barber and other such officers is now extinct" the money allotted to them is to be divided between the Petty Canons and Singing men, "for the betterment of their wages which is now too mean to maintain them, considering their charge of wife and children . . .", but they are not allowed to sublet their duties, "for while the wages are divided between two, the service is commonly undischarged by either". The Accounts show no change whatever in the wages of these people as a result of this Injunction. They continue to receive—Petty Canons £13 0s. 0d. and the Singing men £10 0s. 0d. per annum. Not until 1642 was the pay of the Petty Canons raised to £14.

8. This Injunction, which deals with the repairs of the church, begins with a reference to "the sacriligious and ravenous disposition of those who formerly have been members of this Church", and goes on to warn the Dean and Chapter against appointing a Treasurer who "shall pull down any part of the old building and make any benefit thereof unto himself or take away any of the leads and cover those

places with any other covering than lead"—all of which makes us wonder whether the charge Sir Richard Cotton in the reign of Edward VI brought against the Dean and Chapter of stealing the lead from the Cathedral roof may not have had some truth in it.

9. This Injunction deals with Abbey Court, or Square as we call it now, a subject on which the Bishop, as a resident in the Square, felt very strongly. All the west side against Northgate Street was let to a brewer, Alderman John Ratcliffe, and part of the south side was a communal bake-house and a malt-house and contained only one prebendary's house.

> It is decreed and strictly enjoined [wrote the Bishop] that because the houses of the Prebendaries are base, little, noisome and unfit for habitation both in regard to site, room, decay and manner of building, and the other buildings about Abbey Court (especially towards the street side from the Great Gate . . . up to the brewer's house and so round till you come to the Dean's house) are more convenient for mansions of the Prebendaries and Archdeacons, Lecturers and other members of the Church, they are advised that they never demise . . . any of these buildings . . . unto any person whatsoever but do reserve them to the use of the said Prebendaries and other members of the Church, as the leases shall expire and become void. . . . Because there is daily seen a most shameful and unsufferable abuse (by the demising of some of those buildings) in the Abbey Court and Cloisters and sometimes in the Church itself being profaned or much annoyed by horses, hogs and other means, so as the Court which was formerly kept for the decent and convenient use and refreshment of the Church members is now become most vile and sordid and with the daily noise of brewers with their knocking, cooping, carting and the like all the members of the Church are much annoyed; and the Bishops themselves and their successors [sic] above all others being thereby oft times interturbed in their studies and other business . . . for which cause it is ordered and strictly enjoined the Dean and Chapter that presently [i.e. immediately] they take order that all and such abuses be taken away. . . .

We may here observe that the condition of Abbey Square would not worry a dean who lived at Mobberly or prebendaries who lived at Dodleston or Swettenham or Barrow and that perhaps it was for this reason that this injunction was utterly disregarded until the Bishop brought heavier guns to bear.

10. The Bishop's last Injunction was as follows:

> Lastly, because by presentment (and also by complaint of the best respected citizens) it appeareth that the Gatehouse is become a receptacle of many disorderly people of the city and others who, taking themselves

Lincoln Christian College

to be exempted in that house from the power of the City, do resort thither and much wrong themselves and discredit the Government of this Church by their immoderate drinking, gaming and vain and wicked expense of time;—it is decreed that from henceforth there shall be none Alehouse, Beerhouse or Victualling House kept in the said Gatehouse, nor any of the City or elsewhere shall be admitted or suffered to drink, game or lodge therein, nor any horses taken or permitted to stand in the Gatehouse nor any corn to be measured there for the private gain of the Porter save for the passage of People and other necessaries of the house and members thereof.

The only reference to all this in the Accounts is:

> for perfume for the Chapter house at the Visitation   iiii d.

A postscript to this complaint of the Bishop's about the use of the Abbey Court by those not connected with the Cathedral is to be found in the Assembly Books of the City under the date 17 October of this same year (1623) and gives point to the Bishop's protest:

> This Assembly upon information by petition that diverse persons not free of the Company of Tailors within the said City do exercise the said trade in the liberties of the Abbey to the great prejudice of the said Company,—it is thought fit by this Assembly that the Dean and Prebends of Chester be spoken concerning the same and that if they will not see reformation thereon, then Mr Mayor and his brethren to proceed therein by punishing the offenders according to law.

Almost a year later they complained again. On 23 October 1624, the petition of the Company of Tailors alleged that "diverse meere strangers and forrenors" were retailing ale, tobacco, soap and flax although they "never served seaven yeares as apprentice nor are free of this Cittie". No place is mentioned, but the fact that the Assembly resolved to write to the Dean and Chapter about it shows that it was their property which was concerned in this illegal trade.

The only subject that remains to be dealt with in James I's reign is James himself. He paid a visit to Chester in 1617 of which Webb gives the following account in *Vale Royal*:

> The king rode first to the Minster, where he alighted from his horse, and in the west Ile of the Minster he heard an oration delivered in Latin by a scholar of the free school. After the said oration he went into the choir, and there, in a seat made for the king at the higher end of the choir, he heard an anthem sung; and after certain prayers the king went from thence to the Pentice, where a sumptuous banquet was prepared at the city's cost.[1]

[1] Ormerod, I, 240.

THE SPRISE OR CLOISTER
GARTH

Chidley, Chester

BISHOP
BRIDGEMAN'S
COTTAGES (1626)

The Cathedral Accounts witness to James' efforts to raise money without having recourse to Parliament. First he revived the feudal dues which had lain dormant for a century. These entitled the king to an "aid" from his subjects on the knighting of his eldest son and the marriage of his eldest daughter. James made use of both these opportunities, but Prince Henry, the eldest son, died soon after he was knighted and a few months before the marriage of his sister Elizabeth to the unfortunate Elector Palatine. These two events come close together in the Accounts.

> 1612 Nov. 10 to the Commissioners of the Shyre for and
> toward the Ayde of the Lady Elizabeth   III li. VI s. VIII d.
> (after Nov. 25) payd to the Ringers for ringinge upon
> the prince Henry funerall day   V s.
> payde to the Ayde of the Lady Elizabeth   III li. VI s. VIII d.

It may be, of course, that the second entry of the Aid is a mistake on the part of the clerk and has escaped the notice of the auditors.

In 1620 the Elector Palatine was driven from the Palatinate by the Spaniards, and James, whose policy had always been peace with Spain, was powerless to help him. However, he made a show of raising an army which first of all meant raising money. First he had recourse to a Loan, as it was euphemistically called. To the first one in 1620 the Dean and Chapter contributed £40. The next demand "towards the recovery of the Palatinate" was called a Benevolence. For this the Bishop advanced £30 on behalf of the Dean and Chapter and let them repay him in instalments. He noted in his private ledger under date February 1621–2: "Dean and Chapter . . . £30 0 0 which the Lo. Bp. hath layd down for them but hath yet recd. but £20.[1] For the credit of the Cathedral it is pleasant to be able to record the following extract from their own Accounts:

> 1622 (between Nov. 25 and Dec. 25) paid to my Lord Bp.
> for an addition to our Benevolence for the Palitanate   x li.

Prince Charles was a true son of his father and horrified the nation by going off to Spain to court a Roman Catholic Princess. (It was for this occasion that the conciliatory phrase "Roman Catholic" was coined to replace the more invidious "Roman" or "Romanist".) The relief when he returned home without her was immense and is revealed by the amount of money the Dean and Chapter spent:

> for bonfires and triumphes at the Princes return   XXXIII s.

[1] *Lancs. and Ches. Record Soc.*, XII.

A new organ by Watts was built about this time:

For charges carrying the organ to Chester, by a bill	I li. xiv s.
March 1626. Delivered to Mr. Wats organ maker at sondry times	lxv li. iii s. v d.
To Castro joyner for the back of the organ	ccc s.
To the same for seate for the organ	iii s.
To the smith [for] hinges and curtain rods	viii s. ii d.

CHARLES I 1625–1648

The opening of Charles I's reign was marked as far as the Cathedral was concerned by the great pulpit controversy. On 3 September 1624, the Bishop had given St Oswald's congregation a commission to make the pews in their church more uniform. The document, which is in Latin, said that there had been quarrels over the seats, of which there were not enough, and that the pulpit was not conveniently situated. The parishioners were therefore empowered to move the pulpit and the pews and to add to them, provided that they were all made uniform and that the women sat apart from the men. When the Bishop returned to Chester on 24 October 1626, he found to his disgust that they had moved the pulpit to the middle pillar and had so placed the seat wherein he and the Mayor of Chester used to sit that he was no longer to sit directly in front of the pulpit, "but the Mayor now sat in the midst of that seat and he [the Bishop] was shouldered to the end thereof"; that his servants had had their places taken away from them; that the choirmen were placed so far from the pulpit that they could not hear the sermons; that the Dean and Chapter were "so disrespected" that they had a most unfitting seat assigned to them on the women's side; that the parishioners had given the best seats to their wives and friends and left none for the wives of the prebendaries and of the choirmen, and that the Mayor, Nicholas Ince, had grown so insolent that he claimed that St Oswald's was a parish church in its own right and that the Dean and Chapter had no authority over it. The Bishop thereupon ordered the Dean and Chapter to remove their sermons into the Choir, which they did on 14 January 1626–27. Such was the Bishop's account of the controversy which he confided to the pages of his private ledger at Wigan.[1]

The Mayor must have been thoroughly familiar with the ways of the Cathedral, for he had been a chorister in it and then a lay clerk for some thirteen years. He left it between 1615 and 1617 and was a maltster at the time of the incident.[2] His account of the dispute is to be found

[1] Bridgeman, p. 296.   [2] *Sheaf*, XXX, p. 73.

in the case which he submitted for counsel's opinion, the counsel being no other than the celebrated John Selden:

> The said church . . . being the most eminent and spacious in the City, the Mayor, Sheriffs and Aldermen of the said City have also used to come to the said church to hear sermons and have an ancient pew, wherein they usually sat, which hath convenient places where the sword and mace do stand before the Mayor in his seat,[1] and a desk for his book and cushion to be before him, in which seat also the Bishop for the time being hath usually sat with the Mayor. . . . The Bishop that now is, upon some allegations that the coming into the Mayor's pew in the said church was inconvenient, moved that the Mayor would come into the same at the back door thereof, and remove the irons for the sword and mace to stand in, to that side of the pew, and that the fore door of the said pew might be left for the Bishop to come into the said pew, which for diverse reasons was not thought fit to be yielded unto. Hereupon the Bishop in Christmas last caused the sermons to be moved from the said church and to be in the minster [choir] of the said cathedral church, which is a place of small extent, and hath not a convenient place either to hear or sit in. Since then, for some reasons known to himself, he hath brought the sermons to the west end of the said great Ile of the cathedral church, and near the old belfry [now the Consistory Court] and divers great and ancient church doors for several usual passages those ways, into a new pulpit lately caused to be erected at the side of one of the nethermost pillars of the great Ile opposite to a window of the chapel in his own house [now St Anselm's Chapel] and hath provided some seats with backs and diverse forms to sit on to hear sermons in the said Ile. . . . The Mayor and his brethren have accordingly refused to attend the sermon either in the choir or in the nave, and "during the sermon in the new pulpit many (for want of convenient room to sit or hear in) do walk in the church, some keep at home, and others (which is most of all) go to the alehouse at sermon time".

William Webb, writing for *Vale Royal* just at this time, discreetly ignores what lay behind the erection of this new pulpit, of which he must surely have been aware, and writes:

> Lately the lower end of that [Broad] Ile is graced with the beginning of such a monument as may, to our posterity, be of more fame and worth than all the rest of this ancient Fabric, if either the Right Reverend Father, Doctor John Bridgeman, the now Lord Bishop, or his successors do finish that preaching place which his Lordship hath already begun with the erection of as fair a pulpit of carved work in wainscot as I have anywhere seen.

[1] This mace holder is still preserved in the cathedral.

The Accounts show that the Dean and Chapter provided two pews for themselves:

1627 [after March 25) 2 wainscot pues in the great Ile	LIIII s.	IIII d.
for 2 locks and keys for the same	II s.	

As for "the seats with backs and diverse forms to sit on", which the Mayor referred to, they are mentioned in the Bishop's private accounts for 1627 and I believe that the three in the south transept today are some of them.[1] They are undoubtedly of Bishop Bridgeman's time, for they are identical with the seats in the Consistory Court which he furnished in 1636. In Dean Anson's time they were placed lengthways in the choir and occupied by the King's School boys.

The miserable dispute dragged on for two years and then the Dean held out an olive branch. Addressing the St Oswald's congregation he offered to remove the pulpit to its old position if the parishioners would acknowledge that St Oswald's was part of the Cathedral. But the Mayor was obdurate, and for twelve years he and the Corporation refused to attend the cathedral services. And there for the time being we leave the great pulpit controversy. Though it seems to us a storm in a teacup, it must be remembered that in those days seats in church were much valued possessions, no doubt for social as well as for religious reasons, and many a lawsuit was fought over them.

Here we may anticipate a little and insert a Visitation report on St Oswald's made by three Commissioners of the Archbishop of York in 1633, one of them being John Cosin, then Archdeacon of the East Riding. It is evident from this that the Bishop's instructions to make the pews uniform had not been carried out. It is also evident that here we have an instance of the Laudian revival which insisted on the moving of the Communion table to stand against the east wall of the chancel and the fencing of it in with "a decent rail with pillasters". They reported that:

The said Church was very undecent and unseemly, the stalls thereof being patched and peeced and some broken and some higher than other; and that the said Church was much defiled with rushes and other filthiness. The said Commissioners did order and enjoine the said Ch. wdns. to cause the rushes and other filthiness forthwith to bee taken out of the same Church; and to take present Order that the tops or peeces wh. were added to some stalls should be taken downe, and those Stalls and the rest of the Stalls in the same Church should be made uniforme and decent one yard

---

[1] Bridgeman, p. 298, note.

in height and noe more, and that the same Stalls should bee decently flagged or boarded within. And because the Communion table there was found to bee undecent and unseemely, not befitting soe holy an use, they did Order and enjoine the said Ch. wdns. to provide A decent and seemly table for the Communion, and likewise to pave or flagge the Isle wh. they call their Quire, wherein the Communion table standeth; and that the seats adjoyning to the wall beyond the Communion Table bee removed and taken away and the Communion Table sett upp close to the wall. And that a decent Raile with Pillasters bee made, one yard in height, reaching from the Communion Table to the pillar against which the pulpit leaneth, and soe from that pillar to the other pillar over against that, and soe up to the Communion Table againe.[1] And lastly, forasmuch as yt did appeare that divers sumes of money were and are arrere both to theis churchwardens now being and to the former churchwardens they enjoyned that A Cessment should bee made both for raising of the monies arrere, and for providing of such ornaments and necessaries as are enjoined. Further adding that all the senchions in the same church should forth with bee taken downe, requiring the ch. wdns. aforesaid to provide a convenient seate in the same church for Mrs Salisbury, wife of Fulke Salisbury, alderman .... [2]

Meanwhile the indefatigable bishop had begun a more constructive piece of work, part of which still survives to this day. He erected cottages for the four singing men or lay clerks on the site of the old monastic kitchen which, as we have seen, was occupied by Widow Davies in 1612. The Bishop seems always to have had a soft spot in his heart for the singing men who (he writes in the document which constituted the trust deed of these cottages and which is copied into his Ledger) have "been utterly unprovided of sufficient dwelling houses within the precincts of the Church and Abbey" and have been forced to rent houses in the City, thereby having to pay rents they could not afford and have been rendered liable to serve on juries "under pretence of being subject to the City government whiles they live in the City". He goes on to describe the site of these cottages. They were being built, he said, "where stood once the old great kitchen, that is to say between the porch of the first and utter hall of the Bishop's palace [now the Choir School playground] and part of the monks' hall [the Refectory] now made the Grammar School on the south side; and the Bishop's Registry abutting on the lane or high-way [now Abbey Street] which leads under the new great gate from the Abbey Court towards the Caleyard over against the Dean's garden on the north side, which places do of right belong to the Bishop".

[1] A rail of that period may be seen in St Anselm's Chapel.
[2] Harl. MS., 2103, f. 81, printed in *Sheaf*, 1, 47.

From this it is abundantly clear that the two stone cottages next to the entrance to the cloisters from Abbey Square are two of the four cottages built by Bishop Bridgeman for the lay clerks in 1626. The document goes on to say that they must never be let to any but choir men who must vacate them if they leave the choir, and the Dean and Chapter agree to keep them in repair. It is dated 15 March 1626.

A list of ornaments of the Cathedral in December 1628 gives one a better idea of the nakedness of the land than any amount of description. This is the list which was signed by the new Sexton on taking office. The omnivorous Randle Holme family somehow got hold of it and it is now in the British Museum.[1]

A Note of the Goods of the Church

Imprimis two Bibles.

Item for the Communion Table a red velvet cushion, a red silk covering, one Bible, a large service book with red velvet and silver clasps as above, a woollen carpet cloth and two new linen ones with an old one.

Item, 4 new green velvet cushions, 4 old ones, one for my Lords seat, another for Mr. Dean's, a third for Mr. Subdean's, as also nine sitting cushions and a pulpit cloth.

Item, two lanterns of glass, a brass pullar [?], two loose ones in the great chest in the vestry with good store of lead also.

Item, the Communion cups with covers, two new flagons and an old one in Mr. Treasurer Bispham's keeping which is to be restored.

Item, there is an iron crow taken out of the church by Mr. Subdean Case which yet is not restored to the church again.

More in the Chapter House, a broad wainscot chair, two wainscot forms, a joint stool for the new pulpit in the aisle.

This is a true note of the goods in particular belonging to the cathedral as witness my hand,

David Burches, Chief Sexton.

PREBENDARY WILLIAM CASE

It is unfortunate but inevitable that the least satisfactory members of the Chapter should be remembered while the conscientious and godly have no memorial. William Case is an example of the former. He was evidently of an irascible disposition with an unbridled tongue which was continually getting him into trouble. For example, in 1621 he had to pay £10 damages in the Portmote Court to William Skellington for accusing him of stealing "a gutter of lead that lay in the Minster". The words complained of were: "Thou art a false thief and did steal a

[1] Harl. MS., 2103, f. 68.

gutter of lead, and take heed that I make not thy neck to stretch for it."[1]

Nine years later he was in trouble again, as appears from the Assembly Book of the City Council under date Friday, 30 April 1630:

> At the same Assembly the Company of Painters, Glaziers, Embroiderers and Stationers of this Citty by their petition complained that William Case, a freeman of the said Citty and one of the Prebends of the Cathedral Church . . . laboured to infringe and entrench upon the ancient rights, liberties and customs of the said citty, and [that] because the said Company hath denyed to let him have a key of their meeting house[2] he did . . . affirme and say that the said Company was a factious Company, and cursed them and wished the Devill to take them all, and further threatened that-he would ere long be avenged on them, and that in pursuit of his said threats he had lately caused a petition to be preferred [to the Bishop] and solicited the same for a stranger to keep a stationer's shopp within the Abbey Court and that he had several time given forth in speeches that he would cause shops to be built within the said Abbey Court for any to trade there.

Knowing the strong views which the Bishop held about letting the houses in Abbey Court to strangers, as expressed in his Injunctions, Case must have been bluffing about the petition he said he had presented. But this was not all.

> And also at the same Assembly information was given by several members of the said house, That the said William Case hath given forth very scandalous words against some of the Justices of the Peace of the said Citty, charging them that whatever the Recorder . . . should say, they would swear [to it] whether it were true or false. And also upon Sunday, April 4, (upon which day the Mayor and Aldermen that are Justices of the peace of the said City are by ancient order and custom to wear scarlet gowns) the said William Case, being in company of the Aldermen who are justices of the peace—and then in their scarlet gowns—did in very contemptuous and disgraceful manner say unto the said Aldermen and Justices of the Peace, "I care not for your red coats. Do you thynke I am affraid of you or your scarlet gownes? I am as good and a better man than any of you."

Case was ordered to appear before the next Assembly to answer for his words, but there is no record of what happened.

The impression one gets that he was not a very likeable man is strengthened by the evidence of St Peter's churchwardens' accounts

---

[1] *Sheaf*, VI, 2.
[2] In the actual petition it is called "The Golden Phoenix", i.e. King Charles' Tower.

which begin in 1627 just in time to record the last of their Rector—in these words:

> Rec. of the parishioners for Mr. Cases wages for three quarters of a yeare due at Christmas last   XII li. X s. XI d.
> paid for a quart of sack bestowed upon Mr. Chancellor by the appointment of Mr. Sparke and Mr. Christopher Blease for his councell touching Mr. Case   XVI d.
> (September) Spent in presence of Mr. Blease and Mr. Sparke and other parishioners when Mr. Case promised the Resignation of his place   XIX d.
> paid to Mr. Case the late minister as appeareth by his acquittance bearing date the 7th December 1627   X li.
> paid to Willm. Sparke one of the treasurers of this Citty for the rent of the chamber by the west dore to have beene paid by Mr. Case for II yeres, I say paide for one yeares rent   VI s. VIII d.

That the parishioners of St Oswald's were not much better pleased with him appears from a paper preserved by Randle Holme and now in the British Museum.[1] It is catalogued as follows:

> Draught of an order made by the Parishioners of S. Oswald's in Chester for prosecuting Mr. William Case, Vicar of the same, he having demanded and taken ten shillings as a mortuary, and having grown otherwise very troublesome, dated 11th March, 1629.

Finally there is the Archbishop's Visitation of 1633, preserved in the Diocesan Registry in York, when Case was presented "for not reading prayers on eves of Sundays and Holy Days nor upon Wednesdays and Fridays and also for not usually preaching within his cure nor catechiseth".

The Accounts are scanty during this reign, for they have survived only for the years 1626–8 and 1631, and then there is a gap until 1639.

REPAIRS TO THE FABRIC:

> 1626 for making up a door going down from the dorter to the church   II s. X d.
> to the glazier   VIII li. VII s.
> to the slater for mending over my L's stayre into the church   IIII s. V d.
> to Randol hall setting up 3 munions (mullions?) in one window about the quire   XL s.
> 1627 Mending the way thorow the frater   VIII d.
> the last 5 weekes to slater and carpenter for timber, slates, smith work, lathes, lime and sand   XVIII li. VIII s. VIII d.
> to Smalshaw and his men for work done upon the dorter uncovered and covered again [with materials]   XXX s.

[1] Harl. MS., 2103, f. 185.

to Hugh Shaw carpenter over my L. his staires	III s.
1628 for iron bars for the east window in the quire	XX s.
to masons, carpenters and laborers in clensing the church, and bording up the window and barring the windows laying down the leads and taking down the pinnacles and for nailes	XLI s. VIII d.
1631 to the glazier for glazing the window in the Quire over the pulpit	III li. XVI s.
to the glazier for his work and glass to the great window in the south side of the parish church	VI li. IX s. IIII d.

GENERAL:

the wayts at the audit	II s.
1626 (summer) to ringers at my L. his coming to Chester	II s. VI d.
Oct. 24 to ringers at my L. his coming to town	VI s. VI d.
carying dyrt from the way to the Calliard [Abbey St. ?]	XXVII s. VIII d.
charges disbursed in a sute agst. Mr. Thicknes	XXIII s. VI d.

Thicknesse was Vicar of St Oswald's until December in this year when Prebendary Case took his office.

to London in Michaelmas term in Mr. Dutton's suit	XX li.
1627 for painting Hugh Lupus	II s. VI d.
for charges in London in Mr. Dutton's suit	XLVII li.

At the end of each year there is a list headed "Pauperibus". A few interesting examples may be given:

1607 to one Potinger that came bare out of Ireland a scholar and a musician	II s. VI d.
1612 May 20, given to a Cambridge scholar one R. Davys being a prisoner in the Northgate towards his debt and fees	X s.
1618 To a minister's widow	XII d.
To another Minister's widow that brought the hands [signatures] of all the doctors in Oxford	II s.
1627 Disbursed in farthings	II s.
1627 to a minister that came to look for a place and told me that if he were furnished with clothes he should be received at Taporley	II s. VI d.
to a Scottish merchant that had suffered shipwreck	III s. VII d.
to half a dozen soldiers that lately came out of Germany and the low countreys	III s.
1628 To an Archb. [sic] by Mr. Subdeans appointment	III s.
To a poor Minister that was promised some stay hereabout if he had clothes	II s.
1631 to two poor scholars and a converted friar	III s. VI d.
to a noble gentleman that had lost his eyes in the war, Mr. Dean appointing	III s. IV d.

BISHOP BRIDGEMAN AND ABBEY SQUARE

We have seen how the Bishop in 1623 forbade the Dean and Chapter to lease any more of the houses in Abbey Square to strangers but to reserve them for persons connected with the Cathedral. This order was not obeyed, for when the brewer died his widow, Jane Ratcliffe, was allowed to have the lease of the brewery for three more lives, her own and those of her two sons. Now in 1638 the widow herself died and the Bishop was apprehensive that another chance of ending the nuisance was going to be missed and that another lease of the brewery was going to be granted. So he wrote to his friend, William Laud, Archbishop of Canterbury, and asked for his help. Laud was at this time the most powerful man in the land, for he was the King's most trusted adviser, a sort of unofficial prime minister and he had the despotic powers of the Privy Council with its prerogative courts at his disposal. In his letter to Laud the Bishop set out the situation in great detail so that Laud could copy it in his letter to the Dean, which he obviously did, and thereby provided us with valuable evidence about the condition of Abbey Square in those days. Randle Holme's plan of it is an excellent illustration of this letter and should be consulted.

The Archbishop writes from Lambeth on 29 October 1638, to Bishop Bridgeman:

> Concerning your quadrangle or Abbey-court and the Brewhouse and Malthouse there. I have, as you desired me, written my letters by the King's command, to the Dean and Chapter there; which are here enclosed; and I pray deliver them. I have likewise sent yourself a copy, that you may see what I have written; and I hope they will obey it. If they do not, I promise you they shall smart for it.

The Bishop had to keep this letter until there was a Chapter assembled to which he could deliver it, and that could not be until the annual Chapter meeting on or near St Katherine's Day when the officers for the coming year were elected. And so the letter is endorsed:

> Dd. the Archbishop of Canterbury his letter . . . to Dean Malory, Mr. Ley, Mr. Bispham and Mr. Clark, prebends, Monday, 26th November, 1638, for their consent 2 days before their audit, and till then they had not a number to make a chapter. I dd. to them in presence of Dr. Mainwaring, Chancellor, in the Palace.[1]

Bishop Bridgeman was nothing if not businesslike.

[1] Bridgeman, p. 404.

And this is the letter, with the Archbishop's own spelling and punctuation:

After my hartie Comend; etc. I am informed, that in yor Quadrangle or Abbey Cort of Chester, wherein my Lord the Bp of Chesters and yor owne houses stand, the Bps house takes up one side of the Quadrangle, and that another side hath in it the Deanes House and some buildings for singing men; That the third side hath in it one Prebends house onlie[1] and the rest is turned to a Malthouse. And that the fourth side (where the Grammar Schoole stoode) is turned to a Comon Brewhouse, and was lett into lives by your unworthy Predecessors. This Malthouse and Brewhouse espetiallie must needs by noise and smoke and filth infinitlie annoy both my Lord the Bps house and your owne, and I doe much wonder that any man of Ordinarie discretion should for a little trifling gayne bring such a Mischiefe (for less it is not) uppon the place of theire dwellinge. But hitherto this concerns your predecessors; That wch followes will appeare to be your owne fault, for not long since [1634] the Bruer dyed; and though the kinges letters were then come down unto yow, to forbid letting into lives yet yow did renew it agen into three lives for a poore sum of £30; This was verie il done, and should his Matie be made acquainted with it, yow would not be able to answeare it; Now I heare the Bruers wife is dead, and yow have given me cause to feare, that you will fill up the lease againe, wth another life; And then there wilbe no end of this Mischiefe. I have therefore taken a spetiall occation to move his Matie in this p'ticular, and his Matie hath required me to lay his comandes uppon yow (wch now I doe by theise presentes), That neyther yow nor any of yor Successors doe presume to lett any part of that Cort to any other than some of the Prebends, or other necessary Members of the Church; And that now for the present yow Renew neyther Terme of life, nor Terme of years, eyther to the Brewer or Malster, but that yow suffer them to wear out that Terme, which they have; and then Reserve the Plase and howsing for the use aforesaid; And yow are further by the same Comand of his Matie to Register these letters, so that your Successors may know what they have to doe in this p'ticular. And in all this I require your Obedience in his Maties Name, as yow will answeare it at your perill. So I leave yow etc.[2]

On 1 December the Bishop wrote a letter of thanks to the Archbishop in which he said:

I owe you for this as much as my health and perhaps my life comes to. For truly ever since my being bishop of this see, which is now almost 20 years, I have scarce had a month's health together whilst I lived at Chester by means of the smoke and other annoyances which came thereby.

[1] Occupied by Essex Clarke, Bridgeman, p. 399, note.
[2] *Ledger*, p. 273, printed in *Sheaf*, o.s., I, 5.

The Archbishop replied on 20 December:

My very good Lord,
    About a month since I received a letter from your Dean, in which I find
that he is somewhat sensible of the loss that will come from the Prohibition
sent in his Majesty's name. . . . But yet he promises all obedience, and I
hope will perform it. And if your Lordship gain any Health and content-
ment by it I shall be heartily glad to have been an Instrument in procuring
it. I hope the Dean takes no inward pet at this, nor labours to distemper the
government there, or cast a Bone between the church and the city, thereby
to discontent you. For if I should find this he should hear of me in another
way.

He then passes to the new trouble which has arisen, for which we
must return to the second half of the Bishop's letter. It refers back to
the great pulpit controversy. The Mayor and Corporation continued
to boycott the Cathedral sermon, and in 1637 the Bishop had another
pulpit made for the choir where no doubt it took the place of the one
with the mended foot (1602). This pulpit is still to be seen in the
south choir aisle where it is altered to form a screen between the aisle
and the chapel of St Mary Magdalene. It bears the date 1637 on the
centre panel and on the next panel to it are the letters "JO. BR. EP.
VS." which stand for "John Bridgeman Episcopus". The pulpit is a
very fine piece of Jacobean workmanship and is worthy of more
attention than it receives. The boycott was ended—though not for
long—in 1638 by the then Mayor, Thomas Throppe, who had been
a chorister in the Cathedral from 1610 to 1617 and had been selected
at the age of thirteen to make an oration on behalf of the King's
School in Greek and Latin to Bishop Morton at the Abbey Gateway
on his first coming to Chester. He seems young to have such a responsibility thrust upon him, but then he was the Mayor's son, which
probably accounts for it. We continue the story in the Bishop's own
words which he wrote to the Archbishop on 1 December:

    The Mayor of Chester and his brethren have discontinued from our cathe-
    dral service about 12 years together till this last year, when an ingenuous
    merchant, who had some time been chorister and grammar scholar of our
    church, broke that schism and came diligently to our Choir at the beginning
    of service every Sunday and there continued reverently till service and
    sermon were fully ended. But he sat in the seat on the south side of the
    Choir door [now the Dean's stall] over against the Dean's seat, so oft as he
    came to the Choir, as all his predecessors (for ought I can learn) have always
    done without interruption and ever since the erection of our cathedral, the
    prebendaries sitting, half of them next the dean, and the other half next the

Mayor on the other side, and after them the aldermen and other gentlemen. But on a sudden our Dean (although he have no ecclesiastical jurisdiction) yet without my consent and the votes of his brethren, commanded the sub-sextons to keep the Mayor out of that seat, whereupon he and his successor have since abandoned our Choir service and sermons so as we shall have scarce five lay persons present beside the consistory and my family, whereas formerly the whole city came to it.

He continues that he is loth to trouble the King with this quarrel just when he has got "the Scottish businness" on his hands, but

> if you thought fit to write me a private letter signifying that you hold it meet that the Mayor shall sit as his predeseceors have ever done, since they came to our Choir service, until, upon hearing of both sides, other order be taken, or if you please to command me, upon my peril or pain of censure, to see things ordered as may in most likelihood prevent tumult or confusion, I will be accountable to you herein, whensoever you shall please to call me to it....

The Archbishop replied in the letter which has already been quoted:

> Yet I must confess I am afraid there is something that makes the man forward. And that he should do it at this time [of the Scottish trouble] and by such mean instruments as sub-sextons, and that after a discreet Mayor had brought the city to the cathedral again after a long discontinuance from it, and especially without so much as acquainting your Lordship with it, it seems to me full of indiscretion.
>
> My Lord, you know that I have not jurisdiction there. And yet rather than I would suffer any distemper to increase I have made bold privately to acquaint his Majesty with it; who is not well pleased with the action, especially at this time; and hath commanded me to write unto you, that you forthwith speak with the Dean, as also with the Mayor and his Brethren, that this difference be composed; and that the Mayor be suffered to sit quietly in the seat where (your Lordship says) he was anciently wont to sit. Against which if the Dean have any just exception, there may be a better time hereafter to have it heard than now....

It is surprising that either Laud or Charles should have found time to trouble their heads over the place where the Mayor of Chester should sit in church, for in 1637 they had forced the English prayer book upon Calvinist Scotland and after spending the year 1638 in vain negotiations to bring the revolted nation to obedience, Charles determined to resort to war. It was the beginning, though he did not know it, of the Civil War.

The question must have often arisen in the mind of the reader, "What about the Archbishop of York? Where does he come in?"

especially as Laud admits that he has no jurisdiction in Chester. The same question has occurred to Laud, and he had some qualms about the action he had taken. So he concludes his letter by asking the Bishop to try, if he can, to settle the quarrel without using his letter, but that, if he has to do so, to write to the Archbishop of York and explain, "that he may know what Necessity put you upon calling for his Majesty's power and that you used my assistance in obtaining it". Unfortunately we do not know the end of the story and must remain in doubt whether the Mayor came back or not.

It is abundantly clear from this correspondence that the Bishop thought himself in charge of the Cathedral over which the Dean "had no ecclesiastical jurisdiction", and he certainly spent a great deal of his money on it. The following list of his improvements is to be found in the Baker MSS. in the University Library at Cambridge entitled "The Estate of the Diocese of Chester in the time of the Right Reverend Father in God John Bridgeman, Lord Bishop of Chester" and endorsed "From Sir William Dawes, bishop of Chester, by Dr. Fogg, Prebendary there"[1]:

5. In the Cathedral . . . he bestowed £20 to have it washed all over withinside; within it also he built a fair new pulpit at the west end of the body of the great Church; and bought wainscot seats and other forms for the people to sit there; and then removed the Sunday sermons from St. Oswald's (where the Mayor of Chester, claiming a parish and usurping chief authority in that Church, had displaced the pulpit and the seats of the Dean and Prebends) first into the Choir, where he caused the Stalls to be fairly painted, and some of them gilt, and thence into the Body of the Cathedral. He built the Bishops stall in the Choir, 1635; and a fair new pulpit right against it, 1637; and gilded the organs in the Cathedral, and made a new set of pipes in it. [This is not quite correct, for in 1627 the Dean and Chapter paid "to my L.B. for the organes, li. x".] He raised the steps towards the Communion Table and made the wall and partition there, and tooke in the two highest pillars at the end of it, to enlarge the Choir [i.e. he moved the altar two bays eastward]; and he glazed the east window with the story of the Annunciation, Nativity, Circumcision, and Presentation of our Saviour; and built two lofts behind the north and south sides of the choir; and the partition between the body of the Cathedral and St. Oswald's Church. And he made a fair seat at the south side of St. Oswald's Church, under the great south window, and three stories, the highest whereof was for the Bishop, the Dean and Chapter, and Chancellor to sit in; and the middle seat for the Choir and Consistorians to sit in; the lowest part for the Choristers and Scolars with other belonging to the

[1] *The Palatine Note-Book*, III, 60.

Church and Churchmen. He erected a font at the west end of the Church; and whereas the stone windows of the Church were so eaten out with antiquity and weather as most of them were in danger of falling, and one of them did fall down directly over the Pulpit in the Choir, about half an hour after the sermon, which (had it fallen a little sooner ere the people had gone out of the Church) would have slain men and women—he made new stone windows almost about all the Choir, and in other places of the Cathedral he put in new stances of stone; as he did in the Palace windows, where he floored or planched five rooms with boards, and wainscotted and benched the two windows in the stone chamber; and made wainscot portals for the Abbot's chamber (since termed the nursery), the chamber over the chapel.

But even this does not exhaust his activities, for we must add the ceiling of St Anselm's Chapel and its screens and probably the sanctuary with its Laudian Communion rails; the furniture of the Consistory Court, its tables and seats and the Chancellor's raised seat with the canopy over it. (This canopy has been cut down at some later date, leaving only a fragment of the Chancellor's name, Edmund Main-waring, who was appointed to that office in 1634.) And also the typical Renaissance heavy stone screen which on closer inspection turns out to be lath and plaster. It has the Bishop's arms on the outside and the Mainwaring arms on the inside.[1] The "two lofts behind the north and south sides of the choir" were occupied by the ladies of the precincts right up to Scott's restoration and the late Miss Fluitt remembered sitting there and looking through the pinnacles of the canopies of the stalls. The immense three-decker which the Bishop built under the south window was evidently his answer to the Mayor for turning him out of his seat. The Consistorians, and the Consistory mentioned above, seem to have been officials of the choir. The seat was probably the last work he did in the cathedral, for it was built in 1642. We know this because the Dean and Chapter paid for their part of it on 9 May of that year:

Payd to Mr. Rich. Bennet for the wainscot and dressing
of a seat in St. Oswald's for the Deane and Chapter   III li. xv s. vi d.

There was one further undertaking on the part of the Bishop which must be mentioned and that is his abortive attempt to set up a stone altar in the Lady Chapel after its furniture had been moved to the new Consistory Court. We should not have heard about it but for a letter

---

[1] Bridgeman arms: Sable, ten plates (four, three, two and one); on a chief argent a lion passant, ermines. Mainwaring arms: argent, two bars gules quartering azure six garbs or. See Bridgeman, p. 12, note.

of protest written to the Bishop by the Subdean, John Ley, Vicar of Great Budworth, dated 29 June 1635, but not printed by him until 22 February 1640.[1] A copy of the book in which the letter appears is in the Cathedral Library.

This letter is interesting for the light it throws on the condition of the Cathedral and on the relation of the Bishop to the Dean and Chapter. Ley says that while at Great Budworth he was astounded to learn—and from a Papist of all people—that the Bishop had set up a stone altar in the now empty Lady Chapel. He could not believe it.

> It seemed to me [he wrote] more strange than true, that a Papist, dwelling at least fourteen miles from Chester, and cumming thither seldome, could know better what was done in the Cathedral than I the Sub-deane of the Church, who was there almost every weeke throughout the yeare. (*Note.* By Occasion of my weekly lectures upon Fridaies at Saint Peters.)

However, at his next visit he saw with his own eyes "that new structure of stone at the end of the old Consistorie", and noted that it was "three yards and about an halfe in length, a yard high, and a yard broad". He told the Bishop that if he had had notice of this intended alteration "(and you have sometimes accompted the Deane and Chapter, *a consiliis* to the Bishop) I should have done my best endeavour to dissuade you from it". The result was a complete surrender on the part of the Bishop. In 1640 he kindly repeated to Ley for the purposes of publication what he had said to him in 1635, which was as follows:

> When I caused it to be set up, I protest I had no thought of an Altar; and I meant it only for a repositorie to the Preacher (in the use of a table) in that place; which though it were somewhat neere the Quire, was not used but as a Consistorie Court, and where, (upon removall of all the seats to the west end of the Cathedrall), the materialls (whereof it was made) were found redy for such a purpose; but hearing that great offence was taken at it, I gave order for it to be taken downe, which is done accordingly.

In the same letter Ley gives us valuable evidence as to the state of the east end of the choir at this time. He writes:

> The place was the same which was formerly (for many years) used for the Consistory Court, it is the utmost room of the Cathedrall eastward, betwixt which and the Quire there is an intermediate space more large than it [i.e. the Lady Chapel] which is imployed to no particular use, but lieth open for passage round about it.

[1] "*Defensive Doubts, Hopes and Reasons. For Refusall of the Oath, imposed by the sixth Canon of the late Synod*, by John Ley, Pastor of Great Budworth in Cheshire. Hereunto is added by the same Author *A Letter against the erection of an Altar*, written about five yeare agoe, 1641."

ST ANSELM'S CHAPEL, RESTORED AND FINISHED BY BISHOP BRIDGEMAN

THE REFECTORY USED AS
THE KING'S SCHOOL

This must mean that at the time this letter was written (29 June 1635) the High Altar must have been still standing two bays westward of the Lady Chapel. This would leave the intermediate space spoken of above, which, if the aisles be included, would be a little larger than the Lady Chapel. We learn further from this valuable letter that:

1. The Consistory Court was set up at the west end of the church in its present position before 29 June 1635.

2. That the seats from the Lady Chapel were moved there. By seats is probably meant the furniture and fittings of the Court.

3. That the materials of which this new altar was made "were found ready for such a purpose". We may well ask how it came about that a stone slab measuring 13 ft. 6 in. by 3 ft. was ready to hand, and the only possible answer seems to be that it was the old *mensa* of the high altar pulled down on 13 December 1550. This guess is confirmed by William Prynne, of all people, who wrote in 1641 charging Bishop Bridgeman with erecting "divers stone altars in his Diocese, one in the Cathedral at Chester, used in times of Popery, *which he caused to be digged up out of the ground where it was formerly buried*".[1] So that is what the Bishop meant by saying that the "materials whereof it was made were found ready for such a purpose". There was no love lost between Prynne and the Bishop, who together with his servants had called his crop-eared horse "Prynne",[2] and it is Prynne who has the last word.

THE CHAPTER IN 1634

Since we last looked at the Chapter in 1620 it has almost completely changed and the list is now as follows:

Thomas Mallory, D.D., Dean	1607
William Foster, D.D., Subdean	1618
John Ley, B.D.	1627
William Bispham, M.A.	1632
Charles Duckworth, M.A.	1634
Dove Bridgeman, M.A.	1634
Essex Clarke, B.C.L.	1634

William Foster died this year and was succeeded by *William Chillingworth*, of whom nothing is known unless he is to be identified with the famous controversialist against the Romanists. But the latter was made Canon of Salisbury in 1638, while our Accounts show that our

[1] *Antipathie to the English Lordly Prelatie both to the Regall Monarchy and Civill Unity*, pt. II, p. 291, quoted in *The Palatine Note-Book*, III, 9.
[2] *Nonconformity in Cheshire* (1864), p. 9.

9

Chillingworth did not vacate his stall at Chester until the summer of 1639, which makes it unlikely that he was the same person.

John Ley took his place as Subdean. An M.A. of Christ Church, Oxford, he was an ardent Puritan and must have been a very uncongenial colleague for the rest of the Chapter. He had been Vicar of Great Budworth since 1616. He was a busy pamphleteer in 1640 and besides the book we have already mentioned he wrote a panegyric on Jane Ratcliffe, the brewer's widow, who lived in the corner of Abbey Square. He called it "A Patterne of Pietie, or the Religious life and death of that grave and gracious Matron, Mrs. Jane Ratcliffe, Widow, and Citizen of Chester, 1640".

William Bispham went to Trinity College, Cambridge, in 1618, took his B.A. in 1623 and his M.A. in 1626. He was Rector of Warburton in the following year and became Rector of Eccleston in 1636. He became a Prebendary in 1632 and was made Subdean in place of Ley in 1641.

Charles Duckworth, M.A. of B.N.C., Oxford, was Vicar of Wrockwardine Wood, Salop, in 1617 and two years after he was made Prebendary he was given the Rectory of Dodleston.

Dove Bridgeman, the Bishop's third son, named after his godfather, Bishop Dove of Peterborough, was educated at Magdalene College, Cambridge, whither he went at the age of fifteen. He was thus only twenty-four when his father presented him to a stall in Chester Cathedral in 1634. He succeeded Foster as Rector of Barrow in that year and held also the Rectory of Tattenhall. Three years later he died of a fever.

Essex Clarke, B.C.L. of St Edmund Hall, Oxford, was made Rector of Tilston in 1631.

Dove Bridgeman's death enabled his father to repay the Archbishop for all he had done for him, for into the vacancy thus created he placed the Archbishop's nephew by marriage, Dr Edward Morton, who also succeeded as Subdean. Two years later, however, Ley resumed his old office and Morton appears in his rightful place at the bottom of the list.

Laud wrote to Bishop Bridgeman:

> I thank you heartily for your letters of September 22; and though a fair opportunity be offered for Dr. Morton, yet I am heartily sorry for the death of your son, and I would rather have had any other opportunity than the one so caused. . . . It will be best for Dr. Morton to take the prebend and the parsonage of Barrow; and to exchange the benefice he now hath for Tattenhall. . . . If you go on in this way [that I have suggested]

Dr. Morton must have a dispensation which shall be granted him for the holding of two livings so soon as I hear which are the two he pitches on.[1]

He pitched on Barrow and Tattenhall, but exchanged the former for Sefton, Lancs., in 1639. He was educated at Eton and King's College, Cambridge. His eldest son William, who afterwards became Bishop of Kildare and of Meath, was born in Chester in 1641 and Dr Morton's signature to the terms of the surrender of the City shows that he was there during the siege.

For the sake of completeness mention must be made of one other prebendary who does not fit into the above list. This is William Hellier, who was probably the Bishop's brother-in-law. He occupied the fifth stall from 1624 to 1627 and returned in 1632 to hold the second stall for two years, evidently to keep the place warm until Dove Bridgeman was qualified to take it. Hellier was Archdeacon of Barnstaple.

Ship Money

It was just about this time that Charles I exacted ship money from the inland towns as well as from the seaports, which led to Hampden's famous protest. The Dean and Chapter did not protest at having to pay the tax, but they denied the right of the City to assess them and claimed that their contribution was a free gift. The Mayor complained to the Privy Council as follows:

> So also the Dean and Chapter, having also upon two former [?] paid 20 nobles a time, and having been told that they ought to pay with the City [not with the County], yet Dean Mallory on this last writ wrote unto the writer that, unless they would waive the rigid words "assessing" and "demanding", and accept 20 nobles as a free gift, they would leave the writers to their course and now they refuse to pay with the City, and have lately paid with the Shire.[2]

The next entry of Ship money in the Accounts is torn, but enough remains to show that the Dean and Chapter had their way:

1639, to the Sheriff . . . nty for Ship money   XLV s.

The Bishop upheld them in this action.

THE KING'S SCHOOL

In its early days the King's School had no fixed abode. In 1578 the headmaster complained that "the schoole where he teacheth" was ruinous, but gave no indication as to where that was. A writer in 1638

---

[1] Bridgeman, p. 400.   [2] *Cal. State Papers Dom.*, 1638.

spoke of St Nicholas Chapel as being "anciently called the School house".[1] In 1634 a lease of the west side of Abbey Square to Jane Ratcliffe, the brewer's widow, mentioned "one ground chamber which was sometimes the Schoolhouse" and "that building, room or house over the brewhouse of the said Jane Ratcliffe where the Free School was lately kept", and we have seen that the Archbishop, prompted by Bishop Bridgeman, says "the fourth side (where the Grammar School stood) is turned to a common Brewhouse". All these references to the School are in the past tense. The School had been there, we are told, but is not there now. However, our pursuit is rewarded at last, for in 1612 the School is definitely located in St Oswald's Church, of all places. The St Oswald's Accounts have the following entries:

1612 Paid for mending the partition between the Chancel and
     the School   4 d.
1613 Item payde for making a hole in a pillar of stone and
     sodering a peace of iron therein to houlde upp the
     partition between the chancell and the school   xii d.

That the housing of the School in the south transept of the Cathedral was only a temporary measure until fresh quarters could be obtained is made clear by the following entries in the Cathedral Accounts which show that some other place was being prepared:

1613 payd to a mason for making a Corbell hole in the wall
     of the new schole   ii s.   vi d.
     payd for little neyles for the vawt of the maysters deske   ii d.
     April 24 payd to Arratt Watt and his men for workman-
     ship in the new Schole the firste weeke   xxiii s.   ii d.
     April 30 payd to the sayd Arratt Watt and his men for
     work in the new Schole in the second weeke   xxv s.   ii d.
     Payd to Laborrer for makinge cleane after the wrights
     had ended   viii d.
     payd for a payre of Hinges for the higher desk and for
     2 Hookes to fasten the deske into the wall   xiiii d.
     to the slater for worke done over all the new Schole   xxiii s.   ii d.
     payd for muringe up a little vaule (?) at the west ende
     of the frater with storne and lyme   ii s.
     payd for making up window over the frater dore with
     laths and clay   xii d.

The mention of the frater in the last two extracts suggests the site of this new school. This is confirmed by the following extract:

1614 payd to Sonal Shaw sclater for workmanship over the
     free school or ffratry   vii s.   viii d.

         [1] *Sheaf*, xlii, No. 8924. Harl. MS. 1994, f. 475.

Further confirmation is to be found in Bishop Bridgeman's document about the Singing men's houses (1626) where he speaks of "parts of the Monks' Hall now made the Grammar School".

The extracts establish the fact that the King's School, after moving about between the Abbey Square and St Nicholas Chapel and a temporary sojourn in St Oswald's Church, took up its permanent abode in the Refectory in 1613, and not in the second half of the seventeenth century as had previously been supposed.

THE SHADOW OF WAR

The remaining Accounts for the years 1637–9 and 1641–2 contain indications that the war clouds are gathering, but items of general interest will be taken first.

1637-38. Jan. 13, to a Joiner for mending the forme at wch. the Letanie useth to be read	xvi d.
To the mason for mending breaches in south side of the church. 58 yards of new flags and 40 yards of old	iii li. xviii s. iiii d.
To Henry Hughes for going to Mr. Sheriffe with the ship money ii s. vi d., for his horse hire ii s. viii d., and for his meat being forth all night xviii d.	vi s. viii d.
May 19, To Mr. Watmough for mending the grates in the schoole	xx d.
1639 To the joyner for mending the Lord Derbies pew and for nailes	xv d.
1641 Nov. 29, to the Lady Grenour for the interest on her lxviii li. this last year v li.	viii s.
1642 April 21, to John Johnson and Thomas Ashton pt. of their moneys for whiteing the church	xl s.
April 26, to Henry Hughes for paper to cover the top of the organs while the church was whited	ii d.

This may have been the occasion when Bishop Bridgeman paid £20 to have the Cathedral "washed all over withinside". The total amount paid by the Dean and Chapter was £7.

May 21, to John Johnson for defacing an image in east end of the Quire and plastering it over by Mr. Subdean's appointment	v s.

It is difficult to imagine what image there could have been left to deface by this time, and the Subdean was William Bispham, not the Puritan John Ley. However, it appears from a letter written by the Mayor, Thomas Cowper, to Sir Thomas Smith and Mr Francis Gamul, dated 26 March in this same year, that the Cathedral had also some "scandalous pictures", probably pictures of saints. The House of

Commons had made an order for the removal of all such pictures from churches and the Mayor writes that he believes the order has been observed in all churches in Chester, except the Cathedral. Mr Bispham, to whom he sent a message on the subject, said that he could not move without the Dean and the rest of the brethren.[1]

And now we come to the items which foreshadow war. As long ago as 1608 the Dean and Chapter had been ordered to provide a light horse as their contribution to the militia, but it is not until 1618 that we find Edmund being sent to train one. Bishop Bridgeman in 1625 made some alterations to the apportionment of arms from the clergy which had been made by Bishop Lloyd, and had them all copied into his ledger (p. 189). Perhaps it was as a result of this that the Dean and Chapter in the following year bought a "dragone" for 11s. 6d., a kind of carbine or musket, and in the autumn of 1628 we have:

to Mr. Holford for the light horse	XXXIII s.	IIII d.

After that there is no further mention of armour until the end of 1638 when it occupies a foremost place in the Accounts:

Nov. 26 to Ric. Warmincham for mending the saddle of the light horse	V s.	
to Tho. Malbon for sword, cap, belt, dragoone, girdle, and a knapsacke	XX s.	X d.
to Ric. Warmincham for furniture to the light horse saddle	XII s.	
1638-39 Jan. 14, to Mr. Bisphams man goeing to Latchford heath with the light horse	XXII s.	VI d.
to Mr. Hurleston for a light horse for the Kings sermer	XXI li.	
April 3 Contribution [torn] towards the warres [in Scotland]	XX li.	
to John Malbon for a buff coat	XXXVIII s.	
May 2. payd to make up the hundred marks to his Majesty	XVI li. XII s.	VIII d.
May 21, to Mr. Bispham for keeping the horse 16 weekes after 3s. 4d. the weeke and some charges he had layd out upon him	II li. XIX s.	IIII d.

We have to jump now to 27 November 1641:

to the ringers for ringing upon the newes of his Majestys return out of Scotland Nov. 27, 1641 and November 30	V s.	
to H. Hughes for a bonfire the same day	III s.	VIII d.

Charles had returned from Scotland on 25 November. He had gone there in August to try and win over the Scots to his side against

[1] Hist. MSS. Com., v, 310.

Parliament, who had by this time abolished the Court of Star Chamber, executed Strafford and (23 Nov.) passed the Grand Remonstrance. Charles' failure to make an alliance with the Presbyterian Scots was the cause of the bell-ringing and bonfires on two different days and they show how unpopular this pro-Scotch policy was.

1641-42 Dec. 16 to Ric. Warmingham for mending the light horses bridle	vi d.
In part of the hundred markes due to his majesty upon bond this Hilarie term 1641	xxi li. xiii s. iiii d.
March 9. to H. Hughes for nailes vi d. for mending the bolt of the great gate and the locke of the prison door	xviii d.
1642 June 30 to Mr. Chancellors man for shewing the light horse at Little Budworth and for powder	v s. viii d.
July 11, to Henry Hughes for a bagge for the souldier to carry his shott and for powder	vi d.
July 22, for shewing the light horse at Hartill, and for powder by H. Hughes	vi d.
Aug. 10, to Henry Hughes for a bushell of oates for the light horse	x s. xi d.
to him for a horsecloth at the same time	iii s. ii d.
to him for a collar, sursingle and pillow	iii s. iiii d.

There are several other similar entries, but enough have been quoted to show that the light horse had a prominent place at this time in the minds of the Dean and Chapter. And with reason, for on 22 August in this year the King set up his standard at Nottingham and the Civil War began. In September he reached Chester and stayed with the Bishop in the palace:

Sept. 26, to his Majesty's footmen their fees for the canopie and carpet	iii li.
Sept. 27. to the ringers at his Majesty being here	v s.
to Tho. Bradb. wife for herbes to rub the seates when his majesty was here	xii d.
to one Mr. Barton robbed and maimed by the rebells Sept. 14	xii d.
1642-43 Jan. 27. to Mr. Dean wch. layd out the mending of the churches Dragoon	vi d.
May 10, payd to the City by Mr. Deane for provision as he delivered it on account. [for the siege which began on July 18]	xx li.
Dec. 27, to the ringers upon the Defeate given at Middlewich	ii s. vi d.

This was on 26 December when the Royalists caught their opponents between Middlewich and Northwich, killed 200 and took another 200 prisoners.[1]

[1] F. H. Crossley, *Cheshire*, p. 225.

In 1645 Charles I paid his second and last visit to Chester at the head of a force intended to raise the siege. He entered the City from Wales by the Dee Bridge, sending his troops round by Holt to cross the river there and take the besiegers in the rear. However, the Royalists were defeated at Rowton Moor and Charles had the mortification of watching them in full flight across Hoole Heath while he stood helpless and inactive on the tower on the Wall which still bears his name. Removing from there, perhaps to get a better view, or it may be a safer one, he climbed to the top of the Cathedral tower, where, says a contemporary account: "as he was talking with a capitaine, a bullet from St John's gave him a salute, narrowly missing the King, and hit the said Capitaine in the head, who died in the place. This sorry entertainment forced the King next day to leave us and secure himself elsewhere."[1] Now it is not too fantastic to suppose that it was while Charles was groping his way down those dark and winding stairs in the tower, his heart full of grief for what he had been witnessing and his mind shaken by his own narrow escape, that he made the decision which ultimately led to his imprisonment and death. For he decided to leave Chester next morning and *go back to Wales*. But he had been on his way to Scotland where, if the worst had come to the worst he could have escaped to France and so saved his head even if he lost his crown, and this decision to turn back (though he had no option after Rowton Moor) sealed his fate.

[2] Harl. MS., 2155, quoted in *C.A.J.*, xxv, p. 226.

4

AFTER THE RESTORATION

1660–1701

No time was lost at the Restoration in restoring the Cathedral to its former state and use. Charles II came back from "his travels" on 22 May 1660, and on 13 June Henry Bridgeman, third son of old Bishop Bridgeman, was appointed Dean, for William Nicholls, who had been appointed to succeed Mallory in 1644, died in 1658 before he could come into office. One of his first duties would have been to welcome the new Bishop, an account of whose arrival has been left us by Dr Thomas Cowper[1]:

> Almost all the gentry and clergy of Cheshire [he writes] went out to meet Dr. Bryan Walton, who was coming to take possession of the Bishopric. The militia both of City and County were drawn up along Forest Street, and at the Bars the Mayor and Corporation in their formalities received their new Bishop and proceeded before him to the palace amidst the acclamations of the people, expressing the greatest joy for the restoration of Episcopacy. On his arrival he immediately put on his robes and hastened to perform his devotions in the Cathedral.

Another account[2] adds:

> At his entering the Cathedral he was received by Dr. Bridgeman (the Dean) and all the members of the Chapter, who paid their respects to their Diocesan, and having walked round the Choir in the manner of a procession, they conducted him to his throne.

We have first to inquire who were all the members of the Chapter and how far they were the same as those who were ejected from their

---

[1] Cowper MSS. Note-book marked "VII cc." Also quoted by Ormerod, I, 248.
[2] Ibid., XIII cc.

prebends by Parliament. Old Dean Mallory had died in Chester on 3 April 1644, at the age of seventy-eight. Poor man, he lived to see five of his sons give their lives for the King, but was spared seeing the surrender of the City. Prebendary Essex Clarke had also died and was buried at Tilston, the church from which he had been ejected on 5 January 1653-4. The rest of the Chapter were still alive and could reassemble at Chester full of tales of poverty and hardship, always excepting the Puritan, John Lee, of whom more hereafter.

There would be *William Bispham*, who had been Subdean in 1641-3. He could tell how he had been deprived of his living of Eccleston in 1644 and how he had been accused of joining with Archdeacon Snell, Rector of Waverton, and with Prebendary Duckworth in equipping a man and a horse for the Royal army. (The horse proved to be a most unmanageable brute and it must have been a relief to its rider when it was killed at Edgehill.) Bispham is said to have fled abroad, "*hinc inde agitatus*", as his epitaph on the wall of the north Choir aisle records. His wife, however, remained in Chester in a house in St Oswald's Ward, and so probably in the precincts, and in 1645 there were three in her family, not counting the soldier quartered on her, and she had only two pecks of meal left.[1] In 1646 she was allowed a sixth of her husband's living.

Charles Duckworth, his partner in the horse, was ejected from Dodleston Rectory in 1646, but remained nearby in Flintshire.

Edward Moreton also remained on the spot, for he was in Chester, all through the siege and was one of the Commissioners appointed by the Governor, Lord Byrom, to treat with the enemy and arrange the terms of surrender.[2] He had been ejected from Sephton and from Tattenhall in 1645, but his wife Elizabeth was allowed a fifth of the income of the former benefice.

Robert Morgan, who was educated at Jesus College, Cambridge, had been a member of the Chapter only since 1 July 1642, when he succeeded another Welshman, David Lloyd. (Lloyd's stay at the Cathedral was very brief. Appointed in 1639, he resigned in 1642 in order to become Dean of St Asaph.) Morgan had two livings in Anglesey as well as his Chester prebend, and as he had the foresight to purchase in 1642 what remained of a long lease of the tithes of one of them (Llanddyfnan), he still had something to live on during the Commonwealth although deprived of both his benefices. At the Restoration these were

---

[1] *Cheshire Sheaf*, 3rd Ser., IV, 60, quoting Harl. MS., 2185.
[2] *C.A.J.*, n.s., XXV, 195.

restored to him together with his prebend, *pace* the *Dictionary of National Biography*. He was also made Archdeacon of Merioneth. He left Chester in 1666 to become Bishop of Bangor.

Thomas Mallory would be the only newcomer, joining the Chapter in July 1660. He was the fourth son of the late Dean and had been Rector of Northenden since 1634. The Dean and Chapter presented him to St Mary's, Chester, in February, 1662, and in April of that year he was given a dispensation to hold Eccleston, Co. Lancs., whither he betook himself in 1663. He died there in 1671.[1]

All these would have had a hard struggle to live unless they were possessed of ample private means or could have a chaplaincy in a noble household, for even school teaching was forbidden. *John Lee*, Vicar of Great Budworth, was the one exception, for being an avowed Puritan he fared well at the hands of Parliament. On 3 June 1646, the Committee for Plundered Ministers ordered that he should have the profits of his prebend in view of "his great worth, the services to the Church of his pen and ministry, his extraordinary pains in the Assembly of Divines, and his suffering in estate for fidelity to the cause of God and Parliament". How his estate suffered is not clear, for he was President of Sion College in 1645, he retained his living of Great Budworth until 1648 and in addition had been presented by the House of Commons on 27 July 1643, to the sequestrated living of St Mary's-at-Hill in the London Diocese, and in 1645 to the Rectory of Charlwood in Surrey, which last living he bestowed upon his son. The following year he secured Astbury (Cheshire) for himself,[2] valued at £800 a year, the ejected minister being Thomas Dod, a former prebendary of Lee's own cathedral, and to it he added Brightwell (Berks.). He was also appointed one of the Triers in 1653. The Restoration found Lee in the benefice of Solihull, which he soon afterwards resigned through ill-health and went to live at Sutton Coldfield where he died on 16 May 1662. It may therefore have been ill health which prevented Lee from joining his former colleagues at Chester in 1660, but what the colleagues thought is revealed in a resolution passed in Chapter on 8 April 1662, to the effect that his house in the precincts should be used for someone else, in view of "his continual absenting himself from us, notwithstanding due and lawful summons, not to mention the disservices he hath done us, and his disaffection to us now".

---

[1] *Sheaf*, o.s. I, 90, 95.
[2] "The people would not pay tithes to him, so he returned to Great Budworth in 1649." The Rev. L. M. Farrell in *C.A.J.*, n.s., XXI, 163.

On his death his stall was filled by Michael Evans, Rector of Llan-
faelog, and in 1663 Simon Land succeeded Thomas Mallory.

The Dean and Chapter in 1664 was constituted as follows:

Henry Bridgeman, D.D., Dean	1660
William Bispham, D.D.	1634
Charles Duckworth, M.A.	1634
Edward Moreton, D.D.	1637
Robert Morgan, D.D.	1642
Michael Evans, B.D. (vice John Lee)	1662
Simon Land, M.A. (vice Thomas Mallory)	1662

Lecturer: Thomas Bridge
Petty Canons: Peter Stringer
             Thomas Ottye
             William Ottye
             John Pilkington

Note that there are four petty canons now instead of six.

The new Dean, as we have seen, was Henry Bridgeman. Educated
at Oriel College, Oxford, he became a fellow of Brazenose, but
resigned his fellowship to become Rector of Barrow in 1639 and of
Bangor Isycoed (his father's old living) in 1640. In 1648 his father
appointed him to the Archdeaconry of Richmond, which, considering
the date, could only have been a defiant gesture on the part of the old
man, who died at Kinnerley in Shropshire four years later. During
the Civil War Henry Bridgeman, who owned a house in Northgate
Ward during the siege,[1] was chaplain to the Earl of Derby. At the
Restoration he was rewarded for his services to the Royal cause by
being made Dean of Chester and Prebendary of York, his two benefices were restored to him and he added to them the sinecure living of
Llanrwst. He also became a D.D. The Archdeaconry of Richmond he
vacated on being made Dean. Sir Peter Leycester, writing at Tabley
Hall at this time, says, "He hath beautified and repaired the Dean's
house in Abbey Court very much". Philip Henry, father of the famous
Matthew Henry, who could not be expected to be so sympathetic,
recorded in his diary in December 1661 that Bridgeman was "busy in
repairing the Dean's house as if he were to live in it for ever". It was a
large house, for it paid tax for twelve hearths.[2] That the Dean was not
without his enemies and traducers is shown by a certificate preserved
at the Public Record Office and signed by William Bispham, Charles
Duckworth, Robert Moreton, Thomas Mallory, and Thomas Bridge,

[1] *C.A.J.*, n.s., XXV, 241.   [2] *Lancs. and Ches. Record Soc.*, LII, p. 54.

Reader in Theology, and dated 1 September 1668. It is in Latin and testifies to the high excellence and merits of the Dean, as to his learning, loyalty and conformity to the Church; lauding his attention to the music of the choir, his liberality in improving the Dean and Chapter's houses, and his faithful administration of discipline. An accompanying letter, also in Latin, states that the Dean has been "attacked by the rage of calumny by some mean spirits, as the dogs of Arcadia feared not to bark at the moon".[1]

Michael Evans, B.D. matriculated from St John's College, Cambridge, in 1624 at the age of seventeen, and three years later matriculated from Magdalen College, Oxford, where he graduated in 1627–8. However he came back to Cambridge for his B.D. in 1642. His first living was Tarrant Rawston, Dorset, but in 1636 he returned to his native land to become Prebendary of Bangor with two benefices to go with it. When he came to Chester as Prebendary he retained his prebend at Bangor until his death in 1670. Indeed, he seems to have added a third prebend of Brecknock.

Simon Land, M.A., at the time of his appointment was Vicar of St Oswald's, Chester, and continued as such until he gave way to Laurence Fogge in 1672, a future prebendary and dean. He was, however, also Vicar of Waverton from 1662 to his death in 1677 and Cowper says that in addition he held the living of Pensance, where he was buried.[2]

The minor officials of the Cathedral were not so fortunate as the Chapter, for only three out of the six Petty Canons (Henry Biddulph, William Clark, sen., and John Pilkington) returned to duty in 1660 and only two of the Lay Clerks or Conducts (Mr Maxey and Peter Stringer). The latter had served the Cathedral all his life, beginning as a chorister in 1627 and going on to be a Conduct in 1637. In 1662 he was ordained and made a Petty Canon and in addition was Organist, Chanter (or Precentor) and Master of the Choristers.[3] There is no doubt that all these officials had a struggle to live during the Commonwealth and we have evidence for this. On 2 January 1655–6 the Committee for Plundered Ministers ordered the payment of £5 towards the relief of Peter Warner, "one of the late singing men" in Chester Cathedral, and on 15 July of the same year they directed the treasurer to pay £20 to several "members and officers of the late hierarchy". Again, on 1 December 1657, £10 was paid by the Trustees for the Maintenance of Ministers to six of the officials including Pilkington,

---

[1] *L. & P. Dom. Chas. II*, No. 66.   [2] *Calamy.*
[3] See Dr Bridge in *C.A.J.*, n.s., XIX, Pt. II.

Stringer, and Biddulph, and on 3 February of the following year another £5 was so distributed.[1]

One official remains to be dealt with and that is Thomas Bridge, who held the office of Lecturer created by Queen Elizabeth in 1582. He remained in Chester, living in a house in St Oswald's Ward with seventeen in his household and he shared with Dr Moreton the honour of being chosen to act as a Commissioner to make terms with the besiegers. He was afterwards charged with distributing muskets provided by Lord Cholmondley to any who were ready to serve against Parliament about the year 1642. He was also Rector of Malpas (upper mediety) to which he was restored in 1660. After the fall of the City he was made chaplain to Lord Cholmondley and later on held the same post under the Earl of Northumberland at Petworth in Sussex. In 1654 he seems to have swallowed his scruples and been admitted by the Committee of Triers to the Rectory of Tillington in the same county.[2]

THE CATHEDRAL DURING THE COMMONWEALTH

Very little is known about the fate of the cathedrals in England during the Commonwealth and practically nothing about Chester. We know that the south transept, which was also St Oswald's parish church, continued in use and a Mr Harrison was the incumbent. This may explain why the Cathedral organ was spared. Payments amounting to £470 p.a. were to be made out of the revenues of the Dean and Chapter for the support of preachers at St Oswald's, St Peter's, St John's, and £45 p.a. to the headmaster and usher of the Free School.[3] The fabric does not seem to have been seriously damaged. It is true that Randle Holme in his list of buildings damaged and destroyed by the siege includes "the ruine of the great church", but gives no details[4]; and Sir Peter Leycester, writing in 1660 of Bishop Bridgeman, says "he lies buried, chair and almost church and all, in the said cathedral ruins of St. Werburgh, at Chester", but as Bishop Bridgeman was not buried there but at Kinnerley near Oswestry in Shropshire we may be allowed to doubt the historical accuracy of the old knight's statement. Unfortunately the Cathedral accounts are missing for the years 1660–4, so that we have no means of knowing how much had to be spent in restoration work during those first four years; when they do begin

---

[1] Tatham, p. 284, quoting *Plundered Ministers Accounts*, ed. W. A. Shaw, II, 108.
[2] Walker.   [3] *C.A.J.*, *XXV*, quoting Assembly Book, 664.
[4] *C.A.J.*, n.s., xxv, 205.

there is no suggestion of any extra expenditure caused by the War. The Chapter House seems to be an exception, for the Chapter Minute book records that at the fourth meeting of the Chapter it was decided to move to the Vestry because "the old meeting place for the Chapter is ruynat and in decay", but they were only away from it eight months, February to October 1661. Dr Cowper, writing in 1728,[1] however, says that the Chapter House "fared very ill at the time of the Great Rebellion in England, the roof whereof was entirely stript and the windows taken away". We are also told that the lead was taken from the roof of the cloisters. Be that as it may, the Chapter House was in use during this period, as the following extracts from the Accounts show:

1671	Oct. 24, paid for a carpet for the Chapter House	13	6
1676	Dec. 19, for making up a breach in the Chapter house wall	1	8
1681	May 3, pd. Tho. Rogers for securing old Chapter house windows	15	0
1691	Dec. 8, for coals to burn in the Chapter house last audit		9
1697	Nov. 16, for a carpet for the Chapter house and a cushion for the church	5	0

It is worth noticing in this connection that the Refectory, "lately used" for the King's School, was repaired by the City in 1657. £60 was levied on the freemen and contributions invited from non-freemen. To commemorate this Mr Peter Leigh, the Mayor, had his initials and date inscribed on the wall over the former dais, with two shields, one bearing the arms then used by the mayors, and the other the arms of the Ironmongers Company of which Leigh was a member.

Mr. P (shield) L.M.   16 (shield) 57.

The first shield bears the arms, a sword erect between three garbs, and the second, a chevron between three steel gads, three swivels, the centre one palewise, the others chevronwise.[2]

But if the Cathedral escaped there is no doubt that the Bishop's Palace, which adjoined it, suffered severely. Dr Cowper says that in 1650: "The Bishop's palace, with all the furniture, was sold, Dec. 13, to Robert Moller and William Richardson for £1059." In 1674 Bishop Wilkins took a case to the Consistory Court at York to try and recover some of the cost of dilapidations from his predecessor. Evidence was given there that one Mr Richardson of Boughton "pretended to have bought the palace of the Parliament... about the

[1] Cowper MSS., *A Cursory View of Chester*, 1728.
[2] P. H. Lawson, F.S.A., in *The King's School Magazine* (Autumn, 1951), pp. 37, 38.

year 1646" and had stripped the lead off the Great Hall and the Green
Hall which opened out of it (both on the site of the present Choir
School playground). Also "a great part of the palace . . . was de-
molished and that part of it that was left standing was made use of
for the common gaol of the county, so that when Bishop Walton came
to be Bishop there it was very ruinous".[1] Furthermore the City Assembly Books for 25 March 1651, record: "Ordered that certain com-
mittees shall treat with Mr. Richardson for the purchase of the late
Bishop's palace for the City's use."[2] Bishop Walton had to spend
£1,500 to make it habitable, and Bishop Hall spent £700. In 1664 tax
was paid on 17 hearths, five of which were due to "new building",
not counting the one in "The Lord Bishop's garden house new built"
which was in the Northgate Ward, whereas the palace was in St
Oswald's.[3]

One deficiency that undoubtedly had to be made good was the
Cathedral silver plate, for none of the old plate survived the Civil
War. The legend that it still lies hidden in some secret hiding place
may be discounted; it is much more likely to have been sacrificed in
the Royal cause or confiscated by a victorious Parliament. Anyhow,
none of the plate now in use is earlier than 1662, and it is quite evident
from an examination of it that in that year a set of Communion vessels
was obtained consisting of

2 large flagons	2 chalices
2 large patens	2 candlesticks
2 small patens	2 maces

The flagons bear the arms of Bishop Hall (1662–8) and so were presumably his gift. Peter Stringer, the Precentor, said in evidence in 1673
that he thought the Bishop spent £100 on it. The two small patens
bear the arms of Dean Bridgeman, in one case alone and in the other
impaled with the arms of the See of Chester. One of the two maces
also bears the Dean's arms. The other may have done so, but the top
of it where the inscription would have been has been clumsily replaced
at some later date. The two large patens and the candlesticks bear no
inscription or arms. The large alms dish was made in 1673 and I suggest
that it was bought to replace the original one which was stolen by a
thief in 1672 (see below, p. 138).
Our survey of the Cathedral at the Restoration would not be

[1] *C.A.J.*, n.s., xxxvII, Pt. II.   [2] *Lancs. and Ches. Record Soc.*, LII, pp. 57, 60.
[3] *C.A.J.*, n.s., xxxvII, Pt. II. p. 306.

complete without a statement about the finances. It so happens that a rental of the Cathedral property compiled by Ellis Rycroft in 1663 has been preserved in the back pages of a MS. copy of the statutes.[1] This gives the total income of the Dean and Chapter in that year as £984 12s. 8d., which is almost the same as it was in 1582, the year of the Leicester award. But if we allow for one rental of £40 being counted twice over and a mistake in addition which the good Ellis Rycroft has corrected in a re-cast on the inside of the cover but has not corrected in the text, the total is whittled down to £934 0s. 6d. There follows a list of the annual payments which had to be made exclusive of any money spent on the day-to-day expenses of the Cathedral:

	£	s.	d.		£	s.	d.
To the Dean	120	0	0	Butler	6	0	0
6 Prebendaries	160	0	0	Cook	6	0	0
Divinity Lecturer	40	0	0	Barber	2	0	0
6 Petty Canons	90	0	0	Glasier	6	13	4
6 Conducts	60	0	0	Slater	6	13	4
Organist	12	0	0	Overseer	3	0	0
Master of the Choristers	10	0	0	Bell keeper	1	10	0
8 choristers	26	13	4	Clock keeper	1	6	8
2 schoolmasters	32	0	0	Minister of Shotwick	15	0	0
24 King's Scholars	80	0	0	Minister of Bromborough	4	6	8
6 Almsmen	40	0	0	Minister of Chelford	4	6	8
Subdean (extra)	2	0	0	Minister of Ince	4	6	8
Receiver (extra)	4	0	0	Minister of Wirvin	3	6	8
Treasurer (extra)	4	0	0	Minister of S. Bridget's	4	0	0
Chanter (extra)	2	0	0	Minister of S. Oswald's	1	13	4
Sacrist (extra)	2	0	0	his assistant at Easter	0	13	4
Steward	6	13	4	Procurations to the Bishop	3	13	6
Counsell	2	0	0	Gable rent to the City	0	6	3
Chapter Clerk	3	6	8	King's rent	106	16	5
Auditor	10	0	0				
2 subsacrists (vergers)	12	0	0	The whole paymts. are £910		7	2
2 porters	10	0	0				

It is not surprising that in these circumstances the fabric of the cathedral was neglected and that considerable borrowing took place.

As has already been said, there is nothing in the Accounts for the year 1664 to suggest large-scale repairs of war damage. Moses Dalby was paid £35 for "glazing about the church according to agreement", the north aisle of the choir was re-slated and the plumber and carpenter received £3 9s. 10d. and £4 14s. 3d. respectively for work done over the Broad Aisle, but that was all. The organ, however, was thoroughly

[1] Preserved in the Cathedral Library.

overhauled and decorated. Dr Bridge calls it a new organ, but the prices paid do not bear this out[1]:

	£	s.	d.
1665 Feb. 7, pd. Anne and Richard Meacock for soder for the organ	1	8	2
pd. William Darwell for leather for the organ	1	14	8
pd. Mr. Reas and John Frye for making the organ	19	14	8
April 25, pd. Mr. Basnett for coloure for the organ		8	6
April 26, pd. Mr. Doley for gold for Mr. Hodges use at the organ	1	15	6
May 22, pd. Mr. Hodges for painting the organ and stuffe found by him	36	3	0
June 30, pd. Mr. Bispham wch. he laid out to buy gold to gild the organ and colure	22	0	0
pd. Thomas Dunnin carver for carving about the organ	10	0	0
	£93	4	6

Other interesting items are:

	£	s.	d.
1664 Jan. 1, pd. John Ward for carving the gilt work over the screene	1	14	8
pd. Urian Minshull for dyeing the cloth for the reading desk		6	8
pd. Thomas Bradburne for the use of Mr. William Clark who was sent for to the Quire at my Ld. of Ormond's coming to Chester	1	7	6

Thomas Bradburne was one of the two vergers and the Duke of Ormonde was Lord Lieutenant of Ireland and therefore often passed through Chester on his way to and from that island. He was generally given a present of wine (see p. 139). William Clark may have been the son of William Clark (sen.) who occurs as a Petty Canon on p.131.

	£	s.	d.
1664 pd. for carrying the new hangings from My Lady Calveleyes and to John Ward and others for viewing the carved work		4	6
1666 March 31, paid Ralph Almond for 5 dosen hookes for the new Hangings & putting them up		3	6
May 1, paid Mr. Maycocke for lineing the hangings	2	17	0

These hangings have always been thought to be the Raphael tapestry now on the west wall of the refectory. Lady Calveley, the reputed donor, was the wife of the last of the Calveleys of Lea Hall, now in the parish of Aldford. She was left a widow in 1648 and is said, according

[1] At Wells, immediate repairs to the organ in 1662 cost £80, but the new organ was to cost £800. Quoted by Moore, p. 97. See *A Short History of the Organs of Wells Cathedral*, Wells, 1951.

to a MS. in the British Museum,[1] to have built Calveley Hall on Milton Green in 1674. If this is correct, the hangings which came to the Cathedral in 1664 could not have come from there but must have come from Lea Hall, unless they came from her town house in Chester. For she had a town house in 1662, when on 3 February she was granted a seat in St Oswald's Church. The Chancellor, John Wainwright, pronounced that "Whereas the Virtuous Lady, Dame Mary Calveley, widow, a constant and good Churchman and frequenter of Divine [service], especially at the Cathedral, where her charity hath been eminently extended, is now an inhabitant within the City of Chester, and hath a good and considerable estate lying within the Parish of St. Oswald in the same City etc."[2] Mr Thomas Hughes, who quotes this document, says that Lea Hall in those days was in the parish of St Oswald, Bruera being a chapel of the same.

It is, however, possible that the "hangings" do not refer to the tapestry at all, which may have quite a different provenance. For in November or December, 1907, the late T. Stanley Ball, author of *Church Plate of the City of Chester*, wrote an article in the *Wigan Examiner* on the tapestry and claimed to be able "to throw some additional light upon its history", but unfortunately did not give the source of his information. In the article he wrote: "Bishop Bridgeman purchased a set of tapestries from his Royal Master the King, worked at the Royal Tapestry works at Mortlake from the original designs of Raphael. What became of them is not known, save that he presented one to the Cathedral Church of Chester, one to the Collegiate Church of Manchester and one to his own Church at Wigan."[3] It has been suggested that Ball's special information came from Canon Bridgeman's notes which may have been still in the library of Wigan Rectory when he wrote his article and may have contained extracts from Bishop Bridgeman's private account books. These are the two theories and the reader must choose between them. Certainly Mr Ball must have had some source of information to have enabled him to be so dogmatic upon the subject. Would that he had told us what that source was. And certainly Manchester and Wigan have Raphael tapestries to this day, so that the evidence is manifestly in favour of Bishop Bridgeman rather than of Lady Calveley.

[1] Harl. MS., 2010, f. 43. See *Sheaf*, 3rd Ser., XVII, 36, 47, and XVIII, 32.
[2] *Sheaf*, O.S., III, 250. The house was taxed on 15 hearths. *L. & C. Record Soc.*, LII.
[3] Information contributed by Mr A. J. Hawkes, F.S.A., who also made the suggestion which follows.

                                                                 s. d.
    1666   May 29, pd. for 3 fox tailes   1   0

This, the only entry of its kind, is a strange one to find here.

                                                                 s. d.
    1666   June 9, paide John ffletcher for ringing for the victory
           obtained against the Dutch   8   0
           Aug. 23, paide for ringing the thanksgiving day for the
           victory obtained against the Dutch   10   0

This was the Battle off Lowestoft on 3 June, news of which reached
Pepys in London on 8 June.

                                                            £   s.   d.
    1669   July 4, pd. for cutting the weedes in the sprice   6
           paid for slateing of the South Ile & for slates, lime, timber
           and for all other materialls   16 16   8
           & for tyreing of the same[1]   1   8   4
    1670   April 2, for a quart of sacke to the gentleman who sum-
           moned the Deane about arrears   2   6
           Nov. 14, paid for repairing the staires to the pulpit 15   0
           paid for flagging & tyleing the Ile to the pulpitt   9   0
    1671   March 18, pd. the glazier for mending the places broake by
           by the theife & other places   2   0

    The following December the Cathedral was robbed again and the
thieves proved to be notorious highwaymen. They were arrested and
tried at York, and John Harrison, who combined the offices of conduct
and cathedral barber, was sent to York to identify the silver. The
official report of the proceedings states that on 8 January 1672-3:

    John Harrison, an officer of the Cathedral Church of Chester, saith that, on
    the 15th December last, the Cathedrall Church of Chester was robd of
    two silver candlesticks richly guilt and imbossed, and one large silver
    charger guilt, and that a silver head guilt with a face upon it, now shewed
    him, is parte of one of the said candlesticks, and that he knoweth it as well
    as any friende's face hee was ever acquainted with; and that he likewise
    saith that a peece of silver plate guilt now shewed him he veryly believes
    is parte of the said charger.[2]

It is noteworthy that the present alms dish and the pair of candlesticks
on the high altar are not part of the set presented in 1662, for the alms
dish bears the date mark 1673 and the candlesticks 1683.[3] Highwaymen
when seen at close quarters were not the romantic people we are
accustomed to think them, but just burglars on horseback.

    [1] "Tyreing", pronounced "teering" today, means plastering under the tiles.
    [2] Surtees Soc., vol. 40, p. 190.
    [3] T. Stanley Ball was incorrect in saying that the dates were 1669 and 1662
respectively (*Church Plate of the City of Chester*).

	£	s.	d.
1671 April 8, Given to Dr. John Campsius by Mr. Deane's order	10	0	
Oct. 17 paid for Common prayer bookes	4	3	0
Oct. 28 paid for Wyne and bottles presented to the Ld. Leift. of Ireland coming and goeing		2	3
1673 Dec. 6 Raph Almond for hasps & staples for the stocks		4	0
Dec. 16 pd. Andrew Andrew [sic] for the stocks		9	0
1674 March 18, for bonfire and Ringing when peace was proclaimed		4	6

This was the Peace which ended the war with the Dutch, a war which had been arranged by the King himself in alliance with Louis XIV by the Secret Treaty of Dover and which had always been very unpopular in the country.

	s.	d.
1675 Jan. 17. Wm. Jackson for tyreing the side ile	15	0
April 26 pd. for morning draughts for Jackson and Dunbabin	1	0

These "morning draughts" first appear in the Accounts on 17 Jan. 1674, and continue to the end of the century. Dunbabin was the glazier. A good deal of work was done on the Broad Aisle (nave) during 1675. The materials included 8 loads of sand, 6 loads of clay, and 136 bars of lead costing £12 14s. 6d.; while £14 15s. 1d. was paid to the plumbers and £9 7s. 0d. to Thos. ffoulkes, a carpenter[1]:

	£	s.	d.
1674 Nov. 19. pd. for morning draughts for workmen all the worke	1	9	8
1675 Nov. 7. For making a paire of staires at the west end of the Schoole for the Scholars to goe to a fire		7	8

THE BISHOPS OF CHESTER

Little has been said about the Bishops of Chester so far, for they do not seem to have had much to do with the Cathedral in this period.

Bishop Bryan Walton (1660–1), who was welcomed to Chester with such joy, was one of the most famous scholars of his day. A Yorkshireman by birth and a Cambridge man by education, and Chaplain to the King, he was ejected from his benefices by Parliament in 1641 and spent his enforced leisure in studying oriental languages in Oxford, which resulted in the publication of the celebrated Polyglot Bible in 1657, which he edited. Nine different versions are represented in it. Walton died while on a visit to London and was buried in St Paul's Cathedral, November 1661.

[1] He is described as a carpenter in the Holy Trinity (Chester) registers (p. 112) under date 12 Sept., 1656.

Bishop George Hall (1662–8), who died from a wound inflicted by a knife in his pocket when he fell from a mound in the garden of Wigan Rectory, was buried at Wigan, but a copy of his Latin epitaph, written by himself, is affixed to the south-west wall of the Cathedral nave, near the great west doors. It is, perhaps naturally, self-depreciatory in tone. Bishop Hall, however, will always be remembered for his gift of silver plate (see above, p. 134).

Bishop John Wilkins (1668–72), who followed him, had sided with Parliament in the Civil War and during the Commonwealth was Warden of Wadham College, Oxford. In 1659 he was made Master of Trinity College, Cambridge, an appointment he owed to his nephew, Richard Cromwell, for in 1656 Wilkins had married Oliver Cromwell's sister. It seems surprising that a man with a record like that should have been made a bishop by Charles II. Anthony à Wood, who sounds a little biased, says that it was "by the endeavours of George, Duke of Buckingham, a favourer of fanaticism and athesim",[1] but it was part of the policy of the Government to win over as many Puritans as possible. Wood also says: "He was a person endowed with rare gifts; he was a noted theologist and preacher, a curious critic in several matters, an excellent mathematician and experimentalist, and one as well seen in mechanism and new philosophy, of which he was a great promoter as any man of his time."[2] In fact he was scientist as well as ecclesiastic, and while at Wadham had taken a leading part in founding the Royal Society. Among his writings is an attempt to construct a universal language—a sort of seventeenth-century Esperanto; and also an attempt to prove that the earth is one of the planets and that the moon may be inhabited. He even suggested the possibility of some day journeying to it. "I do seriously and upon good grounds affirm it possible," he wrote, "to make a flying chariot; in which a man may sit and give such a motion unto it as shall convey him through the air". The good bishop was a little before his time. In the midst of his essay on a universal language he digresses to show by careful measurements that the Ark could easily have contained the animals that were put into it together with the food that they would require. A diagrammatic illustration shows how all the different animals were stowed away. The other side of his character is shown by two books of devotion that he wrote, one on *The Gift of Prayer* and the other on *The Gift of Preaching*, the latter accompanied by an exhaustive bibliography.[3]

[1] Wood, III, 968.   [2] Wood quoted by Hemingway, I, 308.
[3] These books are all in the Cathedral library.

Bishop John Pearson was also a Fellow of the Royal Society, but was a theologian rather than a scientist, in fact the greatest theologian of his day. Like Bishop Walton he spent his time during the Commonwealth in study, and it is interesting to consider how much learning the Church of England would have lost if the livings of these two men had not been sequestrated. For the result of Pearson's enforced leisure was the publication in 1559 of an *Exposition of the Creed*, which within its limits is said to be "the most perfect and complete production of English dogmatic theology. The notes . . . are at least as remarkable as the text and form a complete catena of the best authorities on doctrinal points." He also interested himself in the promoting of the Polyglot Bible, which established his reputation as a scholar. At the Restoration he was made Master of Jesus College, Cambridge, in 1660 and of Trinity College, Cambridge in 1662. Arriving in Chester in 1672 the Bishop held a Visitation of his Diocese in 1674 and in the following year "visited" the Cathedral and issued injunctions on the lines of those issued by Bishop Bridgeman. He held a second Visitation of the Cathedral in 1677. He died in 1686 and was buried near the high altar. The place of his burial was forgotten and the grave was discovered only by accident in 1841. The body was then moved to the North Transept and a massive and over-ornamented monument surmounted by a recumbent effigy was placed over it in 1863, designed by Sir Arthur Blomfield.[1] There can hardly have been any diocese in England ruled by three such outstanding scholars in succession.

By 1675 there had been many changes in the Chapter which had been reconstituted at the Restoration. In 1666 Dr Robert Morgan was made Bishop of St Asaph and in 1670 Michael Evans died. Charles Duckworth followed him to the grave in 1673 and Dr Edward Moreton the next year. Dean Bridgeman was consecrated Bishop of Man on 1 October 1671, but retained his Deanery. The Chapter in 1675 was as follows:

Henry Bridgeman, D.D., Dean	1660
William Bispham, M.A., Subdean	1634
Simon Land, M.A.	1663
William Finemore, M.A.	1666
Phineas Bury, M.A.	1670
Laurence Fogge, D.D.	1673
William Thompson, M.A.	1675

[1] I suppose Sir Arthur had good authority for giving the bishop a moustache.

William Finemore was the son of a gentleman living at Hincksey near Oxford. He went to Christ Church at the beginning of the Civil War, took his B.A. in 1646 and his M.A. in 1649. At some date he tutored young Philip Henry, father of the more famous Matthew Henry, who had come up to Christ Church in 1647. Finemore became Vicar of Runcorn in 1662, Prebendary and Archdeacon of Chester in 1666 and died in 1686. He was buried in the Cathedral where there is a tablet to his memory in St Erasmus Chapel. Perhaps the most valuable thing he ever did was to nominate a boy named Thomas Wilson to be a scholar at the King's School in 1683, who became the celebrated Bishop of Sodor and Man. There can be no doubt that the three years he spent at the King's School gave Wilson the start he needed and enabled him to go on to Trinity College, Dublin.

Phineas Bury took his degree of B.A. at Wadham College, Oxford, in 1652, and remained there as Fellow until he came to Chester Cathedral in 1670. His living (in 1675) was the Rectory of Southrop, Glos. He died in London, 28 January 1678-9.

Laurence Fogge was the son of Robert Fogge, the minister who was intruded into Bishop Bridgeman's living of Bangor-on-Dee (then in the Chester Diocese) in 1646. He was ordained first by ministers of the Cambridgeshire Association in 1658, but received Episcopal ordination in Galloway in 1661, at which time he was Rector of Hawarden, which also was in the Chester Diocese. As he explained to Calamy in a letter written in 1702, he was not ejected from Hawarden where he had been among the first to restore the Prayer Book in 1660, but he resigned the living at the end of July 1662, because he "scrupled the declaration against resistance to government required by the Act [of Uniformity]". For three years he remained in retirement, but a judicial interpretation of the "Oxford Oath" given by Lord Justice Bridgeman removed his doubts and in 1666 he became curate of Prestwich. In 1672 he was presented by the Dean and Chapter of Chester to the Vicarage of St Oswald's, a post which he continued to hold after he became a Prebendary in 1673 and only relinquished it when he was made Dean in 1692. He also held the Vicarage of Plemstall which was in the gift of Sir John Bridgeman.[1]

William Thompson succeeded Dr Moreton on 26 July 1675. He was a Cumberland man and went to Queen's College, Oxford, in 1631, aged eighteen. He took his B.A. in 1635 and his M.A. in 1639. He was Vicar of Childwall, Lancs., in 1664 and Rector of St Peter's, Chester

[1] *Notitia Cestriensis*, p. 136, note.

(1663–93). In 1681 he was given the Rectory of Thurstaston. He died on 9 January 1693 and was buried in the Cathedral.

We turn now to the Chapter Minute Book. The minutes are disappointingly short and are concerned chiefly with the granting of leases and the appointing to offices, but now and then they throw a little light on the daily life of the Cathedral. In 1669 Bishop Bridgeman's Injunction relative to the obsolete offices of Cater, Butler, Porter, Cook, Baker, and Barber was at last carried out. The Bishop had ordered that the salaries attached to these offices should be used to augment the stipends of the Petty Canons, but the Chapter confess that "since his Majesties happy restoration [they] have been granted under seale to Mr. Nathaniel Brooke of London, Stationer, and others, who have commenced a suit against the Dean and Chapter". It was now decided to buy out these lessees for the sum of £100, and if the Cathedral funds could not afford it "we engage ourselves to take it up out of our respective salaries",—the income (£22) to be "paid as an augmentation unto the places of 4 pettie Cannons priests, each of which shall in their turns quarterly read morning prayers at 6 o'clock in the Quire". In these degenerate days we may perhaps feel that the Canons fully earned their extra money. It was also decided that the number of the Petty Canons should be made up to six, though this was not done.

In 1670 there was trouble with a Bedesman, one Richard Whitby, who despised the statutes and the "godly admonitions of the Dean, which he hath not only declared by words but confirmed by his contemptuous actions, having neither performed due reverence to his Governor, nor devotion to his God in this Quire, openly avowing that he careth not for the place, and is not only a person of bad example but of an evil life, being much given to excessive drinking, vile detracting and several other vicious habits". In consequence he was suspended, and the King was to be "petitioned to place some other almsman in his room". All the bedesmen in those days were appointed by the Crown.

In 1672 the sexton of St Oswald's was the offender, albeit unwittingly. The Dean and Chapter were very jealous of their rights over St Oswald's Church in the south transept and when the parish appointed a new sexton without their knowledge or consent the poor man had to bear the brunt of the Dean's displeasure. His abject apology was copied into the Chapter Minute Book and here it is:

Whereas I John Deane of the City of Chester Butcher was upon Tuesday was a sevenight being the 12th day of this instant June elected sexton in

place of William Catterall deceased for the parish of St. Oswald's by
Alderman William Ince, Mr. John Radcliff and some others, and by virtue
thereof I thought I had sufficient power to break ground in the Church of
St. Werburg otherwise sometimes called by the name of St. Oswald, which
being part of the Cathedral Church of Christ and the Blessed Virgin Mary
in Chester and the Dean and Chapter of the same maintaining the fabric
of the said Church at their own proper cost and charge, I perceive that I
could not lawfully do so, and therefore when I was going about to make
the first grave in the same after my said pretended election for Richard
Mercer, Clothworker, I was forbid so to do by Dr. Henry Bridgeman the
present Dean of the said Cathedral in behalf of himself and the Chapter
whose right it is alone to nominate and make the Clerk or Sexton of this
place. Wherefore I did humbly on my knees beg pardon of the Dean and
Chapter for my undue intrusion and invasion into the said office, and
utterly renouncing all power, right or title unto the same . . . do humbly
beseech the said Dean and Chapter . . . that they will be pleased to bestow
the same office of sexton in their said Church and Churchyard of St.
Oswald upon mee. . . .

This the Dean and Chapter graciously consented to do.

On 25 November 1671, the Dean's signature is changed to "Hen.
Sodorens; Ep. Dec. Cestriae", and it was while he was residing in his
island Diocese that he wrote a long letter to the Subdean and Precentor
dated 9 June 1673, which throws a good deal of light upon the burial
customs in the Cathedral in those days.[1]

Mr. Subdeane Bispham &
Mr. Chanter Stringer
    There is an hon'ble Maid lately deceased at Mr. John Anderson's, being
the Hope and Anchor in our Northgate Street within the City of Chester,
viz. the Lady Jane Montgomery, sister to the Right Hon'ble Hughe Earle
of Mount Alexander in the Kingdome of Ireland; who being a great lover
of the Ceremonyes of our Church while shee lived desired to bee buryed in
our Church when shee dyed. And since shee had the Quire so much in her
heart living I adjudged it fitt to bury her in the heart of our Quire now shee
is dead, her executors paying to the Cathedral all customarye dues and
justifyable fees which belong unto us. Now by reason of the late distraction
in this Kingdome and my frequent absences from this Church, my memory
not well serving mee in every particular thereof, and the Rt. Reverend
John [Pearson] Lord Bishop of Chester having a great kindness for her
family, as well as a great love unto Justice, desiring that shee may not be
imposed upon by any kind of Exaction; You being the most antient stagers
now resident in this Church, I doe require you upon virtue of your oaths
formerly taken that you declare unto mee in writing what the former fees

[1] Also printed in *Sheaf*, I, 261.

and customs have been in like case; that as I may not impose upon such hon'ble persons, so neither prejudice our successors in this Church; since our late Leiger bookes and other writings and Records of the Church, which should have informed us of former use and customes, have been miserably plundered and by violent hands taken away in the late warres between King and Parliament; and though I have used all manner of imaginable diligence and charg to retrieve them, yet could not regaine them, but do beeleive they were burnt in the late great fire of the City of London. I pray you deale faithfully and impartially, for what you declare in writing under your hands I intend to enter into the Chapter book *in perpetuam rei memoriam*, that it may be a standing rule and direction for our Successors, whom I would not have doe anything unwarrantably. I have sent my Chaplaine Mr. Francis Wood, to you with this letter, that he may have full discours with you about the praemises, by whom I shall expect a full answer thereunto. So commending Myself kindly to you, I rest

Your very loving freind
Henric: Ep'us Sodor et Monae.
Decanus Cestriae.

June the 9th, 1673.

These two ancient stagers took Prebendary Duckworth, who was only two years junior to Bispham, into collaboration and together the three of them concocted the following reply:

Rt. Reverend Mr. Deane,

Wee received your Ldship's letter of the nineth of this instant June, 1673, and in obedience thereunto wee return your Ldship this answer. 1st, That all the burials or Lestalls in the South side of the Cathedral commonly called St. Oswald's Churche doe belong unto the Deane and Chapter of this Church; who have sometimes leased them unto the Vicar of St. Oswald's upon the rent of five pounds a year payable at Easter; as namely to Mr. William Case before the warrs and to Mr. William Boardman since the warrs, and the present Vicar, Mr. Laurence Fogg, doth enjoy them upon the like annual rent. 2ndly, That in the body of the Cathedrall old Mr. Alderman John Radcliff, Grandfather, and Alderman John Radcliff, Father to John Radcliff, Esq. late Recorder of this City, paid unto the Deane and Chapter for their sepulture under the great marble stone in the middle Alley such considerable summes of money as they demanded. And the said late Recorder's wife, Mrs. Dorothy Radcliff, dying in the year after her Mother and Daughter and others of that family, Wee, considering the great mortality that was amongst them, demanded only five pounds of them for breaking up the ground near the place for her to be buryed in, before we would suffer the ground to be broken; and though hee did grumble at it at first, yet your Ldship may remember hee sent his servant, Mr. . . . Jones to your Ldship, that hee would satisfye the Deane and Chapter in their demands. And now that hee is dead himself, considering how kind a neighbour hee hath beene in affording us his Councell upon all occasions, though in your Ldship's absence I demanded five pounds for his burial there of his Executors, yet wee leave it to your Ldship's wisdome to return or abate him what you please.

And for those who, 3rdly, bury in the side Alleys of the Quire, they have usually paid five pound; and we know your Ldship does well remember that you received no less from Mr. Thomas Simons, a Lancashyre man, who dyed at Mr. Thomas Clarke's, the Petty Canon. 4thly, And for those that were buryed in the body of the Quire, they have usually paid ten pounds for the ground or upward, according to the vicinitye and eminencye of the place; only the members of the Church and those that have descended from them have had the Indulgences to be buryed gratis according to their qualityes; which if greater, in St. Mary's Chappel, betwixt he Quire and the East end of the said Chappell, where the Dean and Prebendaryes are usually buryed; as your brother, Mr. Dove Bridgeman was, and your Excellent Mother, Mrs. Elizabeth Bridgeman, and your own two daughters, Mrs. Henrietta and Mrs. Katherine Bridgeman and your daughter Grenhalgh's wife[1] Mrs. Catherine Grenhalgh, all in the vaulted sepulchre which your Father, my L'd John Bridgeman, B'p of Chester did in his life time by consent of the Deane and Chapter build for the buryall of the branches of his family and which your Ldship and wee all of the Chapter have delivered our Assents and Consents to be continued unto your family solely and p'petually. Further Wee certifye that the blacks that cover the Pulpit and Cushion doe belong to the Deane and Chapter. If the Corps bee sung into the Church and at the Grave the least that the Quire men have usually had was forty shillings. There is also due for the use of the bells to the Deane and Chapter for one day twenty shillings besides satisfaction to bee given to the Ringers. There is also due to the Virgers for a passing peale ten groates if they tole the great bell. If the fourth bell, eight groates, from both which the Chanter usually had eight pence.

Your Ldships humble Servants
William Bispham, Subd.
Charles Duckworth, P'bend.
Peter Stringer, P'centor.

We cannot help wondering whether it occurred to the writers of this very informative letter that before long they would be testing the truth of their statements with their own bodies, for Peter Stringer died a few days later and Charles Duckworth a few months later. He, however, was buried at his own parish church of Dodleston and we do not know where the body of Stringer was interred. The Dean and Bispham

[1] The word is "daughter" in the original.

lived for another decade or more. Peter Stringer[1] was a great loss, for he was not only Petty Canon, Organist and Master of the Choristers, but also Deputy Receiver and Treasurer, and being on the spot, did most of the work. This is revealed in the decision of the Chapter to appoint his son, John, to succeed him, in the following terms: "Whereas the late nominated Receiver Mr. William Finmore and Treasurer Mr. Phineas Bury being now both absent and at so great a distance that we presume they are utterly ignorant of the premature departure of their said substitute in those their respective offices", and as salaries must be paid and rents must first be gathered in and there are duties to be paid to the King and others which cannot admit of any delay, they appoint John Stringer to succeed his father in all the offices formerly held by him (except that of Precentor) and allow him his house and garden on a service tenure "for his more commodious attendance upon the duties of the forenamed places". This is signed by the Dean, Subdean, Duckworth, and Finemore on 25 June. At the same Chapter William Ottye, Petty Canon, was made Precentor.

The next volume of the Minute Book which begins in 1674 opens with some interesting regulations for the conduct of divine service, from which we learn that the sermon on Sunday morning was usually preached in St Oswald's because it was impossible to have two sermons, one in the choir and one in the south transept, going on at the same time. So on Sunday morning the Dean, prebendaries, and choir moved into St Oswald's.

Then follows a most interesting order about the cathedral music which throws a welcome light on a very little-known subject. To understand it we must remember that "full services" means settings for the canticle for (usually) four parts without solo passages and that "verse services" consist largely of solo passages, and that "hymns" here mean canticles.

> Whereas every one cominge to the publick services of God ought to join and bear part therein, yet when full services and anthems are sung few of those who either are not skilled in music or have not copies thereof pricked out can join in the said worship or be edified thereby; It is ordered that instead of full services after each lesson either verse services of the hymns shall be sung wherein one or two singing at once, the words may be the more distinctly attended to and in heart joined with by the congregation, or the said hymns shall be sung in the ordinary chanting tune which all who frequent cathedrals may easily bear a part in, and instead of full

[1] For further information about Peter Stringer see Dr J. C. Bridge in *C.A.J.*, n.s., XIX, Pt. II, p. 92.

anthems verse anthems shall be also used for the reason before suggested and before each anthem one of the singing men shall audibly declare what portion of Scripture is then to be sung.

The burden of this is that the Dean and Chapter in their desire to encourage the congregation to take part in the service ordered that either canticles and anthems with solo passages should be sung so that the words would be more likely to be heard or else that an ordinary chant should be used for the canticles instead of a setting.

Bishop Pearson's Injunctions, dated 24 September 1675, follow fairly closely those of Bishop Bridgeman, but the following items are new. Choir practice for the boys was to be for half an hour after morning and for an hour after evening service, and for the men one hour a week.

As there were not enough houses to accommodate all the Cathedral staff: "Be it therefore decreed . . . that the houses betwixt the Deanery and the Kaleyard on the north side of the way [i.e. in Abbey Street] shall be the houses appropriated to 4 Petty Canons and those which are now in the possession of Mr. Garenciers and of Robert Carter (after his removal or other accommodation) appropriated to other two Petty Canons." It would appear from this that in those days there were four houses in Abbey Street, where now there are six. Carter was one of the Choirmen.

Other items of interest from the Chapter Book in this year and the next year are:

(1) "If the Precentor is absent from the choir the senior petty canon present shall supply his place in appointing what service or anthem shall be playd or sung."

(2) The verger, Henry Hughes, is to ride the light horse when necessary, for which he is to receive £4 a year.

(3) "It is also decreed that the second wainscote seate from the choristers seate on the south side of the Quire of the Church be kept for the Dean and Prebends' wives to sit in and noone else."

In 1676 there was trouble with the Petty Canons, of whom there were only three at this time, not counting John Stringer, the organist. They were William Ottey, Thomas Clark, and Dudley Garenciers. Ottey had already been suspended once in 1674 "for that he did by insolent and contemptuous behaviour and words unfit to be mentioned vilify the Subdean & Prebends to their faces in the audience of the Choirmen", but was soon restored. What happened in 1676 can be learned from the entry in the Chapter Book dated 3 May 1677:

Whereas Mr. Thomas Clarke, one of the Petty Canons of this church, hath formerly absented himself from the service of this Quire without procuring any to officiate in his name & hath not performed the conditions upon which some addition to his salary was promised (which promise was made by reason of a strait we were brought into about 10 months since through Mr. Garenciers mutining & drawing Mr. Otty (the only Petty Canon we had beside them) into the same crime, we do declare that he has thereby rendered himself unworthy of receiving any benefits by the afore-said conditional promise especially during his unlycenced absence.

Garenciers was dealt with two days later, when he was "mulcted in the summe of tenne poundes for his neglect and contumacy and if he persisted therein for six months was thereby declared to be expelled". Ten pounds was six months salary paid £5 a quarter. The Accounts show that he received nothing at Midsummer, but was paid his usual £5 at Michaelmas, and on 20 November the Chapter decreed that "we do remitt the mulct and readmitt him into the office of Petty Canon". Ormerod says he was made Rector of Handley in 1684 and of Waverton in 1696 and in that same year was made a Prebendary of the Cathedral.[1] "He is said to have been the only minor canon of Chester that was ever advanced to a prebend stall." In 1690 he had two boys at the King's School named Theophilus and Athanasius. Poor boys!

The other two offenders must have been restored earlier, for in October they "complained in the Chapter House that they were too few to perform the service of the Church", with the result that "wee did appoint Mr. Francis Wood constantly to read six o'clock prayers till Xmas & no longer without further order". The Accounts show that in the last quarter of that year (1677) two new Petty Canons were appointed, Mr Mace and Mr Fearn, but here again the Chapter were unfortunate in their choice, for on 23 June 1679, Mace was expelled for slandering Mr Fogge and the last we hear of him is that on 27 November 1680 the Dean and Chapter ordered two shillings a week to be paid to John Mace, "late Petty Canon of the Quire & now prisoner in Norgate". His successor was Mr James Graham who lasted only four years, for on 8 November 1682 he "hath this day come into the Quire in the time of Divine Service much distempered in drink and there slept during a great part of the Service". He was discharged.

[1] Mr R. Richards, *Old Cheshire Churches*, p. 344, lists him as succeeding Simon Land at Waverton in 1677, the year of his disgrace. Ormerod's date is the more probable and the Accounts show that he continued as Petty Canon until 1683, when there is a gap. Of course it is possible that he might have held both offices at once.

We must at least give the Dean and Chapter credit for trying to preserve discipline, and hope that these men were not typical of the clergy of that day.

THE ACCOUNTS 1676–1683

In June and July 1677, extensive repairs were carried out to the roof of the church involving the use of 2,000 slates and nearly three tons of lead, the latter costing £24 os. od. The carpenter was paid £7 odd and the plumber £14. The total cost was over £64. The Treasurer was authorized to borrow £100 for six months to pay for this work.

	s.	d.
1677 Oct. 23, pd. Jo. Malbone for yron cramps for ten o'clock bell-clapper	7	0

This would be the bell rung for matins.

	s.	d.
Aug. Allowed Mr. Thompson for 6 quarts of canary presented to the Recorder and a tasting pint among them	16	3
Oct. 29 Pd. Thos. Bradburn for Ringing at the good tidings of the contract between the Prince of Aurange and for a bonefire on the account	2	6

The other party to the contract was of course Princess Mary, daughter of James, Duke of York.[1] This Protestant match was naturally very popular with a nation threatened by the Romanizing influence of Charles II (secretly) and of the Duke of York (openly). Mary was only fifteen at this date and was married a month later.

	£	s.	d.
1678 Nov. 26 pd. for Chapter's dinner at Wolfe's Head		13	8
Nov. 29. pd. on the same account	1	4	0
Oct. 30. pd. for certaine stuff, given by consent of the Brethren, to secure our good Bp. from the wind	1	14	0
for silk, rings, tape & making them up		3	10
Nov. 11. pd. Hen. Hughes for 8 quire candlesticks		1	4
Nov. 25. Given Mr. Otty for the quiremen's dinner	1	0	0

The accounts for the years 1679 and 1680 are missing.

	£	s.	d.
1681 March 3. pd. James Mort per note for flagging the broad Isle by the Quier door	10	8	0
Sept. 12. pd. for venison Feast at Bp. of Man's	7	8	2
for 6 bottles of claret		6	6
(Nov.) 2 quarts of canary drunk at the Dean's by Dean & Chapter & 4 pt. of claret at the Dean's dinner		8	4

[1] When the news was announced to her poor Mary cried all that afternoon and the whole of the following day. *Mary II,* Hester W. Chapman (Jonathan Cape), p. 63.

£   s.   d.

Dec. 6 pd. Henry Hughes for a journey in to Wirral & for
ringing to welcome the Bp. of Durham   5   0
1682 Feb. 14. For scouring altar candlesticks   6
(1682) March 3. pd. Tho. Rogers mason for flagging the p'bends
quadrangle cloyster and church   11 8   0
pd. for carrying away Rubbish from Abbey Court cloisters
etc.   7   0

These two extracts taken together make it appear that the Prebends'
quadrangle which was flagged was the Abbey Square.

£   s.   d.

May 5. pd. Isaac Cross for forms in the quire   3   6   0
June 13, for making up the prison wall[1]   1   0   0
July 22. for the Dean's kneeling bench   3   0
Aug. 14. pd. chymney money for Mr. Biddulphs house   3   0
Nov. 9. pd. Jo. Dunbabin for church & school windows   7   7   0

These were the windows broken in the Monmouth riot on 11
September, for which see below.

s.   d.

Nov. 25. for 2 qwt. canary & 2 of claret at Subd' chamber   6   8

Last year the dinner was held in the Dean's house and 4 quarts of
claret were consumed as well as 2 of canary.

£   s.   d.

Nov. 28. pd. Mr. Minshal for a collation at Wolf's Head   4   7   6
1683 Nov. 15. pd. Attorney Taylor for his pains & losses in sueing
a beggarly knavish tenant   3   0

And on this irascible note the Accounts end for the time being and
do not begin again until 1689.

DEAN ARDERNE 1682–1692

Dean Henry Bridgeman, Bishop of Man, died on 15 May 1682 and
was succeeded by James Arderne, D.D., who was the fifth son of Ralph
Arderne of Harden and Alvanley.[2] He went to St John's College,
Cambridge, where he took his B.A. in 1656. He was ordained in 1660
and in 1666 obtained the curacy of St Botolph, Aldersgate, which he
held until he was Dean of Chester. He was also chaplain in ordinary
to Charles II, who gave him the living of Davenham, Cheshire, on 10
January 1681. His attachment to the Crown survived the accession of
the Romanist Duke of York to the throne and "is said to have sub-
jected him to many affronts and indignities in the vicinity of Chester".[3]

[1] The prison comprised the two houses adjoining the Gateway into Abbey
Square (Hemingway's *History of Chester*, II, 15).
[2] His portrait hangs in the Canons' vestry in the Cathedral.
[3] Ormerod, II, 83.

He was installed Dean of Chester on 12 July 1682. His term of office was full of incident, covering as it did the last three years of Charles II, the whole reign of James II and the first four years of William and Mary. He had hardly been in Chester two months before the Duke of Monmouth, illegitimate son of Charles II, arrived, with dire results to the Cathedral.

THE MONMOUTH RIOT

Monmouth at this time was posing as the Protestant Prince in opposition to the King's brother and heir, James, Duke of York, and to this end he arranged a semi-royal progress through Staffordshire and Cheshire. He entered Cheshire from Trentham (where he had passed the previous night) on Saturday, 9 September, dined at the Crown Hotel at Nantwich and reached Chester at six o'clock in the evening escorted by some of the nobility and gentry of the County. He was received by the Mayor, George Mainwaring, at the Bars and lodged in his house in Watergate Street, but entertained to meals at the Plume of Feathers in Bridge Street. That evening, says a report to the Secretary of State, "the Dean sent for the keys of the churches, but the Rabble broke into St John's Church on Saturday through the windows and rang the bells".[1] Breakfast with the Mayor on Sunday morning was accompanied by "a great deal of rabble always shouting and throwing up their hats".[2] Monmouth after breakfast went to church at the Cathedral accompanied by Mr Williams, the Recorder, where one of the Prebendaries—one report says it was a minor canon —made the most of his opportunity in his sermon, "telling him his duty [and] of Disobedience and [of] of Achitophell, Henry 1st of France, and that God would blast all the wicked and mischievous devices against the King, and make the memory of their wicked names stink in the grave". There is obviously a reference here to Dryden's satirical poem, *Absalom and Achitophel*, which had appeared less than a year before this and had created a great sensation. In the poem, Absalom, the son who rebelled against his father, stood for Monmouth, and Achitophel, the young man's evil counsellor, for the Earl of Shaftesbury, who at this time was a prisoner in the Tower. The reference to Henry I of France could not have been obvious to his hearers, for he was an unimportant Capetian king (1031–60), but it appears that for a short time he took up arms against his father, Robert I, and that may have been the reason why he figured in the sermon. After this lecture from the unnamed prebendary Monmouth went back to the Plume of

[1] *Lancs. and Ches. Hist. Soc.*, n.s., x, p. 84.   [2] Hist. MSS. Com., VII, 533.

Feathers for dinner and returned to the Cathedral for another service in the afternoon. This time he probably fared better, for the preacher was Dr Fogge, whose Protestant tendencies were well known and it was noticed that he omitted to pray for the Queen and the Duke of York by name and prayed only for the King and the Royal Family. That afternoon the Duke also found time to stand godfather in Holy Trinity Church to the Mayor's little daughter, who was christened Henrietta. He left Chester next morning (Monday the tenth), slept the night at Peel Hall, Bromborough, and on the Tuesday rode in the Wallasey Races and won a £60 prize, "by contrivance of the man that rid against him", says one report rather unkindly. He sent the silver cup which he won back to Chester as a present for his goddaughter, "at which news the people here grew so mad that all the streets were full of bonfire, the church doors were broken open to ring the bells, contrary to the Dean and the minister's orders, and nothing was heard in the streets but a Munmouth, a Munmouth". The rioting was renewed on Wednesday night when the Duke's horse which had won the race was led through the streets, the Duke himself being at Rock Savage, near Runcorn. It was on one of these nights that the mob "furiously forced the doors of the cathedral church and destroyed most of the painted glass, burst open the little vestrys and cupboards, wherein were the surplices and hoods belonging to the clergy, which they rent to rags and carried away; they beat to pieces the baptismal font, pulled down some monuments, attempted to demolish the organ, and committed other most enormous outrages".[1] We have already noted that it cost seven guineas to put the glass back in the windows.

BISHOP CARTWRIGHT

The next event was the death of Bishop Pearson and arrival of Bishop Cartwright, D.D., for whom nobody has a good word to say. This is not on account of his Romanizing tendencies, but because he appears to have been an unscrupulous time-server, whose great object in life was his own advancement.[2] Like his predecessor, John Wilkins, he contrived to hold office under both Parliament and Crown, and to the latter he professed such ardent loyalty that in 1672 he was made chaplain in ordinary to the King and attached himself to James, Duke of York. When the latter ascended the throne in 1685, Cartwright preached a sermon at Ripon, of which collegiate church he was Dean,

[1] Cowper MS. quoted in Ormerod, I, 248.
[2] Rev. F. Sanders in C.A.J., n.s., IV, 2.

so strongly in favour of the absolute power of the Crown that James
made him a bishop in the following year. Though he was only at
Chester for two years—for he had to fly the country at the Revolution
—he left his mark on the Diocese. His connection with the Cathedral
is recorded in his diary,[1] a MS. copy of which is preserved in the
Cathedral library. Consecrated on 17 October 1686, he entered his
Diocese on 12 November by way of Richmond, reached Wigan on
the twenty-seventh and entered Chester on the thirtieth. On 1 December: "I was sung into the Cathedral by the choir in procession and
enthroned by Mr. Dean, and sung back into the palace for prayers".
It was not long before he made his presence felt in the Cathedral. On
19 January 1687:

> I admonished Mr. Ottway, the precentor, in the church, of his neglecting
> services and anthems, and his teaching of the quire; and he refusing to
> amend, and be the packhorse, as he called it, to the choir and choristers, I
> told him I should take care to provide a better in his room, and one that
> should attend to God's service better, and pay more respect to his
> superiors, he behaving himself very insolently towards the Subdean at that
> very time.

William Ottye appears as Minor Canon and Precentor in 1664 when
the Accounts begin and he is still in that dual office in 1694, so the
Bishop's threat came to nothing. It was not the first time he had been
insolent to the Subdean (see p. 148).

The next person the Bishop had to admonish was Mr Morrey,
probably the Peter Morrey who was Dean Arderne's curate and to
whom the Dean left certain articles of apparel in his will.[2]

> Jan. 31, Mr. Morrey preached in the cathedral, and I admonished him to
> mend his prayer, in which he gave not the King his titles, and to be wary
> of reflecting so imprudently as he did upon the King's religion, which he
> took thankfully and promised amendment.

Even the laity did not escape the Bishop's censure.

> Feb. 13, I preached in the cathedral at Chester, being the first Sunday in
> Lent to the greatest congregation that ever I saw, a sermon on Repentance.
> God give a blessing to it! . . . I rebuked, as they deserved, Mrs. Brown,
> Mrs. Crutchley, Mrs. Eaton, and her sister, for talking and laughing in the
> church; and they accused Mr. Hudleston for being as guilty as themselves.

The diary, however, gives praise where praise is due. On 6 February
Dr Wroe, Prebendary, "preached an excellent sermon on the King's

---

[1] Which was printed by the Camden Soc. in 1840.   [2] Ormerod, II, 40.

inauguration, which I requested him to print, as highly seasonable".
On 4 March: "Dr. Fogg preached an excellent sermon on Repen-
tance". On the twentieth: "Mr. Archdeacon Allen preached an
excellent and seasonable sermon, and he and Mr. Thane [another
Prebendary] dined with me".

VISIT OF JAMES II

Bishop Cartwright spent the summer months of the year 1687 in
London, returning to Cheshire on 27 July, and on 27 August King
James II visited Chester. He was on a progress through the west of
England to prepare the ground for the repeal of the penal laws against
Roman Catholics, which he had temporarily suspended. He had
already visited Bath, Gloucester and Worcester.[1] Cartwright records
in his diary:

> His Majesty came to the palace in Chester about four in the afternoon. I
> met him at the palace gates, attended by the Dean and Prebends, and about
> forty more of the clergy, and afterwards introduced them to kiss his hand,
> Mr. Dean making an excellent speech to him. Then his Majesty went and
> viewed the choir; after that the castle, to which he walked on foot, and I
> waited at his cushion till I saw him in bed.

Perhaps the King viewed the choir in order to see where he was
going to perform on the morrow, and it would be on this occasion
that he observed the unsatisfactory condition of the cloisters, "with
resentment and displeasure", the Bishop afterwards told the Dean and
Chapter. The "excellent speech" of the Dean is worth reproducing in
full both as illustrating the Dean's character and also as showing the
lengths that loyal churchmen would go in support of their belief in the
Divine Right of Kings.[2]

> Allow us, Great Sir, to express our loyal joy in beholding here the face of
> your sacred Majesty. Our eyes are now blest while we see amongst us that
> mighty and wonderful King, who equals in clemency his late Royal
> Brother; in the sincerity of his religious purpose his Father the glorious
> Martyr; in other princely virtues both his grandfathers, the great Henry
> [IV] of France in courage and conduct of wars and King James I of England
> in wisdom and defence of this National Church. And what more recommends
> this generous patronage he preserves that altar from being overthrown

[1] *Samuel Pepys, The Saviour of the Navy*, by Arthur Bryant, p. 222. Pepys
accompanied James as far as Worcester, where he got so absorbed in the manu-
scripts of the Cathedral library that he was left behind and returned to London.
[2] Printed in *C.A.J.*, n.s., v, 323 (1895) and in Ormerod, II, 40. The punctuation
and capitals have been modernized.

at which he does not worship. T'were to be wished true that all who enjoy this protection had returned suitably their thankful addresses.[1] However it be, we humbly hope that your Majesty, like God, (whom in governing power you represent upon earth, and in pardoning-mercy you do imitate) will be kind to the unthankful, and according to your accustomed goodness will spare the place for the smaller visible number of good men therein.

So great grace certainly heals their infidelity and revolt, especially when they are thus united to believe [in] and adhere to a Prince of whom we have had the experience that he will no sooner receed from his promises than he would fly from an enemy in the field.

As for what concerns us of this Royal Foundation, with all humility I undertake for myself and several of my brethren that we will continue to advance amongst your subjects the strictest principles of a mannerly, peaceful and active loyalty making earnest prayers to Almighty God that he would in this world grant your Majesty length of days and hereafter eternal life and glory.

It is small wonder that after this speech it was rumoured that when Cartwright should be translated to Salisbury, Dean Arderne would be the next Bishop of Chester.

The next day the King went into the choir of the Cathedral at nine o'clock, "where he healed 350 persons. After which he went to his devotions in the Shire Hall, and Mr. Penn held forth in the Tennis Court, and I preached in the Cathedral". This was the celebrated William Penn, the Quaker, lately returned from America where he had founded the Colony which still bears his name. He supported the King because he thought his desire for religious toleration was genuine, and the King showed him favour because he found it useful to have an honest man about him who would have influence among the Dissenters.[2] On the third day Chester saw very little of the King, for he rose at six and was in the saddle by 7.30 *en-route* for St Winifred's Well at Holywell where he was presented with the shift which his great-grandmother, Mary Queen of Scots, wore when she was beheaded.[3] In the evening the Bishop took the opportunity to put in a good word for the Dean, recommending him to the King "for better encouragement, because he was daily affronted for his zeal in his service by the Whigs". James left Chester next day (30 August), after

---

[1] Before he left, James expressed his displeasure that there was no loyal address forthcoming from Chester. *C.A.J.*, n.s., IV, p. 16.

[2] The Tennis Court was the Tennis Court Theatre. It stood on the south side of Foregate Street opposite the Nag's Head and next to Astbury's, the monumental mason. *Sheaf*, 3rd ser., XLIV, 42. There is no authority for the oft-repeated statement that James heard Mass in the Castle chapel.

[3] Cowper MSS.

he had "had mass in the presence chamber where he did eat. From thence I attended him into the choir, where he healed 450 people; from thence to the penthouse [Pentice] where he breakfasted under a state [sic], and from thence took horse about ten of the clock. . . . The King left £20 to the house servants."

The Bishop now had time to carry out his Visitation of the Cathedral, which he fixed for 6 September, but adjourned it till 4 October "by reason of Mr. Dean's sickness". On 6 October we are astonished to read "I concluded my Visitation *and suspended Mr. Dean*; the sentence to be published, if not taken off before, on Sunday three weeks". However, the Bishop seems to have relented, for on 24 October he wrote from Oxford: "I wrote to the Chancellor of Chester not to publish the suspension against the Dean till further order from me, according to the Dean's desire, by letter." There is no hint in the diary of what the Dean was accused.

The Bishop's Injunctions[1] are for the most part copied verbatim from those of Bishop Pearson, but No. 5 and No. 6 are new.

No. 5 orders that the Cathedral archives "henceforth be kept and secured in a strong chest, on which are to be three locks of different work, of which the Dean to have one key, the Subdean another, and the Senior Prebendary the third. . . . " There is little doubt that this is the chest now used as a collecting box standing in the south transept. Only one of the three locks is the original one.

It is strange that the Bishop should have ordered this, for only the year before, on 26 November 1686, the Dean and Chapter had ordered: "that a convenient way be made to the room over the Abbey Gate and that the Common Chest be brought thither and that the same room be used for the service of the Church and that all books and writings relating to the Dean and Chapter be brought to the Common Chest there and not to be delivered out without an undertaking for the restoring of them again". In November 1698, the great room over the Abbey Gate was ordered to be fitted up as an Audit Room. This was done in 1690 at a cost of about £24.

No. 6 deals with the fabric of the Cathedral and singles out the Cloisters for criticism:

And for that the cloisters of the said Church are much out of repair and become rather scandalous than useful to it, which the King's Majesty lately observed with resentment and displeasure upon his own royal view; it is enjoyned and decreed that the Dean and Chapter take all convenient,

[1] They are to be found copied into a book of leases preserved in the Muniment Room.

speedy and effectual course for repairing and covering of them above with lead or slate and purging and securing them below from sordid prophanation and indecencies before the 24th of June next ensuing and that the Treasurer do not pay any portion ... or dividend to the Dean or any of the Prebends till this be done and the Church be out of debt,

to which has been added later "except their annual stipends as by statute".

It was in this year (1687) that the marble font which stands at the west end of the Cathedral was given by Bishop Moreton of Kildare, a son of that Prebendary Moreton who was Archbishop Laud's nominee. On a slab on the west wall near it is a Latin inscription to say that as an infant he found it brick and later as Bishop had changed it into marble.[1] As he was baptized in 1641 the "brick" font would be the one given by Bishop Bridgeman, which would have been "beat to pieces" in the Monmouth riot.

Meanwhile William Bispham had died in 1686; his memorial is on the wall of the north aisle of the choir and his gravestone lies in the Abbot's Passage covered at the time of writing by a pile of beams out of the roof. It is said that it is an old tombstone with another inscription on the reverse side.

VISIT OF WILLIAM III

William and Mary were proclaimed King and Queen of England on 13 February 1689. On Sunday, 10 June 1690, William paid a hurried visit to Chester on his way to the reduction of Ireland. It is interesting to contrast his visit with that of the King whom he had just displaced.

King William came to Combermere [writes Dr Cowper], and the next day to Col. Whitley's at Peel Hall, and on Sunday morning arrived at Chester and went immediately to the Cathedral where, being seated in the Episcopal throne, he heard divine service and a sermon preached by Dr. Stratford, the then Bishop; after which the Bishop desired of his Majesty to accept of a dinner at the Palace, but the King declined and set out immediately for Gayton Hall in Wirral, the seat of William Glegg Esq. upon whom the King was the following day pleased to confer the honour of knighthood; and all things being ready for his embarkation, from thence proceeded to the reduction of Ireland.

No mention is made of the Mayor and Aldermen being presented to him, perhaps because some of them had ridden out to Peel Hall on

[1] An obvious reference to Augustus Caesar's boast that he found Rome brick and left it marble.

the seventh to wait upon the King there,[1] and we get the impression of a soldier whose mind is fixed on the campaign ahead of him and who has no time for ceremony, as indeed he had not, for he left on Monday morning for Hoylake where the fleet awaited him while his army lay encamped at Leasowe, and they sailed at midday with the tide. Macaulay's account agrees with Dr Cowper's in the main, though of course it is much shorter. He says the King set out from London on June 4 and in four days (i.e. on Friday, 8 June) "the King arrived at Chester where a fleet of transports was awaiting the signal for sailing".[2]

Further confirmation is obtained from the Accounts for 10 June:

> For ringing Fryday Saturday and Sunday for the King's
> and Prince George's coming to Town   10 0

Prince George of Denmark, Queen Anne's husband, accompanied the expedition to Ireland and had to make his own way to Chester. He had hoped for a seat in the King's coach, but William managed to give him the slip for he was a crashing bore.

One other event of a less martial character occurred about this time which should be recorded. In October 1689, Bishop Stratford ordained in his private chapel (now St Anselm's) Thomas Wilson, a former King's School boy and a native of Burton, Wirral. Wilson was at that time acting as assistant curate to his uncle, Dr Sherlock, Rector of Winwick, but afterwards became the famous Bishop of Sodor and Man (1697–1755).

Dean Arderne "died unmarried at his new house at Kelsale near Delamere"[3] on 18 September 1691. He bequeathed all his property to the Cathedral:

> I give to the glory of God and the service of the Cathedral Church of Chester, more particularly for a small beginning of a public library of books; but if a library cannot be had, that the Fathers of the first three hundred years that I have, together with the commonplace book which I made out of them, of controversies, may be set up in the Chapter House for the use of the dean and prebends; and if this doe not take place a further use hereof is, that this may be kept as a stock whereby they may defend the

[1] See the Corporation Accounts for 7 June: "To moneys spent wn. sent severall to wait on ye King at Peele—3s. 6d."; and the Assembly Book, 6 June: "Ordered that a deputation (there named) be appointed to wait on their Majesties at Poole and learn whether his Majesty will be pleased to take this city in his way" (Hanshall, p. 210).

[2] History of England, II, p. 176 (1873 ed.). Is it possible that Macaulay pictured the fleet lying off Crane Wharf in the River Dee?

[3] Cowper MSS.

rights and privileges of this ecclesiastical corporation and that it may serve to defray the expenses of procuring an Act of Parliament for disposing of the great lease, when it shall fall, called Jollive's lease, so as shall be most conducive to the welfare of this Cathedral and to the public good. Excepting only, out of this my whole grant to them, my best suit, as gown, cassock, hat, silk stockings, doublet and breeches, which I desire be given to my curate, Mr. Peter Morrey, and that my executors do take care of his preferment, he leaving a very good place to come to me.[1]

Dean Arderne was given the Vicarage of Neston in 1689 by the Chapter which would necessitate the services of a curate, and his executors carried out his wishes by letting Morrey succeed him there as vicar. The Dean in his will also desired to be buried in the choir, near the foot of the altar, with an inscription upon a cheap stone or brass, set up in the wall, to the effect that he left his money to the Cathedral because he considered it "a sort of sacrilege to sweep away all from the Church and Charity into the possession of their lay kindred who are not needy". This inscription can be found today on the wall of the south choir aisle.

DEAN LAURENCE FOGGE 1692–1718

Laurence Fogge, the Subdean, succeeded Arderne as Dean, and the Chapter was now constituted as follows:

William Thompson, M.A.	1675
Richard Wright, B.D.	1677
Richard Wroe, D.D.	1678
John Allen, M.A.	1686
John Thane, D.D.	1686
Edmund Entwistle, D.D.	1691

All these except William Thompson are new since we last looked at the Chapter in 1675.

Richard Wright was born in 1640 in Nantwich and went to B.N.C., Oxford in 1657 where he took his B.A. in 1660, his M.A. in 1663, and his B.D. in 1672. He was "curate or minister" of Bidston (Wirral) in 1667 and in a case brought by him in the Consistory Court in that year he stated that he had been for five years past "clerk in Holy Orders" and "curate".[2] He was actually ordained deacon in 1663, but was not ordained priest until 1669. In September of that year he was instituted

---

[1] Ormerod, II, 83.
[2] He was prosecuting one of his congregation for not paying the eight shillings he had promised for a free-will offering—"Other times, other manners."

to Holy Trinity, Chester, by the Archbishop of York. He was Rector of St Mary's-on-the-Hill, Chester, in 1673 and Rector of Malpas (Higher Mediety) in 1683. He married Mary, daughter of Chancellor Wainwright. He died in 1711.

Richard Wroe was the son of a yeoman, born in 1641 at Prestwich. He went to Jesus College, Cambridge, in 1658 and was a Fellow of it from 1662 to 1669. He took his B.D. in 1672 and his D.D. in 1686. He was Vicar of Bowdon from 1674 to 1690 and Fellow of the Collegiate Church of Manchester from 1675, becoming Master of it in 1684, and at the same time Vicar of Garstang. Bishop Pearson appointed him his Domestic Chaplain in 1678 and also a Prebendary of the Cathedral. In 1696 he relinquished Garstang for the living of West Kirby. He died in January 1717 and his epitaph is in the Cathedral. He had a great reputation as a preacher and earned the title of "silver-tongued".[1]

John Allen was made Prebendary in 1686 and almost immediately married "Madam Margaret Bridgman". He died in 1700.[2]

John Thane was the son of a physician in Norfolk and was born at King's Lynn, but when his father moved to Shrewsbury he finished his schooling there and proceeded to Trinity College, Cambridge, where he graduated M.A. He came to Chester with his uncle, Bishop John Pearson, in 1673 and was collated to a vacant stall on 17 April 1686. In 1690 he was given the living of Northenden by the Dean and Chapter, and in 1693 married Penelope Hide. During the vacancy after Bishop Stratford's death Queen Anne appointed Thane Archdeacon of Chester, when he took his D.D. He died on 30 June 1727 and was buried in the Cathedral, where his inscription can still be seen. His wife was among the ladies who founded the Blue Girls School.

Edmund Entwistle was the younger son of John Entwistle, armiger, of Ormskirk. He matriculated at Brazenose College, Oxford, in 1676 at the age of sixteen, took his B.A. in 1680 and his M.A. in 1682. He was made Prebendary in 1691 at the age of thirty-one, becoming at the same time Chaplain to the Bishop, Dr Stratford, and Rector of Barrow. He took his D.D. in 1693 and was appointed Archdeacon of Chester two years later. His first wife was a daughter of Bishop Stratford and on her death he married Priscilla, daughter of Sir Thomas Bunbury, Bart., the Bishop officiating in his private chapel. Sir Thomas Bunbury lived in Abbey Square. Entwistle died on 15 September 1707, and was buried in the Cathedral, where a tablet to his memory is to be found on the south wall of the nave. Edmund Entwistle was responsible for

[1] See *Notitia Cestriensis*, I, 30.   [2] Cathedral Registers.

inaugurating the present Warrington Institutions in aid of Clergy widows and orphans in the ancient Diocese of Chester, for it came into being as a result of a sermon he preached in Warrington Parish Church in 1697.

The new Dean had the same disciplinary problems as his predecessor, as the following extract from the Chapter Book will show. At a special Chapter meeting held on 16 October 1693, it was recorded:

> That whereas Henry Hughes, one of the vergers of this Church, did on the 14th of this inst. October not only impute to Mr. Dean the giving orders which he gave not, but in a most rude, irreverent and impudent manner, in the Broad Ile of the said church (tho' commanded to forbear and to go about his employment) yet did reproachfully and clamourously pursue Mr. Dean with the said false imputation often repeated . . . he shall acknowledge his offence before the members of the Quire, in these words, distinctly and respectfully pronounced by him after the Precentor reading them to him" and is to have no pay until he has done so.

Thus did the Dean try to "save face", but the picture of him being pursued through the nave of his own cathedral by an irate verger must have caused considerable amusement to those who witnessed it.

THE ACCOUNTS, 1689–1701

		£	s.	d.
1690 Feb. 19 pd. for making cleane the free school stairs after the great snow				6
1690 April 19. To Tho. Rogers for worke done about the church in full to this day		7	15	0
May 22, for timber and carpenter work done at the back of the Quire		7	10	0
May 30, For searg (serge) cotton and silk to face the Bps. throne		1	5	0
July 10, for ringing for K. Williams successe at the Boyne and before for his arrival in Ireland			10	0
Nov. 3, pd. the Mayor's officer for attendance when the vergers were arrested and their expenses at Mr. Tithers			4	2
ffor 6 Russia leather chaires for the roome over the Abbey gate		1	?	?
ff scowring and sufting [sic] the 6 chaires				?
ffor the grate and nigerd irons		1	12	0
1691 Dec. 8, Paid for ringing when Genl. Ginkill came to Town from Ireland			2	0
May 24, Paid for ringing on the news of our beating the French fleet			1	6

This was the Battle of Cape Le Hogue which was begun on 19 May and not finished till 24 May. By this victory all fears of an invasion by the French were removed.

	£	s.	d.
May 30, Paid for carrying away the dungill from the Bps garden door		1	0
1695 For ringing for the taking of Namur		3	6
1696 July 27 Pd. for mending a bench whereon the Poor sit			9
Aug. 1 Jo Ambrose for cleansing the leads and pulling up the elders etc.		1	6
Oct. 15 Lost in putting Church money into the Mint which was received before the 4 of May			
I put in £3 and received £1 13 0	1	7	0

This refers to the renewal of the coinage undertaken by the Government in this year. The old coinage had suffered so much by being clipped that it was ceasing to be a medium of exchange. The Government undertook to replace all coins at their face value which were handed in before 2 May, the loss being paid for out of revenue. It looks as though the Treasurer thought the date was 4 May and was penalized for being two days late.

	s.	d.
1697 April 3 Payd Tho. Jones for work about the pentice by the Maiden Ile	9	0
for carrying into the Chapter House the timber and slates that fell over the Maiden Ile door		6
April 24, pd. Cradock for slating over the Maiden Ile door as per note	4	6
Aug. 19 for pulling up weeds over the Cloyster and cleansing the gutters		6
Sept. 17 for ringing for news of the Peace	3	0

This was the Peace of Ryswick by which Louis XIV was forced to acknowledge William III as King of England and to surrender all the conquests he had made since 1678 (Nimwegen).

	s.	d.
April 24 Given to a distressed merchant sent to me from the Dean	1	0
To a distressed man and woman		6

For some reason the accounts for this year have been written out again and in the second version there is a significant change in the above item, as follows:

	s.	d.
April 24 Given to a distressed merchant and a woman who pretended they were sent by the Dean	1	6

The cloisters seem to have been in a very bad state of repair at this time, and what follows is the natural sequel to the elders and weeds which had been allowed to grow on the roofs.

	£	s.	d.
1699 Jan. 25, for carrying away the slates that fell from the Cloyster		1	0
March 19 To Tho. Hancock the mason for making up the ends of the Cloyster	8	13	0
to labourers for levelling the rubbish		7	11
More to Ambrose for work		3	0
April 28. To Ambrose and his wife and two others for cleansing the Tabernacle work		1	6
For cleansing the Tapestry at the altar	1	10	0
July 31 payd two workmen for clensing the top of the Cloysters, being about 10 days work		12	10
Nov. 28 To Thomas Hancock mason, glaziers and other workmen in full for work over and above my lords gift	9	16	3

Apparently Bishop Stratford had taken a hand in restoring the Cathedral and his lead had stimulated the Dean and Chapter to do likewise. And now follows a headache for historians, for it was Bishop Bridgeman who in 1626 built four stone cottages for the conducts.

	£	s.	d.
Sept. 30 Payd to Alban Grey for timber etc. for the Conducts houses given by Bp. Hall	7	5	4
Nov. 4, payd Math. Badders note for slates for the Ch. and Bishop Halls houses	7	16	0

Can it be that the Commonwealth had made such a gap in men's memories that the origin of these houses was already forgotten and that Bishop Hall was credited with them?

"The Exposed Child"

By Elizabeth's Poor Law each parish was made responsible for its own poor; the Cathedral precincts being extra-parochial would have had to do the same. It was not likely that there would be any poor in need of relief in such a respectable quarter, but it did sometimes happen that an unwanted baby was left on the doorstep of one of the Chapter houses and thus became a charge on the Cathedral until it was seven years old and could be apprenticed. Here are two examples:

	£	s.	d.
1699 Jan. 11 to Edward Gibbons for the exposed child		15	0
Dec. 12 Payd Edward Gibbons for clothes for the exposed girl	1	0	0

1700 July 24 To Edward Gibbons daughter for Midsummer Qr.   £   s.   d.
for the exposed girle and the odd time to her putting to
apprentice and 1/- given her   1   1   0
Sept. 11 for clothes, linnens, etc for Eliz Abby the exposed
girle, and the Indentures and bond for putting her apprentice   2   5   0

And so the poor little mite was sent out into the world with a
fictitious surname and a real shilling, the first money, probably, that
she had ever possessed.

                                              £   s..   d.
July 18. To Mr. Lea for a horse and charges of his journey to
Conway to search after the mother of the exposed boy   10   0
Nov. 21 For 19 weeks nursing the exposed boy from July
the 6th when it was found to Nov. 23, besides 2/- received
of Mr. Dean towards it   1 16   0
1701 A note of Wilson the Joiner for a coffin for the exposed boy
and work in the choir   5   4

St Thomas' Court

A peep at life in Abbey Square during the last decade of this century
is afforded us by the records of St Thomas' Court,[1] the private court
of the Dean and Chapter which they inherited from the Abbot:

October 25, 1693. Wee the Grand Jury etc. doe present . . . Mrs. Swift,
widdow, for not keeping the Abbey Court well in repaire, and do
amerce her in the sum of ten shillings. . . .
We present the Dean and Chapter for not repairing the Court-house;
and also for a dunghill before the Register office and we doe amerce
them in 13s. and 4d.
We present Mrs. Swift, widdow, for suffering part of her house in the
Abbey Court, which she holds from the Dean and Chapter, to go to
ruine and decay; and we order her to repaire the same before the next
Court Leet to be held for this manor, upon paine of six pound. . . .
April 1695. We present the Deane and Chapter for not keeping the
stocks in repaire, and amerce them in one shilling. . . .
We order that Mrs. Elizabeth Swift do keep the common well in the
Abbey Court duly enclosed, to prevent the danger of persons being
drowned or hurt in said well, upon paine of twenty shillings.

The well which Mrs Swift, the brewer's wife of that day, neglected
to enclose, is now built over by No. 7 Abbey Square. The Courthouse
in Randle Holme's plan is next to the Abbey Gateway.

[1] *Sheaf*, o.s., I, 28.

5

IN THE EIGHTEENTH CENTURY

PART I

1701–1740

THE beginning of the eighteenth century conveniently corresponds within a year or so with the beginning of the reign of Queen Anne (7 March 1702), which in its turn ushers in a period with a marked individuality. The Age of Anne somehow seems far removed from the seventeenth century, though of course the transition was a gradual one. It conjures up before our eyes a vision of prosperous, bewigged, full-skirted citizens, living in "Queen Anne" houses, frequenting coffee-houses and reading there the latest *Tatler* or *Spectator*. Marlborough of course is the dominating figure both at home and abroad, while Defoe, Swift, Steele, and Addison are the big names in the literature of the period. The whole reign is taken up with the war with France, ending with the Treaty of Utrecht (1714) which laid the foundations of our overseas empire. During the rest of our period the Hanoverians, George I and George II, occupied the throne, and thanks to Sir Robert Walpole, peace was maintained.

Religiously, it was an Age of Reason, introduced by John Locke's *Reasonableness of Christianity* (1695), which led to a certain amount of latitudinarianism among the higher clergy, which in its turn led to erastianism on the one hand and a spirit of toleration on the other. Religion became more and more equated with morality, the sermon continued to be the most important feature of the service, and the square pew, the three-decker pulpit and the gallery at the west end became the normal furniture of a parish church. "The social gulf between rich and poor clergy was still almost as wide as in medieval times."[1] It is against this background that the doings of the Dean and Chapter of Chester Cathedral must be placed.

[1] G. M. Trevelyan, *Eng. Social History*, p. 359.

The Dean and Chapter at the beginning of the century were constituted as follows:

Laurence Fogge, D.D., Dean	1692
Richard Wright, B.D.	1676
Richard Wroe, D.D.	1678
John Thane, D.D.	1686
Edmund Entwistle, D.D.	1691
Peter Lancaster, M.A.	1694
Dudley Garenciers, M.A.	1696

All these except the last two have been dealt with in a previous chapter.

Peter Lancaster was the son of the Rector of Winston, Co. Durham, and went to St John's College, Oxford, in 1676 at the age of eighteen. He took his B.A. from Balliol in 1684, though why he took eight years to get his degree and changed his college in the process does not appear. In 1690 he was Rector of Nantwich, was made Prebendary of Chester Cathedral in 1694 and exchanged Nantwich for Tarporley in the following year. He lost a daughter Mary in 1707 and died himself in 1709, being buried in the Cathedral on 17 May.[1] His family was left very badly off and had to be relieved from time to time by the Cathedral.

Dudley Garenciers has already been dealt with as a Minor Canon (Ch. 4, p. 149). He died in 1702 and was buried in the Cathedral. The Registers also mention that John and Elizabeth Vanburgh were his executors,[2] and Thomas Hughes adds a note to say that he wrote a book called *A History of Christ's Sufferings*. There were at least four boys in his family. Theophilus and Athanasius were at the King's School in 1690, Thomas was his father's nominee in 1697 and remained at school

---

[1] The Bishop (Sir Wm. Dawes, Bart.) had to leave his dinner to attend the funeral, but did not let that event cast a gloom over his party. Deputy-Registrar Prescott noted in his diary: "May 17, 1709. I dine with my Lord Bishop. A select number (including) Lord Gower, Sir Ric. Grosvenor, Sir Roger Mostyn, Sir Hen. Bunbury, Mr. Cholmley Egerton, Dr. Thane etc. fill the table. Here is an elegant dinner, good wine and free conversacon. About 4 my Lord recedes to Mr. Lancaster's funeral. . . . My Lord returns about 5, and the conversacon improves very cheerfully." *Sheaf,* XI, 65.

[2] John may have been the famous Sir John Vanbrugh, who in 1702 was in London busy writing plays. He was born and educated in Chester (? at the King's School), but *The New British Traveller* (1819) says he was privately educated.

until his father's death in 1702, when the new Prebendary, Dr Fogge, nominated John in his place.

THE FINANCIAL POSITION

At the turn of the century the financial position of the Cathedral must have been giving cause for considerable anxiety. The reason is not far to seek and is to be found in the Leicester Award of 1580, which confirmed the possession of the Cathedral estates in the hands of those who had obtained them (illegally, as the Dean and Chapter claimed) by purchase from Sir Richard Cotton in return for a fixed annual payment of rent to the Cathedral. The result was that the annual income of the Cathedral was much the same as when it was founded in 1541—i.e. about £1,000—although money had depreciated enormously in value since then and the Dean and Chapter had no power to raise the rents. Furthermore, the holders of the land were very backward in paying, so that the income of the Cathedral was always in arrear and it was difficult to find a remedy. The average annual income from 1694 to 1701 was only £901 10s. 10d. The result was that there were serious deficits at the end of each year and considerable borrowing had to take place. It was therefore decided to apply to the King for a brief. This was eventually published on 13 April 1701, and it is interesting to see what an expensive and complicated business it was; amongst other things the help of Mr Cumberbach, the City Recorder, had to be obtained and one of the Chapter had to make a journey to London. The Brief itself, a framed copy of which hangs in the Chapter House, states:

> That such is the present ruinous condition of the said Cathedral Church in Chester, and of the Buildings thereunto belonging, by reason of the perishable nature of the stone wherewith they were built, and the damage they received in the time of the Civil Wars, that the said Dean and Chapter (though they have run themselves much in debt) have not been able with all their care and the utmost of their ability to prevent the continual and increasing decay of the said Buildings. [The cost of restoration is estimated at £7000,] which the said Dean and Chapter are utterly incapable of raising themselves, by reason of the mean endowment and extream poverty of the said Church. [All parsons, vicars and curates are commanded] deliberately and affectionately to publish and declare the tenor hereof to our said loving subjects, and earnestly exhort them to a liberal contribution on this occasion. [In addition the churchwardens are to conduct a house to house collection, accompanied by the incumbent.]
>
> April 13, 1701.

The expenses were as follows:

		£	s.	d.
Expended about the Brief				
1700	A treat to Mr. Cumberland and Mr. Adams	0	4	7
	for paper		1	0
	for 3 sheets of stampt paper for Mr. Fowkes [the Chapter Clerk]		3	6
	for 3 sheets of large paper			6
	to Mr. Adams for procuring £50 and making the bond		5	0
	To Mr. Jackson the scrivenor		10	0
	To Mr. Cumberback for procuring a Court and Counsel	1	1	6
	To Mr. Adams for his pains		5	0
	To the Cryer of the Court		2	6
	At Dr. Entwistles parting in wine		3	0
	To Dr. Entwistle for his journey	15	0	0
		£18	1	7

In the following year we have further payments:

	£	s.	d.
Disbursements on Account and Credit of the Brief			
For a book in which they are entered		3	0
To Mr. Wait Diocesan Registrar for his care at London	1	1	6
To Mr. Bowcher which he has laid down for carriage of briefs		2	0
For carriage by wagon		2	6
For printing letters to the Archdeacons		8	10
To Will Cook for dispersing Briefs		18	0
Tho. Cradocke Note [bill] about the side Ile being all new mended next the green ch. yard	11	18	0
Nat. Badders note for slates laths etc.	7	3	6
and Payd in part of Tho. Jones the Carpenters note for work done in the Broad Ile	5	0	0
To John Jepson for dispersing Briefs		5	0
For Letters to and from Stafford		2	0
To Will Ratsdall for carrying the deputations to Stafford		5	0
To Ald. Allen for return of £100	1	5	0
	£28	19	8
Overcharged myself fourteen shillings last year		14	0
To Mr. Fowke for stamps that have been used hitherto		10	0
	£30	3	8

It is to be regretted that there is no record available of the parishes which subscribed, but the following have been recorded in the *Cheshire Sheaf* at various times:

	£	s.	d.	
Llanyblodwell		14	6	(I, 198)
Llanymynech		4	6	

	£	s.	d.	
Ormesby, Norfolk		2	2	
St. Oswald's, Chester		15	7	(III, 53)
St. Michael's, Chester	13	18	0	(n.s., I, 76)
Cuckfield, Sussex	1	5	6	(n.s., 88)
Bunbury, Cheshire	2	18	$11\frac{1}{2}$ [1]	

The money seems to have come in very slowly, for there are two further mentions of the Brief in the Accounts several years later:

	£	s.	d.
1706 Aug. 21, to Evans for carrying two packs of Briefs to the Audit Chamber			6
1708 May 6 To Mr. Heatley and his clerk for Searching the Brief 7 days	1	5	0

And in a history of Chester written in 1815 we read that the choir roof was "new planked from money raised by a brief in 1708".[2] The Accounts do not record how the money was spent.[3]

A memorandum in the Accounts for 1710 sums up the financial position at that date:

	£	s.	d.
In^d that the Church is now indebted			
To Mrs. Plumley by bond under Chapter Seal	100	0	0
To Mrs. Wood by like bond	100	0	0
To Dr. Fogge as above [being the deficit for the year]	141	12	1
Note that the salaries unpaid for the last year and rent due to Sir John Werden at Mich. as last above taxes allowed out of the same are	388	12	$5\frac{3}{4}$
Note also that the arrears of rent now due, only of which taxes have to be deducted, amount to	410	18	$8\frac{1}{2}$

In November 1711, it was decided to borrow another £200 on account of the non-payment of rents, and in 1714 another £200 was borrowed from Gabriel Wettenhall Esq., and Matthew Meakin, gent, making £700 in the course of six years. An economy was effected by paying the Lecturer £1 for each sermon he preached instead of paying him the usual stipend of £40 a year.

BISHOP STRATFORD'S FUNERAL

In February 1707, Bishop Nicholas Stratford died of an apoplexy in London and his body was brought to Chester for burial in the Cathe-

[1] Bunbury Churchwardens' Accounts.
[2] Pigot, p. 60.
[3] A very belated response came from Mansfield where included in a list of briefs in the Churchwardens' Accounts is: "Returned May 11, 1713 Chester Warminge, 1/2."

dral which he had helped to repair in 1698. He is best remembered for his share in founding the Blue Coat Hospital for the maintenance, instruction, and apprenticeship of thirty-five poor boys. He gave £100 to begin with, promising to bequeath a like sum at his death, but he died intestate. "His son, Dr. Stratford, finding one hundred pounds wrapped up in a piece of cloth upon a shelf in the Bishop's study, gave it to the said Charity, imagining it had been his Father's intention that it should be so appropriated."[1] The following account of his funeral was printed in the *Cheshire Sheaf* in 1878 from a MS. scrap found among some papers of Dean Cotton of Bangor and gives a vivid picture of the funeral customs of that time:

All the bells in Chester began to toll at six of the clock in the morning; and about one o'clock all the company went out to meet the Corps at the Glass House, where the undertakers who attended delivered out the gloves, scarfs, hat-bands, etc. Between four and five o'clock they returned into the town in the following order—first, the Captain of the City Militia, followed by his company two and two, as slow as they could march; after them all the livery servants in the same order; after them the gentlemen; all these had pepper coloure'd gloves, seamed with black. Then followed the Blue Boys on foot; after them the constables; next came the sword and mace, covered with black, preceding the Mayor and the Recorder with scarfs, hatbands and Shammy gloves; then the Aldermen; after them eight of the Bishop's servants on horseback in cloaks; then came forty or fifty clergymen, the last of whom were the six Prebends, who were the bearers, with scarfs, hat-bands, girdles and gloves; and lastly, the Dean and the Chancellor. Then followed the hearse decorated with black plumes and escutcheons, as were the horses' heads, their backs cover'd with velvet; on each side the horses were three porters in black gowns and caps, and black staves, to carry the coffin. Then several mourning coaches and others, to the number of between twenty and thirty. When they came to the Exchange, the Captain drew up his Company of Militia. The coffin was then taken out of the hearse, and the pall was supported by the bearers to the great door of the Broad Ayle. As soon as they entered the Church the bearers walked before the corps, and the choirmen and choristers chanted the services. The Choir was hung with black and escutcheons from the throne to the pulpit. The grave was at one end of the Communion Table. The coffin covered with velvet, the Ringes and plates of Prince's mettle. The Dean preached from *Daniel* chap. xii, verse 3, "And they that be wise shall shine as the brightness of the firmament, and they that turn many to righteousness as the stars for ever and ever."

Bishop Stratford's monument is now to be found on the south wall

[1] Cowper MSS., XIII cc.

of the west end of the nave. It consists of a marble tablet bearing a long Latin inscription, surmounted by three cherubs' heads with a skull at the foot. The only references to the funeral in the Accounts are to the setting up of the tablet and the taking down of the mourning, which last was not done until the new Bishop was elected in January 1708–9, eleven months after the funeral.

	s.	d.
1708 Oct. 29. A Beerage to the stone cutter at setting up the late Bishop's monument	2	6
1709 Jan. 23. To the Virgers for wax when the Lord Bishop was elected		6
Jan. 31. To James and another man for taking down the mourning	1	0

THE ACCOUNTS

As in previous chapters we propose to extract only those items which throw light on (i) events of national importance, (ii) the social life of the times, and (iii) the condition of the Cathedral and its precincts. Also those which call for an explanation which possibly some readers may be able to supply. As it is the reign of Queen Anne (1702–14) it is natural that ringing for Marlborough's victories should figure largely in them. I have decided to include them all, as they give us some idea of how the War affected the minds and lives of the people of those days. There were three scales of payment—2s. 6d., 2s., and 1s. 6d.—depending no doubt on the length of time the bells were rung, so that we get a clue to the importance attached to the different events. It is rather startling to find that in one or two cases the victory was celebrated before the battle had been fought, attributable no doubt to forgetfulness on the part of the Treasurer rather than to his power of clairvoyance, and we happen to know that one Treasurer wrote up his accounts from the notes he made in his pocket book, so that he might easily make a mistake over a date (see p. 175).

	£	s.	d.
1700 May 20 to James Evans for helping about pulling down the towers		2	0
July 18. For redeeming the Captives in Barbary	10	0	0
1702 Dec. 24. To Mr. Sayer for laying of water pipes to the Preb. houses	8	18	0
1703 March 6 item to Mr. Thane wht he had paid for his pipe	12		0
Feb. 24. To Tho. Pickmore for mending scarlet and purple hangings, viz. the hangings about the Com. Table, Pulpit, Cushions		9	8
May 4. To Tho. Pickmore for a Chest to put the hangings in	10		0

	s.	d.
Dec. 4. Pd. Hugh Hand the Joyner for four boxes to empty		
the sinks wth	8	0
1704 For ringing on St. George's Day [First mention]	2	6
For ringing on account of the news of the victory at Dona-		
wert [July 2]	2	0
For ringing on account of the news of the victory at		
Hochstett [Blenheim, Aug. 13] and taking Gibraltar [Aug. 4]	2	0
1704 To four torch bearers	2	0
For ringing on account of the victory obtained at sea	1	6

We have here preserved the memory of a nameless and almost forgotten victory won by Admiral Rooke over the French fleet on 24 August 1704. It was fought in defence of the newly acquired Gibraltar and was successful not only in protecting that place from attack but also in giving us command of the Western Mediterranean, for as a result of the engagement the French fleet retired to Toulon and did not risk another battle.[1]

	s.	d.
1705 Sept. 2 to Evans for two days Ringing for forcing the		
French lines	3	6
pd. for four torches, but not used	4	0

In 1705 ... the French threw up a defensive line known as "The Lines of Brabant", forty miles long, protecting Brussels and the Low Countries against the Army of the Allies, which had now returned from Bavaria. But by a brilliant manœuvre Marlborough broke through this line at the first attempt, pushed the French beyond Louvain, and, but for the interference by the Dutch Deputies and generals, would in all probability have won another victory south of Brussels.[2]

	s.	d.
Nov. 26. to Ald. Page's servant who brought Mr. Shacker-		
ley's present	2	6
1706 March 18. To three poor people for giving light into Mr.		
Jolliffe's lease	1	6

Here is a puzzle indeed! Jolliffe's lease was the lease of the bailiwick of Chester, i.e. of all the Cathedral property in that City, and that there was some difficulty about it is clear from a clause in Dean Arderne's will (1691) in which he directed that his money might be used, if desired, "to defray the expenses of procuring an Act of Parliament for disposing of the great lease, when it shall fall, called Jollive's lease, so as shall be most conducive to the welfare of this Cathedral and to the public good".

I can only suggest that those three poor people were "oldest

[1] *Camb. Modern Hist.*, v, 413.
[2] *The Art of War on Land*, A. H. Burne, p. 100.

inhabitants" supplying evidence of what they remembered about the property in times gone by.

	£	s.	d.
1706 May 25 to Evans for Ringing upon the news of the victory in Flanders [Ramillies, May 23]		2	6
Aug. 26. To Mr. Lamb for his journey to Chester, when designed to be organist	1	0	0

Unfortunately he was not appointed and the post was given to Mr White, who was to cause a great deal of trouble later on, as we shall see.

	£	s.	d.
Sept. 18. To Evans for ringing on account of the victory in Italy. [Battle of Turin won by Prince Eugene Sept. 7]		2	0
Dec. 2. To Wid. Ambrose for a brush for the Tabernacle work		1	2
1708 May 8. To Rathbone by the Dean's order for supplying the organist's place the last half-year ending at Lady Day	2	0	0
Oct. 23. To Mr. Rathbone by the Dean's order, for being at the organ the last half-year ending at Michaelmas	3	0	0

Rathbone was one of the choirmen, and the vacancy he was suddenly called upon to fill was caused by the sad behaviour of Edmund White, the organist, who (says the Chapter Book under date 16 September 1707), "being entrusted to instruct a young gentlewoman (of an antient and right worshipful family) in musick, endeavoured to engage her affections by kissing courting and the like dalliances unknown to her parents, and mentioned a match with her, which particulars when convened he doth deny, onely frivolously pretended the mention of marriage was in jest". White was dismissed forthwith but was restored to his post the following May although, as we have seen, Rathbone continued to "be at the organ" until Michaelmas. The leniency of the Chapter proved to be misplaced, for in 1715 White was finally expelled since "a bastard child hath been lately filiated upon him". The organist's salary was £12 a year and Rathbone having filled the post for 14 months should have received £14 if he was being paid at the same rate, whereas he actually received only £5, in addition of course to his Salary as Conduct (£5).

He does not seem to have complained until four years later when he was dismissed from his post as choirman for "many very great misdemeanours and enormities by him committed" (Chapter Minute of 31 May 1712). He at once proceeded to get what he could out of the Chapter.

	£	s.	d.
1712 Aug. 12 to Rathbone by Mr Deans order, declaring solemnly that he never recd more than 40s. from Mr. Lancaster who had entered £5 in his accompts	2	10	0

This is possible, for Lancaster died suddenly in May 1709, and the page of Expenditures for that year is headed "By Mr. Lancaster, late Treasurer, as appear by his Pocket Book", but Rathbone had been a long time in claiming it.

	£	s.	d.
Sept. 22 to Rathbone, by the Bp's order, in full for officiating at the organ 14 months during Mr. Whites' suspension	9	0	0

Evidently Rathbone had appealed to the Bishop and got a decision in his favour.

We now return to the year 1708.

	s.	d.
1708 May 11. To ringing May 9 for the preventing the intended invasion of Scotland	2	6

Louis XIV had fitted out an expedition to take James Edward, son of James II, to Scotland, but the luckless Prince was delayed a week by an attack of measles, which gave Admiral Byng time to intercept him at the mouth of the Firth of Forth and the Chevalier with some difficulty escaped back to France.

	£	s.	d.
May 28. To Giles Peck for leading the Muck out of the Abbey Court Lane [? Abbey Street]		2	6
July 15. For ringing on the 9th [sic] for the victory in the battle near Audenard [July 11th]		2	6
1708 Sept. 3. To Susan for a mop to wash the floor about the altar			7

In this year a gallery was erected in St Oswald's:

	£	s.	d.
1709 Sept. 8 to Evans for ringing for the victory near Mons [unidentified]		2	0
Nov. 9 to Evans for ringing upon the surrender of Mons [Oct. 20]		1	6
Nov. 23 to Evans for ringing upon Thanksgiving Day for the victory at Blarengnies [Battle of Malplaquet]		2	6
Paid by Dr. Thane to Mr. Walker for Mrs. Lancaster and family	1	1	6
1710 Jan. 3. To the Master of the House of Correction, Constable and Beadle for correcting Darwell for defiling the Church		2	0
1710 April 19 to Evans for ringing on account of forcing the enemies lines		2	6

This was a line of fortresses on the French frontier. Evans was a little early with his bell, for the allies did not begin to move until 20 April, when Marlborough wrote: "I hope to date my next on the other side of the lines".[1] Sieges occupied the rest of the year in Flanders but battles were being fought in Spain.

	£	s.	d.
Aug. 16 to Evans for ringing on news of the victory in Spain [Almenara, July 27]		2	6
Aug. 26 to Evans for ringing on the news of the surrender of Bethune [Aug. 29]		2	6
Aug. 30 to Evans for Ringing on news of the second victory in Spain [Saragossa, Aug. 19]		2	6
Sept. 25 to Evans for ringing on K. Charles arrival at Madrid and surrender of St. Venant [in France Sept. 30]		2	6
1711 Dec. 4 to Mr. Peak for Mr. Lancaster's children	10	0	0
Sept. 17 to Evans for Ringing at the taking of Bouchain [Sept. 12]		1	6

On 31 December Marlborough was dismissed from all his offices, and opportunities for bell-ringing ceased. The English army was treacherously withdrawn from France, leaving Prince Eugene to face the enemy alone; and an armistice was made with Louis XIV by which he surrendered Dunkirk.

	£	s.	d.
1712 July 14 to Evans for ringing on the news of our having possession of Dunkirk		2	6
July 16 to John Carter for pulling down and building up the wall at the end of the cloister	3	2	6
Nov. 19 to Mr. Wishaw his bill for sueing Mr. Glaseur and Darwell	10	12	0
To Totty for worke about the Church and stoneworke for the Turnpike		10	0
Nov. 20 to Jonathan Pickering for timber and making the Turnpike in the Ch'yard		3	9
Dec. 12 to Evans for ringing on the occasion of setting up the Queen's effegies		2	0

As far as is known there was only one statue of Queen Anne, which was set up on the south front of the Exchange in Northgate. For some reason it always attracted the attention of the mob at election time, so that by 1815 "she is now much mutilated, having lost the globe and sceptre which she formerly held".[2]

	s.	d.
1713 March 25 to Evans for ringing upon Dr. Sacheverell's restoration	2	6

[1] W. Churchill, *Marlborough, His Life and Times*, IV, 240.

[2] Pigot, p. 48. Misfortune continued to follow the unhappy Queen, for the statue was removed to the Water Tower Gardens when the Exchange was pulled down and was there broken by hooligans during the Second World War (1939–45).

Sacheverell was impeached by the Whigs in 1710 for a sermon he preached against them and was suspended from preaching for three years. The Dean and Chapter's politics were evidently Tory.

In this year the Audit Chamber was restored at a cost of £29 7s.11d., and the next item gives us a clue as to where it was situated:

	£	s.	d.
(1713) May 16. For slating part of the Palace broken by the workmen at the Audit Chamber		1	6
Nov. 22 to Mr. Stratford a Bill of Court fees in prosecution of Mr. Darwell	3	0	0
1714 Feb. 3 the Society for Propagating [*sic*] Christian Knowledge per Mr. Callis	10	0	0
April 4. A letter of thanks from the Society above mentioned			4
Aug. 5. Evans for ringing and gorse for a bonfire on the proclaiming his present Majesty [George I]		3	6

This year £78 18s. 6d. was spent on the broad aisle and the steeple roof.

And here with the death of Queen Anne we may conveniently leave the Accounts for a while and look at the Chapter. Of those who composed it in 1701 only two remained, Wroe and Thane. Entwistle had been succeeded by Samuel Shaw in 1707; Garenciers by Arthur Fogge, the Dean's son, in 1702; Lancaster first by Richard Clutterbuck in 1709 and on his death by Charles Blake in 1710, and Richard Wright by John Oliver, in 1711. The Chapter in 1714 was therefore constituted as follows:

Laurence Fogge, D.D., Dean	1692
Richard Wroe, D.D.	1678
John Thane, D.D.	1686
Arthur Fogge, D.D.	1702
Samuel Shaw, M.A.	1707
Charles Blake, M.A.	1710
John Oliver, M.A.	1711

Samuel Shaw, M.A., was Rector of Warrington. He was presented to West Kirby on 16 January 1718 in succession to Richard Wroe, but died in the following year. He was buried in Warrington Church.

Arthur Fogge, D.D., who was installed in the Cathedral on 20 April 1702, had been Vicar of St Oswald's since 28 November 1699 and became Rector of Heswall on 9 February 1702, and of Dodleston, 6 July 1716. He died on 8 January 1738–9 and was buried in the Cathedral. He was remarkable even in those days for the size of his family. His first wife, Anne, died in child-bed in 1692 and her baby son soon followed her to the grave, but the Doctor married again and from 1698 to 1718 there were only five years in which a little Fogge was not brought to the Cathedral font. Altogether his second wife bore him 15 children, of whom 5 died in infancy, and she herself survived her husband two years, dying in 1740.

Richard Clutterbuck, D.D., Fellow of St Catharine's, Cambridge, only lived a few months after being installed.

Charles Blake, M.A., was the son of John Blake, of Reading, gent. He was educated at Merchant Taylors' School and gained a scholarship at St John's College, Oxford, at the age of nineteen. He took his B.A. in 1687 and became a Fellow of his College, where he appears to have remained until he came to Chester in 1710. His benefice was St Sepulchre, London, from 1712 to 1716. In 1715 he left Chester to become Sub-Dean of York.

John Oliver, M.A., was Vicar of Audlem from 1696 and collated Prebendary on 7 May 1711. He was also Curate of St Peter's, Chester from 1710, and in 1717 received the valuable living of West Kirby. He died in 1730 and was buried in St Peter's.

THE BISHOPS

The Bishop who succeeded Nicholas Stratford was Sir William Dawes, Bart., D.D. He was consecrated Bishop in February 1708, and translated to York in 1714, so that he was in Chester Diocese for a few years only and had very little to do with the Cathedral. However, his character as recorded by Ormerod is worthy of mention here. "Sir William Dawes is said to have been most scrupulously laborious in discharging the duties of his high offices, uniting easiness of manners with the most dignified deportment, and recommended by all the qualifications of personal gracefulness." With this agrees Dr Cowper, who writes: "This Prelate was of a noble and gracefull Personage, and a sweet engaging behaviour, kind and respectful to his clergy, and humane to everyone." He and Charles Blake were probably school and college friends, for he too was at Merchant Taylors' School, won a scholarship at St John's College and became a Fellow there. This may account for the fact that Blake followed the Bishop to Chester and later followed him to York.

Bishop Francis Gastrell, D.D., who succeeded Bishop Dawes, was consecrated Bishop of Chester on 14 April 1714, and was allowed to hold his canonry of Christ Church *in commendum.* He died on 24 November 1725, and was buried without memorial in Christ Church Cathedral, Oxford.

We owe him a debt of gratitude (i) for having helped to preserve the invaluable historical collection of the Randle Holme family after it had been refused by the Corporation of Chester, by inducing Robert Harley, Earl of Oxford, to buy it and add it to the collection which bears his name, and (ii) for having compiled his *Notitia Cestriensis*, an historical record of his Diocese. He was Bishop from 1714 to 1725. His death is referred to in the Chapter Book only because the mourning which was hung up in the Cathedral was by resolution of the Chapter given to the Sacrist who that year was Minor Canon Dockerill.[1]

More Trouble with the Choir

The steps taken at this time to improve the discipline and singing of the choir reveal that there was some difficulty in attracting sufficiently qualified men. We have seen how they had to suspend and ultimately get rid of an organist and a choirman; soon afterwards they had trouble with another choirman. On 28 November 1711, they record that William Webb, who "hath been hitherto admonished concerning misdemeanours" without any effect, was now suspended from the Choir, and it is ordered "that in the meantime he doe not presume to sit in the stall that he was accustomed to sit in, or to wear his surplice, but that he constantly attend the services of the Church in some other visible [this inserted] place". Though this resolution was annulled the next year, he was ultimately dismissed in July 1713. In the following November at the Annual Chapter when all the members were expected to be present the question of the Choir was taken in hand and the following decision was come to:

> Whereas some of the Quire-men by reason of age or other infirmity read the service so as not to be heard throughout the Quire, others by indecent or ill-ordered pronunciation give offence to the hearers and help not but hinder their reverent atten'on, It is decreed that those whom the Chapter judge to be such, shall hire some others of their rank in the Church to supply their Courses at such rates as the parties shall agree upon.
> And whereas the Chapter through want of candidates qualified for singing according to statute have been necessitated to admitt sundry persons too meanly skilled in that faculty upon condition or promise to fitt and accomplish themselves in some reasonable time, yet when entred on their office either wilfully or through incapacity have not improved so as to perform that part of the duty not to the help but hindrance of Devotion; It is

[1] The accounts kept for Bishop Gastrell and his successors by the Deputy-Registrar, Mr Edward Roberts, are preserved in the muniment room, and some account of them is given in the *Cheshire Historian*, No. 4, p. 4 (1954).

decreed that such Probationers shall have not more than one year from the date hereof allowed tryall and in the meantime make such allowance to a teacher as the Chapter shall appoint who shall also perform their office in singing verse Anthems for them when conveniently required and allow such rates to their teachers as the Chapter shall appoint not exceeding a fifth part of their salaries. And if their Proficiency in that time give not assurance that their Performance will be devout laudable and answer the the end of their Institution, they shall be dismissed and the Church be no longer burthened with them.

L. Fogg	Decan^d
Joe Thane	Preb.
Arthur Fogg	Preb.
Jo. Oliver	Preb.

1715. This year the Treasurer (Dr Arthur Fogge) made the following note:

"N.B. Whereas the Almsmen's salaries are here mentioned six at £6 each, Their salary is properly £6 6s. 8d., which six shillings and eight pence is given by them to the sweeper of the church."

This is a queer business. If Dr Fogge had turned back to the year 1700 he would have read in the Accounts

	s.	d.
The Sweeper of the Ch. for the Almsmen out of their Salarys	13	4
The toler of the bell for the Almsmen out of their Salarys	6	8
	£1 0 0	

At the same time the salary of the almsmen is reduced from £6 13s. 4d. to £6 0s. 0d. What happened was that the organ blower in that year was given the title of Sexton and took over from the almsmen the duties of sweeping the church and ringing the bell for which the unfortunate almsmen had to pay him 13s. 4d. a year. Where the other 6s. 8d. came from does not appear. The feelings of the almsmen can be imagined when they found that they had to "give" a portion of their very inadequate wage to a man who was much better paid than they were. For James Evans, the Sexton, under this arrangement received

	£	s.	d.
for organ blowing	4	0	0
for "towler of the bells"	2	12	0
for sweeping	2	13	4
	£9	5	4

not to mention the 2s. or so that he pocketed for ringing the bells every time Marlborough won a victory.

The salaries of the rest of the staff are added for comparison:

Headmaster of the King's School	£22	0	0
Minor Canons	£15	0	0
Organist	£12	0	0
Conducts	£10	0	0
Usher of the King's School	£10	0	0
Vergers	£6	0	0
Almsmen	£6	0	0

When Evans died in 1720 the fee for organ blowing was reduced from £4 to £2 by resolution of the Chapter (p. 109) but it was restored again to £4 in 1728.

On 16 January 1718, old Dean Laurence Fogge signed the Chapter Book for the last time in very tremulous writing. He died on 27 February following at the age of eighty-eight and was buried in the Lady Chapel, his wife Mary having preceded him on 30 January, also aged eighty-eight. His epitaph in Latin, not now extant, recorded that he was Vicar of St Oswald's for twenty-seven years, Prebendary for nineteen, and Dean for twenty-six. Born in the reign of Charles I, in residence at Oxford during the Civil War, he was Minister at Hawarden during the Commonwealth and received episcopal ordination in 1661 at the hand of Thomas Sydserf, Bishop of Galloway.[1]

The funeral sermon was preached by his son. Henry Prescott noted in his diary: "March 9. Dr. Fogg has a good discourse in ye Quire on the words of Ely—It is the Lord, let him do what to him seemeth good. In his prayers, omitting the Dean, he is moved with pious affection into tears."

DEAN OFFLEY 1718–1722

Dr Fogge was succeeded on 6 March by Walter Offley, D.D.,[2] a nephew of the John Offley (d. 1658) of Madeley, Staffs., to whom Isaak Walton dedicated *The Compleat Angler*. He was born at Broughton Hall in 1680 in a house which still stands, and was educated at Lichfield Grammar School and Oriel College, Oxford. He was made deacon at Eccleshall, the seat of the Bishop of Lichfield, on 23 May 1703, and ordained priest on 24 September 1704. The same year he was presented

[1] Mr W. F. Irvine writes: "He seems to have been busy in 1660–1 ordaining Cheshire folk, including the Rev William Colley, Vicar of Bruera. Tillotson the Archbishop was another of his ordinations."

[2] Prescott wrote in his diary: "March 7. The more private news is of the disposition of the deanery. It affects many with inexpressible admiration." (*Sheaf.* XI, p. 97.)

by his relative, Mrs Crewe, to the Rectory of Bartholmey, Cheshire, where we are told "he built a very handsome parsonage house". In 1715 he was made a Prebendary of Lichfield Cathedral, coming to Chester as Dean three years later. In 1721 the Crewe family gave him the Rectory of Mucklestone, Staffs. (which he held in plurality with Bartholmey) but he did not live long to enjoy it, dying the following year at the early age of forty-two and being buried there.

THE ACCOUNTS, 1718–1722

> 1718 April 8. Mr. Jones for flagging Lady Maries Chap. £33, of which Dr. Fogg paid £15 15s. 10d., the balance due from his Father, the late Dean, to the Ch. on account of Collections; and the last year's Treasurer advanced him £8, vide last year's accounts   £11 4s. 2d.

Last year's accounts have "Mr Dean for his garden £10", which must be the transaction referred to. We gather from this extract that at his death Dean Fogge held in his hands a considerable ammount of money collected at Communion Services. This no doubt prompted the Chapter to pass the following resolution:

> Sept. 19, 1718. Memd. It is this day agreed that all Sacrament money received in the Choir of Chester [Cathedral] by the Sacrist or in his absence by the Prebendary that officiates be delivered to the Treasurer, who shall disburse the same, first providing for the poor belonging to the Cathedral, via. to Mrs. Lancaster, the widow of Preb. Lancaster decd., Elizabeth Harrison, the Widow Pickmore and such like.

On 1 May the Chapter contracted with Mr Anthony Vater to repair the organ for £20, a work which was duly carried out.

	s.	d.
Aug. 6. Cleansing the water course under Mr. Thane's house	1	0

Unfortunately we do not know where Mr Thane's house was, but probably the watercourse means the culvert which still runs across the green opposite the houses in Abbey Street, and is monastic in origin. It was in 1275 that Edward I granted the Abbot permission to pierce the City wall and let his culvert drain into the Town ditch.

	£	s.	d.
1719 Nov. 10. Pd. the Churchwardens of St. Peter's by order of the Dean and Chapter	6	6	0
1720 Jan. 9. To Ald. Puleston and Bingley for the Sub-Dean's curtain and cushions	1	1	4

At a Chapter meeting on 6 September 1720, an interesting reference was made to Bishop Bridgeman's houses which he built for the choir-men in 1726:

> Whereas Benjamin Lowndes, one of the Conducts of this Church, having dwelt in the house that was Ternals and paid him five pounds per annum for the same as long as he lived, and having continued to dwell there ever since his death without paying any rent at all, the Treasurer is hereby order'd to stop the said Lowndes's salary or pension as Conduct till the rent of the said house be paid into his hand and to take care of the house till the Bishop's pleasure be known how it shall be dispos'd, that being one of the houses that were built by Bishop Bridgeman.

A few weeks later this same Lowndes was up before the Chapter again for having pilfered for several years past the collections taken at the Communion Service in St Oswald's, of which he was "the late parish clerk". He was ordered to be suspended from the Choir; and it is rather surprising to read that on 2 January 1721, he was made Sexton of the Cathedral, which comprised the posts of organ-blower, sweeper, and bell-ringer. He seems to have made good, for in 1728 he was made Verger, but died before the year was out.

In 1722 we get a hint of the way the Cathedral clergy lived in those days and where they lived: "Agreed that the cellar betwixt Doctor Thane's cellar and the School yard be assigned for the use of the two Prebendal houses now belonging to Mr. Henchman and Mr. Maple-toft." The School was the Refectory, but where was the school yard? Much depends on that. And was this an old monastic cellar?

The Arderne Law-suit

When Dean Arderne bequeathed all his estate to the Cathedral in 1691 he could not have forseen that it would some day be considerably augmented by the property bequeathed by Mrs Jane Done. It followed that Dean Arderne's will was "the means of wresting from his family a very large share of one of the most antient estates in the County, and has involved the representatives of two of his brothers in a series of law expenses, which compelled them to alienate a considerable portion of Mrs Jane Done's bequest and the successive turns of presentation to the Rectory of Tarporley".[1]

The Dean and Chapter were not slow to put in their claim:

> Sept. 22, 1718. Mem^m. It is this day in Chapter agreed that the Treas-urer for the time being shall disburse all necessary sums in prosecuting

[1] Ormerod, II, 83.

and recovering of a reversionary title to some lands in this County
Palatine bequeathed to the Dean and Chapter of this Church and their
predecessors by the late Revd. Dr. James Ardern, late Dean of this
Cathedral.''

They must have known that they were letting themselves in for considerable expense, but no doubt they thought it was worth it, and the
event proved that they were right.

	£	s.	d.
1719 March 25, Paid Adam Chadwick for a journey about Dean Arderne's will		5	0
Oct. 28, Pd. Mr. Wishaw's bill in D. Arderne's cause	24	12	0
1720 Oct. 1. Repaid the Dean money laid out in the suit with Mr. Arderne	3	0	0
1721 May 22. Mr. Wishaw's bill	8	18	0
Aug. 26, 27, 28. By Mr. Henchman at the Commission in Norwich	3	6	1
By Mr. Henchman at the Commission in Chester pd. the Commissioners	4	4	0
By Mr. Henchman at the Commission in Chester	1	4	0
Pd. the Commissioners	4	4	0
1724 Aug. 1. To the messenger who brought the Survey of Utkinton and for Tarporley		2	0
Nov. Spent at the meeting of the Commissioners in Chester to settle the return of the Utkinton Commission		11	6
1725 Paid Mr. Henchman for his attendance on the Commission for discovering and dividing the Tarporley estate			
For his attendance at Northwych, Aug. 24, 25, 26, 1721 for examining witnesses	3	8	0
Pd. him for spent in treating the Commissioners at a Meeting to settle the opening of the Commission for partition Chester, Oct. 2, 1723		8	0
for his attending the Commission at Tarporley Dec. 14, 1723	1	1	0
for pd. by him to Mr. Edwards, one of the Commissioners at that time	1	1	0
for pd. by him to a Messenger into Lancash. Dec. 7 ⎫ to enquire		7	6
It. a Messenger to Middlewych Dec. 8 ⎬ after		4	0
It. a Messenger to Tarpurley Dec. 9 ⎭ Surveyor		2	6
for his own attendance and for spent on the Surveyors at Torpurley Dec. 9	1	4	0
Itm at Sandyway, July 27, 1725	1	1	0
It. Sept. 3 and 4, 1725 at Sandyway	2	2	0
It. Oct. 25, 26, 27, 28, 29 at Northwych	5	5	0
pd. Mr. Prescott for attending the Commission Sept. 3 and 4, 1725 at Sandyway	2	2	0
Oct. 25, 26, 27, 28, 29 at Northwych	5	5	0

After long-drawn-out and expensive litigation lasting about six years the Dean and Chapter were successful in obtaining "a considerable portion of Mrs Jane Done's bequest".[1]

DEAN ALLEN 1722–1732

Thomas Allen was born at Kingsley in Staffordshire and educated in the village school of Dilhorne. He must have been a brilliant boy, for he eventually proceeded to Emmanuel College, Cambridge, and was for twenty-five years Rector of Stoke-on-Trent a few miles away from his birthplace. He was also Archdeacon of Stafford. He was instituted to the Deanery of Chester on 13 July 1722.

One of the first events of his reign was the restoration of the Chapter House, which was undertaken by Prebendary Charles Henchman in 1723. No record of it appears in the Accounts because it was done by voluntary subscription, the first example of a method with which we are so familiar today. Dr Cowper, writing in 1728,[2] tells how the Chapter House lost its roof and windows during the Civil War, but as the Accounts show that it was in use in the latter half of the seventeenth century he may have been exaggerating, as also when he writes: "it was afterwards so utterly neglected that it became a Common Receptacle for Filth and Rubbish". He continues:

> In this condition it lay till the year 1723 when the Rev. Mr. Charles Henchman, one of the Prebendarys of the Cathedral, was elected Treasurer [actually he was elected in 1721], a gentleman of great knowledge and learning and an admirer of antiquity, well noted and esteemed for a generous public spirit, who ... covered it with a new roof, secured the windows and inletts to the weather, to prevent its further decay, [and] carefully reformed it into a decent order and condition in which it now remains.

1726. The Chapter Book corroborates this, for on 20 January 1726 it was "Agreed that whereas the Rev. Mr. Henchman hath received by contributions towards the repair of the old Chapter House £107 3s. 1d., and hath expended £118 2s. 11d., whereby the balance of £10 19s. 10d. remains due to him", he should be paid it out of Cathedral Funds.[3]

1726. While restoring the Chapter House Henchman let his

---

[1] They sold the land in 1920, but still retain their share in the advowson of the living of Tarporley.

[2] *A Cursory View of the City of Chester.* Cowper MSS.

[3] Bishop Gastrell contributed £20 on 13 Oct. 1723. See his account book.

admiration of antiquity lead him to excavate beneath the floor, where he found a stone coffin containing the body of a man:

> wrapt up in sear-cloth and stitched over with strong black leather from head to foot and at some distance resembling a man lying in armour; upon the right breast was the form of St. Andrew's Cross of yellow galloon [braid] or fervetting very fresh and stitch'd to the leather. . . . In diverse other parts of the Chapter House were skeletons found, but whether of Earls or Bishops or other ecclesiastics is uncertain, there remaining no monuments thereof to clear the doubt.

THE ACCOUNTS

	£	s.	d.
1723 April 2. Mr. Parker Upholder[1] for Curtains for the windows and mending the cushions		1 7	6
April 25. Ringing on the thanksgiving day for Deliverance from the Plague		5	0
Dec. 31. John Johnson for 7 days and an half shewing the Surveyors the lands and houses belonging to the Dean and Chapter in Lord Vane's lease		11	6
Mr. Grantham for abstracting the Inquisition of King James the first, and the Parliamentary Survey, and taking a particular of the premises in the Lease made to Mr. Jollife and comparing that with the Lease made to the Lord Vane		2 2	0
1724 Oct. pd. for mending the wall between the School back side and Dr. Fog's garden		1	1
Nov. 27. Paid Mr. Prebend Prescott by order of the Chapter for assisting the Surveyors of Ld. Vane's lease		2 2	0
Dec. Spent at Mr. Willoughby's at settling the valuation of Ld. Vane's lease		15	0
Dec. 8. To Mr. Kennick for his opinion and drawing a clause to be added to Ld. Vane's Lease		1 1	0

This was a lease of the bailiwick of Chester called "Jolliffe's lease" mentioned in Dean Arderne's will, which was evidently due for renewal. The Chapter on 28 June 1725, in the absence of the Dean resolved that whereas £1,400 was fixed in Chapter on 25 November last to be the fine payable for a new lease, and whereas Lord Vane "had not yet offered to pay the said sum", if he did not pay by 3 August next the agreement would be null and void. Evidently he did not do so, and when in 1726 he approached the Dean and Chapter again he found they had raised their price. At a Chapter meeting on 8 May "a letter from Mr. William Mills on the Lord Viscount Vane's

---

[1] An upholsterer was originally an upholder, one who holds up goods for inspection (*Concise Oxford Dic.*). This is the only place in the Accounts where the old spelling is retained.

behalf was read wherein he proposed to pay the sum of £1,600 for the renewal of his Lordship's lease". The Chapter agreed to accept this offer, but as the Dean was not present he was written to for his approval. He replied:

> The sum abovementioned is in my opinion too little, but to obviate all objections of hardship if all the Prebendaries agree to it, they shall have the concurrence of their and your humble servant Tho. Allen.

Viscount Vane was an Irish Peer who had a lease of part of a messuage in Parsons Lane, consisting of four rooms, two up and two down.

		s.	d.
1725	Nov. Tolling for the Bishop [Bp. Gastrell]	—	
1726	Jan. 9. To Ringing for the King's landing [from Hanover ?]	5	0
	March 5. To Ringing at returning the Conge d'elire [electing Samuel Peploe as the new Bishop]	5	0
	To given to Mr. Mayor's servant when we met the Mayor and the Recorder about their intended Act of Parliament	1	0

This was probably the Navigation Act for canalizing the River Dee (see below, p. 192).

		£	s.	d.
	Sept. 7. To a roller for the Saint's bell [Sanctus bell]		1	0
	Oct. 15. To Mr. Parker Upholsterer for 1725 and 1726	7	0	0
	To Charles Boswell for paving in the Abbey Court by Sir Henry Bunbury's	3	8	0
1727	July 4. The address to his present Majesty		3	6

This was George II, who had succeeded to the throne on 11 June. In this year the head verger, Charles Hughes, was admonished a second time for immorality and drunkenness. The old reprobate had been in the service of the Cathedral since 1690 and was old enough to know better. The third admonishing, which was usually followed by dismissal, took place on 17 June 1728, but instead of being dismissed he was retired on pension, the pension being taken out of the wages of the incoming vergers! Peter Parry, cordwainer, and William Taylor, had to sign an agreement that they would each pay £3 a year (half their wages) to Charles Hughes and his wife as long as one of them was alive, so that the old man continued to receive as pension the same amount as he had been receiving in wages. The vergers appear to have been allowed to take the "Sacrament Money" in compensation.

The *Cursory View of the City of Chester* quoted above was written by Dr Cowper in 1728 and from it we can get a description of the Cathedral at the point we have reached in its history. We learn that it

had "an excellent organ, sonorous and musical", the tapestry now in
the Refectory depicting St Paul and Elymas the Sorcerer covered the
altar, or so he says, and "contiguous to, and on each side of the Altar,
are several handsome monuments of marble". There were:

> five large bells of such weight that formerly with difficulty but of late years
> at no time having been rung in a peal; the tenor, which weighs 44 hundred,
> is of a sweet musical tone in which respect and for bigness compared to the
> large bell of St. Mary-le-bow, London, and like that, is rung at nine every
> night, thereby useful not only to the City but to all the villages adjacent.
> The Cathedral was lately made clean and whitewashed within,[1] and at the
> same time beautified with the arms of the former earls and barons of
> Chester, and of the Bishops of this See, painted over the Choir door orna-
> mentally enough; the charge whereof was defrayed by the executors of the
> late famous mathematician Mr. John Ward deceased, a native of this City,
> who by his will gave a legacy of [blank] for that purpose.

The Choir door was in those days set in a wall, the remains of the old
pulpitum, at the west end of the choir: the arms which were displayed
on it are now on the south wall of the refectory. We are here given
an indication of their age and date. The Doctor goes on to describe
Abbey Square: "a pleasant square plot of ground which was lately
planted with lime trees growing in regular order, the spaces between
which are formed into delightful walks which from their agreeable
retiredness are much resorted unto by gentlemen and ladies in the
summer season".

In this connection we may note the following item in the Accounts:

	£	s.	d.
1727 June 2. To 19 loads of red gravel, laying the walks and pruning the trees in the Abbey Court	2	2	0

Of St Oswald's the Doctor comments that the congregation "enjoye
the benefit of the Choir organ", and of the Abbey Gateway that it
was used by the Dean and Chapter for a court, "therein holding a
Court Baron, whereto all the tenants of the Church lands pay their
suit".

The ringing of the curfew in 1728 is interesting evidence of the age
of the present custom, unless indeed it has been discontinued and
started again in modern times. Further evidence on this point would
be of value.

The Chapter House, which was restored in 1723, was fitted up as a

---

[1] The whitewashing was done by Bishop Gastrell, whose accounts for 1725
contain the item "To whitewashing of the Church, £25 os. od."

library in 1728 with money from Dean Arderne's estate, the law suit having at last been terminated. A single manuscript preserved in the Muniment Room records that the Dean and Chapter received a sixth part of the estate in question which produced a yearly rent of £67 2s. 3d., together with the sum of £500 and "have desired the same may be applyed to the repairing and fitting up the old Chapter House (being a beautifull and antient Building, but now useless . . .) and to convert the same to a Library and to furnish it with books. . . ." Then follows an estimate of the cost:

	£	s.	d.
Estimate of Expenses of repairing the intended Library.			
Carpenter's work: Floor timber, Board, Nails, carriage and work	85	17	0
Joyner's work: Wainscot, locks, hinges and nails	309	10	0
Glazing	40	0	0
Iron bars and putting in with lead	30	0	0
Roof over Ante Room leading to the Library	50	0	0
	£515	7	0

	£	s.	d.
1728 Dec. 4. Mr. Potter for Dr. Croft's Anthems, Mr. Tey's prayer book, etc.		3	8	0

Dr Croft, M.D., who had just died, was organist at Westminster Abbey and the Chapel Royal. Two volumes of his anthems are still preserved in Chester Cathedral. Mr Tey was one of the Minor Canons.

	£	s.	d.
1730 July 15. To a bottle of wine with Mr. Ch. Foulks when we took possession of the buildings behind the Wolf's Head		2	0
Dec. 1. To Mr. Bingley Upholsterer for 8 Turkey work cushions; new curtains to the Bishop's Throne, and two matts at each end of the Communion Table		3	11	0
To John Davis for his horse and self going to the Dean [? to Stoke-on-Trent]		10	0
1731 Nov. 27. To Mr. Wm. Tailour [Under-Verger] towards paying for the cure of his collar bone broken in a journey on the Church's business		11	6

On 1 April 1730, the Dean and Chapter paid the late Prebendary Thane's widow £105 for her husband's library, he having died in 1727.

In November they passed a most revealing resolution to the effect "that no member of the said Cathedral Church inferior to Prebendary shall walk in the Broad Isle of the said Church while the Dean, Sub-dean or any of the Prebendaries are there". They evidently took themselves very seriously in those days.

A year later they resolved "that the Vergers be ordered to take care for the future that no leather nor linnen be suffered to hang upon the Church walls, which make an indecent and unseemly aspect, and that they draw the nails and other things on which they hang".

DEAN THOMAS BROOKE 1732-1757

Dean Allen died on 31 May 1732, and was buried at Stoke-on-Trent where he had been Rector for twenty-five years. He was succeeded on 18 July by Thomas Brooke, LL.D., the son of Benedict Brooke, of Brereton, gent.[1] Thomas was born at Brereton on 27 February 1692, and went to Brazenose College, Oxford, in 1710. He took his B.A. degree in 1714 and seems to have moved to Cambridge, for he took his M.A. degree from St Catherine's Hall in that University in 1719. His first living appears to have been Winslow, Bucks., but on 30 June 1720, he was instituted to the Rectory of Nantwich, a benefice which he continued to hold for the rest of his life. He was made Dean of Chester in 1732, and took his LL.D. the same year. In 1738 he took to himself the living of Dodleston which had fallen vacant through the death of Prebendary Arthur Fogge.

The Chapter over which the new Dean presided was constituted as follows:

Arthur Fogge, D.D.	1702
John Prescott, M.A.	1715
Charles Henchman, M.A.	1718
John Mapletoft, M.A.	1719
Samuel Peploe, LL.B.	1727
Christopher Sudell, M.A.	1730

John Prescott, M.A., was the son of Henry Prescott, Deputy Registrar of Chester and a "learned and judicious antiquary". If John was educated at the King's School it must have been as a fee-paying pupil, for his name does not occur among the King's Scholars at the appropriate date. He matriculated at Christ Church, Oxford, in 1709 at the age of eighteen. He took his B.A. on 20 March 1713, and the following year became Rector of Waverton at the early age of twenty-four. On 27 January 1715 he was installed Prebendary of the Cathedral, surely the youngest Prebendary on record. It was evidently not for nothing that his father was wont to dine with the Bishop. He was deprived of his stall in 1746 and died in 1767.

---

[1] His portrait hangs in the Cathedral Parlour. J. Hall, *A History of Nantwich*, 1883, p. 302, says he was of Buglawton and Handforth, Co. Cheshire, and graduated from Queen's (*sic*) College, Cambridge.

Charles Henchman, M.A., was son of Thomas Henchman, of London, gent., and a grandson of Dr Humphrey Henchman, Bishop of London. He matriculated at Christ Church, Oxford, on 29 June 1688, at the age of seventeen, and took his B.A. in 1692. In 1700 he was presented by his College to the Vicarage of Great Budworth, a benefice which he held until his death. In 1707 he was appointed to assist the Headmaster of the King's School who was old and infirm, and he succeeded him as Headmaster in 1714. He combined this office with that of Prebendary from 30 January 1717-18, having previously added the Rectory of Alderley to his list (1714). Thus he held a prebend, a vicarage, a rectory and a headmastership at one and the same time. He died in 1741 and was buried in the Lady Chapel of the Cathedral.

John Mapletoft, M.A., of Cambridge University, was collated to a stall in Chester Cathedral on 27 June 1719, and made Vicar of Neston in 1719, to which benefice he added the Rectory of West Kirby in 1730. He died at his house in the Abbey Court on 11 June 1761. Before coming to Chester he had been Rector of Broughton, near Kettering, and in 1719 leased from Bishop Gastrell the tithes of Vicarage of Mottram.[1]

Samuel Peploe, LL.B., son of the Bishop of Chester, was collated to a prebend in the Cathedral on 4 July 1727, on the death of Prebendary Thane. He was also made Chancellor of the Diocese. In 1748 he was appointed to the Rectory of Tattenhall where the Communion plate he presented is still preserved.

Christopher Sudell, M.A., was collated on 27 August 1730, in place of John Oliver, deceased. Before coming to the Cathedral he had been Rector of Holy Trinity, Chester, from 1707, but appears to have resigned this living on his appointment as Prebendary. With it he had held another one, Leyland, Lancs., from 1720 to 1733, and North Meols from 1733 to 1735. His note-book is still preserved at Holy Trinity Church, from which we can learn what his stall at the Cathedral was worth:

				£	s.	d.
Received from my Prebend of Chester, 1731						
Nov. 25 Year's Salary				26	13	4
Sam Ayre, rent				1	10	0
Benjamin Glover				2	0	0
Mr. Coker	3	2	6 ⎫			
	2	12	6 ⎭	5	15	0
Leases—Mr. Hullen				7	10	0
J. Pery, the Verger				5	0	0
Mr. Calert				6	10	0
				£54	18	4

[1] *Notitia Cestriensis*, p. 55, n.

THE ACCOUNTS

	£	s.	d.
1733 May 29. To bells, etc., and on June 11, and for passing the Navigation Bill	1	4	0

This bill empowered the City Corporation to make the new cut which now exists from Chester to Queen's Ferry. There had been much opposition to it by those who had vested interests outside the City, and there was general rejoicing in Chester when the bill became law. Nathaniel Kinderly was the engineer and the work was completed by 1737.

	£	s.	d.
June 5. To Charles Boswell in part for paveing in the great Abby Court	20	0	0
Dec. 12. To Mr. Boswell in full for paveing the great Abby Court	22	18	8
Dec. 7. To John Cross for a new Board, and for mending an old one on which the Prebendaries kneel		1	4
Gratuity to Mr. Mapletoft's servants on account of the Chapter holding several meetings at his house		7	6

This is the first instance of the custom of beginning a Chapter meeting in the Chapter House according to statute and then adjourning it to the house of the Treasurer for the time being, which no doubt was warmer and more comfortable.

	s.	d.
1734 Aug. 6. Given to a Greek priest and an Archimandrite [Abbot]	10	6

In 1735 "the Wellhouse" was leased to the Bishop for £6 p.a. It is described as "all that bay of building lying on the north side of the Abby Court", and it is evidently the building opposite the well marked in Randle Holme's plan—now No. 7.

	£	s.	d.
1736 Jan. 19. Interest for £550 due to Girls Charity School [i.e. at 5%]	27	10	0

This money had been borrowed to pay the cost of the law-suit over the Tarporley property. As soon as the rents from this land began to come in and the library had been fitted up, they were used to pay off this loan.

In 1738 the tenor bell was sent to London to be recast by a Mr Knight for the sum of £20. On 29 April it was taken down and weighed and conveyed to the Crane Wharfe, whence it was taken by boat to Parkgate and shipped from there to London. It was returned in December.

		£	s.	d.
1738 Dec. 1. To the Freight of the new Great Bell from London to Parkgate		4	0	0
To the River Freight from Parkgate to Chester		1	0	0
To Craning it a'shoar			10	0.
To the men that helped to gett it a'shoar				6
Dec. 4. To the workmen and Ringers the day the Great Bell was putt up			5	0
To two men for watching the Great Bell all night after she was a'shoar			1	0
Dec. 15. To John Wheavel for his Horses drawing the Great Bell from the Crane			10	6
1739 Mar. 20. To Mr. George Prescott for the use of the Owners of the ship called the King's Fisher, the Freight for carrying the old Great Bell to London		1	15	3

Altogether the bell cost the Dean and Chapter £86, and when they got it back they did not make much use of it, for Mr Clarke writes, "except for the service bell and the tolling funeral bell, ringing had ceased by 1754, and the bells lay derelict for sixty years".[1]

	s.	d.
1737 Oct. 29. To the Sacrist for the nursing and burying of a child born in the church porch	17	0
1738 June 4. To Peter Parry and Wm. Carter for taking down etc. the fence of the trees [? in Abbey Square]	4	6
1740 Jan. 11. To John Walker Joyner to making a door to the stair leading up to the Bishop's throne	13	0

In 1738 the Chapter "ordered the Treasurer pay Mr. Prescott four pound ten shillings towards the expense he had been at in making seats in St. Mary's Chapel for prayers at six in the morning", and on 8 October 1740 they decided that "the Treasurer cause the wall at the west end of the public school [the Refectory] belonging to this Church to be built quite up to the roof and such alterations made as may be by him thought necessary in and about the chimneys of the School and the inside of the School to be cleared".

The Choir and Others

The Chapter Book apart from recording the granting of leases devotes a disproportionate amount of its space to the doings of the Choir and other Cathedral servants. There is no doubt that many of

[1] *Cheshire Bells*, by J. W. Clarke in *Lancs. & Ches. Ant. Soc. J.*, IX, where he gives a full account of the episode.

them were unsatisfactory, as might be expected from the low wages they were paid. £6 to a verger and £10 to a conduct (choirman) seems very little even in those days, although a minor canon received only £15. They had a better organist than usual just now. Edmund Baker, who had been a pupil of the famous Dr Blow and organist of St Chad's, Shrewsbury, was appointed organist *and* conduct in 1727. How he could hold both these posts at once is not clear, and his dual rôle led to trouble in later years as we shall see.[1] In 1730 he had trouble with one of the conducts (Wm. Davies) who "did on the 15th day of June in a very rude manner strike Mr. Baker on the face" and it was a week before he could be induced to apologize. He was evidently a difficult person, for on 16 December 1732—to quote from his sub-mission written down in the Chapter Book—"upon the Sub-Dean sending to me to sing an anthem [I] not only obstinately refused so to do, but also went immediately out of the Church and upon the Sub-Dean sending after me to return and do my duty did rudely and saucily refuse so to do and thereby did occasion confusions in the service". Very likely, though one may be permitted to doubt whether the Sub-Dean handled the situation very tactfully. However, on 17 May 1733, he again refused to sing an anthem. The Prebendaries who were present as soon as the service was over went at once to the Chapter House and there "in full Chapter assembled" pronounced sentence of expulsion, which was confirmed by another Chapter two days later. Next year one of the boys had to be expelled by another Chapter for ill-behaviour and non-attendance. In 1735 William Davies turns up again and is allowed "to officiate as a probationer for a singing man or conduct—and to hold the house he living yet in (though since his expulsion he has no right thereto)". Incidentally, it is mentioned that he has to provide his own surplice. He gave no further trouble and went on drawing his salary till 1744. In 1737 we are surprised to find that Mr Baker himself refusing to sing an anthem which by order of Chapter (9 March 1736) were now to be sung in the Choir "and not in the organ loft unless it be upon a tryal of any new one".[2] Dr Bridge says it must be remembered that the time was now past for organists to be singing as well as playing, but why then did Baker receive a conduct's pay if he would not do the work? He received £12

[1] The Rev. P. C. Moore writes: "This, I think, was merely a means of augmenting his income. At Carlisle John Howe was both lay clerk and organist and subsequently also a minor canon."

[2] "It was doubtless considerations of space rather than any musical reason which resulted in the banishment at some cathedrals of the choir into the organ loft." (Moore, p. 89.)

as organist, £10 as Teacher of the Boys and £10 as Conduct together with a Conduct's house. "In time of divine evening service—in the absence of the Precentor and Dean and Sub-Dean, [he] was sent to by the Senior Prebendary to sing an anthem (which he had some times before done) and absolutely refused so to do." Immediately after the service the three Prebendaries who were present at it—John Prescott, Charles Henchman, and John Mapletoft—sent for him and admonished him to be of better behaviour for the future. It was all they could do. One wonders why the singing of the anthem was not arranged before the service began but apparently even at Westminster Abbey towards the end of the century it was customary on a weekday to choose the anthem during the service.[1]

Prebendary Prescott, who was very musical, did more for music than he could possibly have imagined by giving a free place at the King's School at Christmas, 1739, to a boy of 13¾ named Charles Burney, who had just come with his father, a portrait painter, from Shrewsbury to live in Chester. He became the great Dr Burney, famous not only for his writings on music, but also for being the father of Fanny Burney, the novelist. He remained at the School till Michaelmas 1742, when another boy takes his place in the Accounts.

[1] Percy A. Scholes, *The Life and Activities of Sir John Hawkins*, p. 162. The Rev. P. C. Moore writes: "The choice of music was not made until service began because until measures were taken to enforce the attendance of lay clerks in the next century, it was uncertain who would actually appear."

6

IN THE EIGHTEENTH CENTURY

PART II

1740–1787

THE natural way to divide the century would be to make the division at 1750, but there are several reasons why 1740 is a more suitable date:

1. It marks the end of a long period of peace and the resumption of the struggle with France and Spain, a struggle which did not really end until the defeat of France and Napoleon in 1815.

2. It marks the beginning—so far as it is possible to do that in any one year—of the Industrial Revolution with its accompanying enclosure of commons, the moving of cottage industries into the "dark satanic mills" and the consequent extremes of wealth and poverty.

3. In the world of literature and art it marks the beginning of what is often called the Age of Johnson, with such a galaxy of talent as has seldom been equalled at any other period, as, for example, Richardson, Fielding, Smollett, Goldsmith, Gray, Garrick, Reynolds, Handel, yes, and Boswell—to name only a few.

From a religious point of view this half-century has a bad name, though it produced John Wesley at the beginning of it and the Evangelical Revival at the end. We associate it with time-serving and worldly-minded clergy, neglected parishes and decaying buildings. But all generalizations are dangerous and we will take refuge in the kindly judgement of Prof. G. M. Trevelyan and say that though a parson might be as eccentric as he liked, more often he was a "typical Englishman, kindly, sensible, and mildly pious. . . . But little pressure was exerted by episcopal authority or by public opinion to compel the clergy to exert themselves more than they wished."[1] An exception

[1] *English Social History*, p. 358.

must be made for the Isle of Man, where Bishop Wilson, an old King's School boy who was ordained in Chester Cathedral, exercised a discipline unknown in this country.

The Dean and Chapter in 1740 were as follows:

Thomas Brooke, LL.D., Dean	1732–1757
John Prescott, M.A.	1715–1746
Charles Henchman, M.A.	1718–1741
John Mapletoft, M.A.	1719–1761
Samuel Peploe, LL.B.	1727–1781
Richard Milward, M.A.	1735–1744
Roger Barnston, M.A.	1739–1782

All these except the last two have been dealt with in the last chapter.

Richard Milward was a Staffordshire man who went as a sizar to Emmanuel College, Cambridge, in 1699 and matriculated in 1701. He seems nevertheless to have taken his B.A. the following year. He was Vicar of Eccleshall, Staffs., and then Vicar of Wybunbury, Cheshire. He was made Prebendary of Lichfield in 1730 and continued to hold this office when he was made Prebendary of Chester in 1735. He died in 1744.

Roger Barnston was a younger son of Roger Barnston of Churton in the parish of Farndon. He was baptized at St Michael's, Chester, on 19 July 1709, which suggests that he was born at the Barnston town residence. He went from Sedbergh School to Trinity College, Cambridge, at the age of seventeen in 1727 and took his B.A. in 1730–31. After ordination he held the livings of St Michael's, Chester (1737–1782) and Condover in Shropshire before being made Prebendary in 1739. He was twice married, first to Elizabeth March in 1748 and on her death in 1767 to Anne Egerton of Oulton. However, he died childless and was buried at Farndon on 19 December 1782.

THE WAR WITH SPAIN

Our story begins with the outbreak of the war with Spain in 1739, commonly called the War of Jenkins' Ear. The proclamation of it in Chester led to a last effort on the part of the Cathedral clergy to insist on their rights and preserve the independence of the Precincts. Dr Cowper has recorded that on:

October 27, 1739, the Mayor and Magistrates etc. on horseback with all wonted ceremonies proceeded to proclaim War against Spain in all the usual places of the City; but coming to the great Abbey gates they found

the same barrackadoed and admittance denied by the Clergy who protested against the Corporations coming there. However, the Magistrates
ordered the gates to be forced open and entered the Abbey Court, and read
the Declaration there.[1]

The Cathedral did not ring its bells on the proclamation of war,
though according to Sir Robert Walpole many churches did so,[2] but
did its best later on in a war which provided very little occasion for
bell-ringing.

	s.	d.
1740 March 16. To ringing for the taking of Porto Bello	5	0
1741 May 22. To ringing on the news of taking several forts near Cartagena	5	0
1743 To ringing on the news of a victory over the French	5	0
1745 Sept. 14. Pd. the Sexton for ringing upon hearing the acct. of the Grand Duke of Tuscany being chosen Emperor	5	0

Porto Bello on the coast of Central America was surprised by Admiral
Vernon and captured with the loss of only seven men, but his attack
on Cartagena nearby failed, and only a few outlying forts were taken.
The victory over the French in 1743 was the Battle of Dettingen,
where George II distinguished himself, and the Cheshire Regiment
won their oak leaves. The Grand Duke of Tuscany, whose election as
Emperor set the bells of Chester ringing, was the husband of Maria
Theresa, daughter of the last Emperor, head of the House of Hapsburg
and ally of England.

In this same year took place the rebellion in favour of the Young
Pretender, commonly called The Forty-Five. As there was no occasion
for bell-ringing in it no mention of it occurs in the Accounts while the
rebels were in England, but on their retreat to Scotland we find:

	s.	d.
1746 Feb. 7. For ringing on the news of the Rebels leaving Stirling	5	0
April 27 and 28. To the Ringers on Sunday and Monday for the victory at Culloden	10	0

The rebels had been besieging Stirling and had defeated the English
relieving force at the Battle of Falkirk on 17 January, but they made
no use of their victory and retreated before the approach of the Duke
of Cumberland, who defeated them at Culloden on 16 April. The fact

[1] Cowper's MSS., Book VII. Hemingway (II, 248) says it was Bishop Peploe
who did this, but does not give any authority for this statement.
[2] Giving him the opportunity for his famous pun, "They now *ring* the bells, but
they will soon *wring* their hands."

that the Cathedral bells were rung for such an apparently trivial reason as the raising of a siege is an indication of the fear caused by the English defeat at Falkirk and the relief felt when it was known that Stirling was saved. And Culloden set the bells going for two days.

	s.	d.
1746 Aug. 20. To the Ringers on the news of the Victory in Italy	5	0
1747 May 19. Ringers this day on the news of a French fleet taken	5	0

The victory in Italy was an Austrian success in which our troops were not concerned. The naval engagement took place off Cape Finisterre, where Sir Edward Hawke with 14 ships met the French with 9, escorting a convoy of 250 sail. He captured 6 ships out of the 9, but the convoy escaped.

We must now go back to 1744 to mention a battle which had an indirect effect upon the Cathedral choir. This was fought with the combined fleets of France and Spain off Toulon and was indecisive, if not a defeat for England, Admiral Matthews in command of the British fleet being badly let down by his subordinate, who deliberately kept out of the fight. And now for its effect upon the Cathedral choir, which we will let the Chapter Clerk tell in his minute book:

April 9th, 1744. Whereas Thomas LLewis of the parish of Saint Peter in the City of Chester Gent. appeared before us this Day in Chapter and informed us That George Robinson, one of the Conducts of this Cathedral, and Francis Comberbach being on Easter Monday last in company with him, the informant, at the house of John Darwell at the sign of the Lamb in the Eastgate Street in Chester where some talk happening about the late sea fight or engagement between Admiral Matthew's Fleet and the combined Fleets of France and Spain, the said Robinson there said That he *wished that the English ships had been sunk and Admiral Matthews had been taken.* And that upon the Informant's saying he ought not to have said so before him being an officer and eating the King's bread and that he ought to take notice of such seditious words, Robinson replied he would say the same before the best officer in the Town, repeated it several times over, and further, That upon the Informant saying he would inform against him Robinson then said He ought to be damned if he did not.

The Dean and Chapter took a serious view of the case, suspended Robinson from the choir until the November Chapter meeting when "on further consideration of his great enormity it is agreed that he be immediately expelled". He was given £5 to take with him, and we shall meet with him again only too often when we come to deal with

14

the subject of Poor Relief. Nothing is said in the Chapter Book about George Robinson's companion in The Lamb, Francis Comberbach, who had just joined the choir as a probationer. Probably he got off with a warning, but if so it was all in vain, for in June 1746, it is recorded that: "He has lately been guilty of an high crime and misdemeanour by which he gave great offence to many of his Majesty's good subjects and was indicted for the same and has been upon his Tryal convicted thereof, and imprisoned for the same." The result was that he too was dismissed from the choir and ordered to give up his house, and he was to be paid "up to this day and no longer". However, the Chapter must have relented, for on 18 December he was given his quarter's salary and a bonus of £5.

HANDEL AND THE CATHEDRAL

The visit of Handel to Chester on his way to Ireland and his rehearsal of the *Messiah* at the Golden Falcon is well known, but can hardly be omitted in a history of the Cathedral, especially as our authority for the following story is the celebrated Dr Burney, who was at that time a boy of sixteen at the King's School. The Golden Falcon is now the Northgate Brewery, but, says Dr Bridge, "the Falcon is still on the spouts which were put up at the back of the house a few years after Handel's visit".[1]

> When Handel went through Chester, on his way to Ireland, this year 1741, I was at the Public School in that city, and very well remember seeing him smoke a pipe, over a dish of coffee, at the Exchange-Coffee-House, for being extremely curious to see so extraordinary a man, I watched him narrowly as long as he remained in Chester; which, on account of the wind being unfavourable for his embarking at Parkgate, was several days. During this time, he applied to Mr. Baker, the organist, my first music-master, to know whether there were any choirmen in the cathedral who could sing *at sight*; as he wished to prove some books that had been hastily transcribed, by trying the choruses which he intended to perform in Ireland. Mr. Baker mentioned some of the most likely singers then in Chester, and, among the rest, a printer of the name of Janson, who had a good bass voice, and was one of the best musicians in the choir. At that time Harry Alcock, a good player, was the first violin in Chester, which was then a very musical place; for besides public performances, Mr. Prebendary Prescott had a weekly concert, at which he was able to muster eighteen or twenty performers, gentlemen and professors. A time was fixed for this private

[1] *C.A.J.*, XIX, Pt. II, p. 106.

rehearsal at the "Golden Falcon", where Handel was quartered but alas, on trial of the chorus in the Messiah, "*And with his stripes we are healed*", poor Janson, after repeated attempts, failed so egregiously, that Handel let loose his great bear upon him; and after swearing in four or five languages, cried out in broken English: "You schauntrel, tit not you dell me dat you could sing at soite?" "Yes Sir," says the printer, "and so I can, but not at *first sight*."[1]

The unhappy Janson joined the choir at Christmas 1731 as a probationer in accordance with the resolution passed by the Chapter in 1713, and it was 1738 before he was admitted to full membership, although the resolution allowed only one year for probation. In 1743 he was admonished for his poor attendance at church, but he remained in the choir until his death in 1764. He was buried in the Cathedral on 1 February but his place in the choir was not filled until November 27.

Charles Burney must have proved an apt pupil, for Baker had no regular assistant, and he taught the schoolboy to play chants enough "to keep the organ going" while he was absent, when he was attacked by gout.[2]

THE ACCOUNTS

Unfortunately the Accounts are not as informative as they used to be, for from now onwards few details are given of the nature of the work done, but only the name of the tradesman who did the work.

	s.	d.
1740 May 28. To Peter Parry's son for a journey to Nantwich	4	6

Peter Parry was the Head Verger. The vergers were generally used as messengers and the journey would no doubt be to Dean Brooke, who was Rector of Nantwich as well as being Dean of Chester.

	£	s.	d.
1740 June 3. To Sam Davies, Mason, for work at Mr. Baker's house, the Cloysters, making and putting up a new sun-dial	2	12	0
Nov. 11. To Mr. Edward Orme for painting the cupolaes		8	0
Dec. 17. To Mr. Smith carpenter for repairing the Cupolaes; for work in other parts of the choir, and in Mr. Baker's house	14	2	0

Orme was a heraldic painter who afterwards became the Cathedral organist. He died of gout in 1777 and was buried in the Cathedral. A tablet to his memory is in the North Transept.

[1] Percy A. Scholes, *The Great Dr. Burney*, p. 13, quoting Ellis in preface of *Early Diary*, I, p. xix.
[2] C.A.J., quoting Burney's *Sketch of the Life of Handel*, p. 26.

£ s. d.

> 1741 March 10. To John Davis for carrying rubbish out of St.
> Mary's Chapel and a cart to take it away   5   0
> Nov. 20. To Mr. Baker for writing anthems and services into
> the organ book   2   2   0
> 1742 Jan. 12. To Mr. Nevit his Bill for candles for the choir, 1740 13   6   6
> Feb. 3. To Councillor Falconer for his opinion concerning
> our having a title to any of Mr. Henchman's effects at Hare
> Hill   10   6

William Falconer was Recorder of Chester and a prominent member of St John's congregation.[1] In 1728 the Dean and Chapter had granted a twenty-one years' lease to Prebendary Henchman of "a cottage called Tapley's cottage with a garden thereto belonging and a parcel of common or waste ground in and about Hare Hill . . . in Utkinton". Now Henchman was dead and presumably had died intestate.

The year 1742 ended with an adverse balance of £216 12s. 9¼d. and as if in explanation, the Treasurer has inserted in his book a list of rents in arrears at the 1742 audit amounting to £224 9s. 6d. Then follows the rent roll as it ought to be, giving a total of £995 19s. 2d., which is about what it was exactly two hundred years ago when the Cathedral was first started. Prices could and did rise, but rents were fixed by the Leicester award of 1580.

£ s. d.

> 1744 Jan. 20. To Wm. Carter for rubbing and cleaning the books
> in the Library   2   6
> Jan. 21. To Painter the Plum[ber]   16 18   6
> April 20. To Mrs. L. Bunbury for a lock for the Turn Style   1   6
> April 23. To Dr. Green's anthems and carrage   3   9

Maurice Greene (1695–1755) was organist of St Paul's Cathedral and the Chapel Royal and also Professor of Music at Cambridge. Six of his anthems are still sung in Chester Cathedral.

£ s. d.

> 1745 Jany. Pd. the man that came from Lichfield as a Candidate
> for a Conduct's place, but was returned   1   1   0
> May 30. pd. the Sexton for carrying the old organ out of the
> room over the Porch [then the Song School]   2   0
> 1747 April 2. Dr. Andrew's opinion about the Chancellor's claim
> to a stall   1   6   0
> Oct. 20. The Carlisle Singing boy for his trouble in coming
> over   1   1   0
> June 10. Mr. Richardson for mending Ashbrook's virge   5   0
> 1749 March 10. Gave the Virgers on account of fewer candles
> being burnt in the choir   1   1   0

[1] Rev. S. Cooper Scott, *Lectures on the History of S. John Baptist's Church*, p. 151.

This probably marks the introduction of lamps, which made the vergers' perquisite of candle-ends a wasting asset.

A summary of Expenses "when the Church was beautified", i.e. from April 29, 1749, to January 9, 1750:

	£	s.	d.
Henry Boxby for whitewashing (in 4 payments)	29	6	4
Henry Cowduck "for repairing the images upon the Bishop's throne" (in 6 payments)	9	8	6
Charles Nichols, mason, in 6 payments which included taking down "the old monument"	2	17	0
Jo Carney, labourer, for 6 days carrying stone from the monument, and 6 days carrying it to the cellar		12	0
Jo Cross, joiner, for work done in the choir	18	16	6
Thos. Johnson, "for 4 days work for scraping the whitewash of some woodwork"		6	0
Mr. Jervis of W'hampton for sconces	6	9	0
Mr. Hervey, Upholsterer, "for making cushions etc."	29	12	0
Mr. Ladsham, Bookseller	4	3	0
"Mr. Borough for lamps and sconces for the Broad Isle"	9	16	0
Mr. Totty, whitesmith	17	3	0
Mr. Aldersey	3	7	0
Mr. Peers	6	4	0
Mr. J. Henley for making the almsmen's gowns	1	11	6
Mr. Edwd. Warrington, Carpenter	11	11	6
Mr. Williams, carpenter	11	13	6
Mr. Geo. Lindsey for timber etc.	20	5	0
Mr. Bayley Junr. for Manchester velvet for the cushions	9	6	0
Mr. Ed. Ormes for painting the choir	80	0	0
Labourers at various times	1	0	6
S. Ashbrooke for making several cushions		14	10½

Towards the cost of all this £130 was voted from the Tarporley account and £500 was borrowed at 3 per cent from Prebendary Peploe to be repaid from the above source. This £500 was to be used "for the Broad Isle, the roof of S. Oswald's and the public Grammar School" as well as for the choir.

Henry Cowduck could not have done his work very well, for later historians have been unanimous in their condemnation of it. "The figures were much mutilated," says Dr Pigot in 1815, "either at the Restoration or during the civil wars, but were restored in a bungling manner about the year 1748."[1] *The Stranger's Companion* (fourth edition about 1828) says: "The beautiful statues of the early kings and saints of Mercia ... were sadly mutilated, and being given to an un-skilful artist to repair, he put some of the heads on wrong shoulders,

[1] Pigot, p. 63.

which gives a whimsical effect." On the other hand Dr Cowper
writes:

> The Chapter of Chester having lately begun to beautify their Cathedral,
> the decayed decorations on the Episcopal Throne engaged their attention.
> This fine piece of antiquity had been ornamented with carving and statuary,
> both which had suffered, not by time but by violence. They have therefore
> endeavoured to repair the one and restore the other, so that the little Images
> which have for so many centuries guarded, as it were, this ancient
> monument, and were so injuriously defaced, are, by a commendable care,
> now made whole again.[1]

This is clear proof that Mr Cowduck replaced the missing heads and it
would be interesting to know who removed them again, for they are
not there now. As they were still giving a whimsical effect in 1828 the
removal probably took place when the shrine was restored in 1888.[2]

		£	s.	d.
1750 April 18. A labourer levelling the ground in the Little Abbey Court			5	9
June 27. To the workmen laying the marble in the choir			2	0
Sept. 9. To Mr. Boswell for paving in the Little Abbey Court			15	0
1751 Jan. 7. To workmen for repairing the Sprice, levelling the ground and sowing it with hay seeds		2	12	6
Oct. 28. A brush and wings for the Church			1	4
1752 Nov. 22. To Mr. Jeynson for printing the prayer for the cattle			1	0

This refers to the cattle plague. Jeynson is our old friend Janson
who distinguished himself on Handel's visit. He was a printer by
trade.

	s.	d.
Painting and cleaning lamps	2	0
Oil for the lamps	3	6
1755 March 25. To Andrew Pugh when going to Shrewsbury Infirmary [Chester Infirmary was not opened till 1756]	5	0
March 17. pd. Mr. Batho's horse hire and expenses in going to Nantwich for Mr. Mainwaring to attend a Chapter	7	0

We do not know what Mainwaring was doing at Nantwich, for the
Dean was Rector of it and Mainwaring's livings were St Michael's,
Chester, and Coddington. However, the Dean did not attend any
Chapter meetings after 23 January 1754, so perhaps he was ill and

[1] *Summary of the Life of St. Werburgh with an Historical Account of the Images upon
her Shrine (now the Episcopal throne) in the Choir of Chester*, dated 31 July 1949.
[2] The heads are all in position in the illustration in Lyson (1810), p. 444.

Mainwaring had taken his place temporarily. Batho was second verger.

	£	s.	d.
1756 Sept. 11. To two constables for taking into custody the disorderly coachman		2	0
1757 Mr. Boswell for the Abby Court	40	0	0
Ringing for the K. of Prussia's Vict'y [either Rossbach or Leuthen]		5	0

THE CONDITION OF THE CLOISTERS

By the end of the century the cloisters were in a ruinous state and the south walk next the Cathedral had disappeared altogether. There seems no doubt that the Chapter, being always in debt, kept what money they had for the church and let the cloisters go. The extract mentioned above about repairing the Sprice (Garth garden) might seem to contradict this, but it is as a matter of fact the exception that proves the rule. A resolution passed by the Chapter on 25 November 1549, makes this clear.

> Whereas a generous Benefactor yet unknown to us has made an offer to us of fifty pounds towards the keeping up and repairing the Cloysters of the Church, at present in great decay, on condition that what that sum shall fall short of doing in that respect we will ourselves provide to finish, We therefore think fit to vote our thanks to be given to our said Benefactor and promise to make good the condition aforesaid.

It is evident, therefore, that the work done on the Sprice was in fulfilment of the above condition. We must now add an extract from the Cathedral Registers, which completes the story:

> 1751. This year the Choir layd with Marble, and the Cloyster covered with a new Roof, by William Stradford, L.LD., Comissary of Richmond.[1]

In the 'forties the then Bishop left his mark on the Cathedral by erecting two galleries in the choir—it was the great age for galleries and no church was complete without them—one on the south side in 1745 and the corresponding one on the north side in 1749. This was Bishop Samuel Peploe, who occupied the see from 1726 to 1752. He was buried in the Cathedral on the south side of the altar and his white marble tablet with its Latin inscription is now in St Erasmus Chapel. No doubt the north gallery formed part of the scheme for the beautifying of the Cathedral which took place in 1749. When that work was

[1] Parish Register Soc., LIV, 1904, p. 27, transcribed by the late Thomas Hughes.

completed the Dean and Chapter (on 28 November) issued the following instructions to the vergers:

> Whereas the Church especially the Choir part thereof hath been lately
> handsomely adorned and beautified and the seats therein made uniform and
> decent, It was thought proper that the Virgers should be admonished
> To keep the stalls wainscote floor in the Choir and broad Isle clean. To take
> care that the Cloysters and the several avenues leading to the Church within
> the precincts of the Abby be kept clean. That the door at each end of the
> Deanery and prebendary stalls be kept locked and none but Gentlemen and
> Magistrates of the City, Clergymen and the better sort of Tradesmen (not
> Mechanicks) be let in, and that the door entering into the Archdeaconry
> seat also be kept locked for the same purpose, and never at any time so
> many to be let in as to incommode the Dean and Prebendaries and
> Archdeacons in their stalls when they are expected to come to the service.
> That the several pews appointed to the Bishop's Lady, the Deanery, the
> Prebendary and Minor Canons wifes, be also kept locked, and opened to
> none except Mistress Bunbury and Mrs. Falconer of the Abby Court,
> Mrs. Hulton and such persons as inhabit either the houses of Prebendaries
> or Minor Canons, and
> That no servants be admitted into either of the two great pews in the Choir
> which are also to be kept constantly locked for Gentlewomen, and Lastly
> That they take care that one of the Almsmen stand at each of the small doors
> in the Side Isles to prevent them being kept open in the winter especially.
> All which rules are to be strictly observed on Sundays and Holy daies and
> the gates leading into the Churchyard are constantly to be kept locked
> saving from the first opening of the Church doors for Divine Service to the
> shutting of them again, and the Virgers and under Sacrists and Sextons
> were called in and admonished to observe the said rules and orders strictly
> and had a copy delivered to them thereof.

These instructions, or at any rate the spirit of them, seem to have
been carried out until almost within living memory, for up to Dean
Howson's restoration in the 'seventies the locking of these doors
continued. Miss Bellamira Payne, who lived in Abbey Green, used to
relate how her place in the Cathedral in those days was in the Ladies'
Gallery above the stalls on the south side. The first lady to arrive was
given the key by the verger, who locked herself in. The next to come
knocked at the door of the short staircase, and after being let in by the
first lady retained the key in order to open the door to the next comer.
So the key was passed on to each new comer until the gallery was filled.
Just before the service began the Dean's footman would arrive and
unlock the Dean's stall and place his service books on the desk. He
was always escorted from his house by a verger.[1]

[1] Information from Mrs Paget, 17 Jan. 1954.

THE TARPORLEY ESTATE

On 23 June 1747, it was decided to borrow £400, to be repaid out of the Tarporley estate, because

> the allowance for taxes at four shillings in the pound and the payments for the relief of the poor settled upon us are at present so great that the rents and revenues of the Church are (if duly paid by the tenants who are for the most part slack in their payments) greatly deficient for discharging of the same and the salaries and repairs and other necessities of the Church.

This leads us to inquire how the income from the Tarporley estate was used. Fortunately the accounts of this property for 1744–57 and 1763–1825 have survived and they show that the money was used in the following ways. After paying the expenses of management

1. To pay the interest on the loans and by degrees to pay off the loans themselves, which had been raised to finance the litigation which took place over Dean Arderne's will.
2. To provide articles for the Library which had been set up in the Chapter House in accordance with the terms of the will.
3. To make grants from time to time from the accumulated residue towards the annual deficit in the Cathedral accounts.

For example, in the two years ending November 1746, £515 18s. 8d. was received and £364 3s. 4d. was used to pay arrears of interest and for the repayment of loans. £4 6s. 4d. was spent on the Library, £3 of which went on Calnett's dictionary, and the rest was accounted for by expenses. Again, in the 2¾ years ending 29 June 1750, £792 3s. 1d. was received, £228 15s. od. was spent on interest and loans, only 12s. on the Library (10s. for a lock from Wolverhampton and 2s. for a brush) and £360 paid to the Cathedral, £30 of which was for cleansing and beautifying it (May 1749).

DISCIPLINARY MATTERS

In this decade the Dean and Chapter were concerned with disciplinary matters—not for the first time. It must be remembered, however, that these would be exceptional and must not be taken as examples of the normal behaviour in the Cathedral. On 23 July 1746, all the bedesmen were admonished for not doing their duty properly "and not to exceed in drink for the future". But worse was to come, for on 9 December of that year John Prescott was deprived of his prebend by the Bishop "for immoralities". This was regrettable, but such things did happen and the scandal would no doubt have been hushed up had not Prescott refused to go quietly and (says the Chapter Book) "has frequently since presumed to intrude and sit among the Prebendaries there in Prebendal habit", with the result that on 23 April his former colleagues actually took the extreme step of ordering the vergers to exclude him. They "do hereby order that in case the same Master Prescott do again (and as often as he shall attempt to) intrude and come into the said church in a prebendal habit, the vergers of the church, without using violence shall prevent his doing so and keep him out". We hear no more of Prescott's attempts to come into his stall after this, but he still retained his prebendal house, and on 29 October 1750 the Dean and Chapter had the unpleasant task of ordering him to be ejected.

On 6 October 1747 it was Edmund Baker, the organist, who was up before the Dean and Chapter. The charge against him was that he was not teaching the choristers properly. Baker's defence was that he taught them several times a week. "The Dean replied that it plainly appeared and was a general complaint that they knew but little and could not be well taught, and therefore he expected from and admonished him for the future more diligently to teach them and fitt them for the service of the choir upon pain of being discharged from being Master and Teacher." Baker did not lose his place, but died in harness in 1765, so that the Dean did not carry out his threat. Indeed five years later we find him appointing Thomas Spence, one of the Conducts, to teach the boys for £10 a year, to be paid out of the Tarporley estate. He must not be confused with William Spence, also a Conduct, who was before the Dean and Chapter on 1 March 1751 for being absent from the choir for a fortnight without leave. It must be admitted that his excuse was an original one. He said "he was obliged to follow a person to Holyhead and thence to Dublin that owed him money". He is probably the only Conduct who has been honoured with a tablet in the Cathedral on his death. It will be found on the north wall of the Choir aisle and tells us that he: "quitted this earthly stage on the 16th of June, 1785, in the 59th year of his age, Near 50 of which he served as a Chorister in this Cathedral and was allowed to have one of the strongest and finest toned Bass Voices in the Kingdom". The Accounts record that a boy named Spence was a member of the choir from 1732 to 1744 and then became a Conduct, retaining that office until 1785, so that he must have joined the Choir when he was six years old.

Two years later (23 January 1754) the Chapter considered a complaint that the Headmaster of the King's School had been charging the scholars more than he ought to do, and they took the opportunity of laying down some rules about the conduct of the School which throw an interesting light on education two centuries ago.

School hours were to be from 7 to 11 and 1 to 5, but in the winter months school was to begin at 8. The under-master was to read prayers at the beginning and end of each day and to teach the boys the rudiments of grammar and the contents of the following books: *Sententiae Pueriles, Cordericus,* Castatio's Latin Testament and Phaedrus' *Fables,* "and that once a year after their Breaking up at Christmas, the head form, having read such books, shall be removed under the care of the Headmaster". The following payments were authorized. For every King's Scholar who came into the Headmaster's class immediately on entering the school 5s., but nothing for those who came up from the Under Master's class, "but from all under his care he shall take 2s. 6d. Fire money and 2s. 6d. Cock money and no more". The Under Master was to have the same from each scholar entering his class. Both masters were "to attend Divine Service in their stalls, wearing a surplice, upon Thursdays and Saturdays and vigils in the afternoon and upon Sundays and Holy Days both morning and evening—to inspect and take care of the behaviour of the said King's Scholars during Divine service".

Cock money was a small sum of money contributed on Shrove Tuesday by every scholar, with part of which the master procured game cocks to provide sport for the scholars.[1] The payment of this money is no evidence that cock fighting was still a sport of the King's School in the middle of the eighteenth century, for customary payments have a way of going on long after the reason for them has ceased, and we note that the Under Master received it too.

Fire money was presumably to pay for the heating of the school, and the mention of it makes one wonder how this was effected. There are no fireplaces in the refectory today, but there is a payment in the Accounts every year for sweeping the chimneys of the School and some fires they must have had. In later days they used stoves.

Benjamin Nicholls, the headmaster whose exactions caused these regulations, was admonished in October 1756 for neglecting the School for several months and on 30 March 1757 he resigned and the Reverend Thos. Woolright, B.A., took his place.

On 2 April 1752, Bishop Edmund Keene, who had been consecrated in January of that year, was enthroned by proxy. As the Dean was

[1] *Notitia Cestriensis.*

absent, Prebendary Roger Barnston was enthroned by the Vice-Dean, John Mapletoft, which must have seemed a curious and unreal proceeding. Dr Keene did not have much to do with the Cathedral but he rebuilt the Palace at a cost of £2,200. He was translated to Ely in 1770. Five years after his arrival in Chester Dean Brooke's long rule of twenty-five years came to an end with his death in 1757. He was buried at Nantwich, his own parish church, on 20 December of that year.

Bell-ringers may claim him as an early member of their fraternity, for Dr Pigot records that: "He was so remarkably athletic a man, as to be able to raise the great bell of the Cathedral without assistance, in which he was very fond of exercising himself."[1] This tenor bell was sent to London to be recast four years after Brooke became Dean, and the ringing of the bells is said to have ceased only three years before he died. May we not see in these two facts evidence of his great interest in bell-ringing? Perhaps Dr Pigot overestimated the difficulty of ringing up the tenor bell, or perhaps bells were not so well hung in those days, for today the raising of it is not reckoned an athletic feat.

POOR RELIEF

In the 'forties of this century we begin to be aware of an increase in poverty, or else of an increased sensitiveness to it on the part of the Dean and Chapter. In the past they had expended on the poor the money received at Communion services as the rubric in the prayer-book directs, and had perforce made themselves responsible for any foundlings who had involuntarily effected a legal settlement by being laid on a prebendary's doorstep or by being born in the church porch. But now there comes a change. On 31 March 1740, the Chapter decided that the Sacrist should be reimbursed "what money he has paid towards the maintenance of such poor who have a right to be and are provided by the Chapter more than he has received from the Sacrament money". In consequence the Sacrist received £2 0s. 7½d. over and above the money he spent on pensioners and foundlings, who are entered separately in the Accounts. The former in that year were two women and one man. The Sacrist did not overspend himself again until 1746 and then the figures tell a tale. The nineteenth was not the only century to have "hungry forties", apparently.

1746	£8 12s. 2½d.	1749	£28 0s. 0d.
1747	£27 12s. 9d.	1750	£22 1s. 6d.
1748	£43 4s. 7½d.		

[1] Pigot, p. 57.

The poverty in the Precincts in 1740 was an indication of the poverty in the whole country, for in that year the price of corn which from 1713 to 1764 averaged 34s. 11d. a quarter soared to 46s. 5d. and in the following year the export of corn was forbidden.

A few extracts from the Accounts will illustrate the situation:

	£	s.	d.
1743 Feb. 3. To Mr. Carter for a pr. of shoes and 2 pr. of stockings for the poor boy		1	2
To Carter for his care of the boy three nights and other trouble		2	6
Feb. 19. To Couns. Falconer for his opinion concerning the poor boy's settlement		10	6
1746 Aug. 21. To Mr. Batho for a suit for little Andrew Firlow		16	6
1747 Jan. 20. To warrant against several persons to appear at the pentice about Galespey's girl left in Abby Court and the Virgers and Beadles for their trouble		3	6
Mr. Fisher for carriage down of Chas. Jones and for his meat at the Wool hall for two days	1	8	6
April 15. Wm. Spence a pair of shoes for Charles Jones		3	0
June 29. Martha Owens a quarter for Charles Jones	1	10	0
Aug. 26 For Charles Jones' carriage up to London again	1	2	0

Poor lad, sent from pillar to post until it could be decided who was responsible for him.

William Carter was a sort of Cathedral Pooh Bah, for in that year he was head verger, the Dean's servant, organ blower, sweeper of the church and "toller of the bells". He also rode out from time to time to collect the Chapter rents.

We now come to the sad case of Martha Macarthy. She first appears in the Accounts in 1739 when she received 1s. 6d. a week spasmodically and continued to do so until in 1745 she is paid regularly. Then we get:

	s.	d.
1745 March 29. Sent Martha Machartey by the hands of her Nurse tender she lying in	2	6
30. Pd. Jno. Pritchard the Sexton of St. Mary's for making a grave for Machartey's child, wch was stil-born	1	0
30. pd. Machartney's midwife, Mrs. Gough	5	0
April 6. pd. Martha Machartney by her nurse tender another week's stipend she being ill	2	6
8. pd. for a coffin for Machartey's child	2	0
12. pd. for her churching at St. Mary's	1	10

		s.	d.
April 13.	Gave the woman that look'd after her whilst she was confin'd	5	0
13.	pd. Martha Machartey another week's allowance she being still weak and ill	2	6
15.	pd. the Clark of St. Mary's his bill for burial of another of Machartey's children	5	10
19.	pd. Hor. Rowney for ale at the Funl. of Machartey's child	1	0
June 1.	pd. for a coffin for another of Machartey's children	5	0

and with that item the unhappy woman disappears from the pages of the Accounts, except that she had her rent paid for her in 1754.

Another sad case was that of the Robinson family. George Robinson, it will be remembered, was dismissed from the choir for treasonable talk in the bar of the Lamb Inn in 1744.

		s.	d.
1746 Jan. 4.	Gave Mr. Carter to give to Robinson's family, being sick	10	0
13.	Gave Mrs. Robinson five shillings more, their family remaining (?) ill	5	0
18.	Gave Robinson's family more	5	0

We hear no more of them for three years and then they become a constant liability. In January and February of 1749 George received five payments for his wife amounting to 12s., and 6s. for blankets for the children. Then:

		s.	d.
1749 May 30.	Gave George Robinson, he having hurt his arm	1	0
Dec. 18.	pd. Wm. Carter for shoes for Robinson's family	14	10
	pd. Ely Poynton for stockens for ditto	3	3½
	pd. Mrs. Aldersey for wares for ditto	12	2
	pd. Mr. Ch. Croughton for wares for ditto	8	7½

In 1750 Robinson's wife received weekly payments in February and March amounting to 10s. 3d. She seems then to have recovered sufficiently to do a little work and on 27 August she was paid 1s. for cleaning the Choir. But next year she was in trouble again:

		s.	d.
1751 March 7.	To Mary Robinson's funeral	18	2
18.	A pair of Bodice for Robinson's wife	7	6
May 29.	Bleeding Robinson's wife		6
Aug. 19.	To two constables for attending twice on the Mayor and conveying Robinson and wife to House of Correction	2	6
	To Mistress of Poorhouse to redeem Robinson's wife's gown which she had pawned	3	0

	s.	d.
28. To the Master of the House of Correction for releasing Robinson and wife	5	0
Two pairs of shoes for Robinson's children	5	0
1752 April 21. To a midwife for Robinson's wife	5	0

In 1753 Robinson received 6s. 6d., and his son John was apprenticed at a cost of £8 6s. od. and his daughter Mary at a cost of £5 6s. od. In 1755 another daughter was apprenticed (£4 os. od.) and £1 11s. od. was spent in making an outfit for her. In 1756 his rent was paid for him (£1 1s. od.) and besides three payments for sickness (£1 4s. od.) his children received 5s. a week for board from 11 October onwards. Then a whole year passes without any payment until we come to:

	£	s.	d.
1758 Oct. 23. To cash paid Thos. Coppack Slater and plasterer for taking Willm. son of Geo. Robinson apprentice	3	0	0
1759 July 12. pd. the expenses of George Robinson's funeral	1	12	6
Nov. 7. paid Mr. Batho the consideration money on taking Margaret Robinson an apprentice	4	0	0

Mr Batho was a barber. This is the last we hear of the Robinson family. George was buried at the Cathedral as "a Pauper", 11 July 1759.

THE POOR HOUSE

Poor Houses or Workhouses are generally thought of as the creation of the Poor Law of 1832, but parochial workhouses were authorized by an Act of 1723, under which a parish could "purchase or hire a house in a parish and contract with persons for the lodging, keeping and employing of poor persons; and there to keep them and take the benefit of their work and labour for the better maintenance and relief of such poor persons". The author of *The Practical Justice of the Peace* (1756) is loud in his praise of this system. "This statute", he writes, "has had such excellent effect that I have now by me a true and full account of no less than 130 workhouses already set up and established in England and more are setting up every day." The other side of the picture is to be seen in the verse of a Norfolk parson who takes quite a different view:

> Theirs is yon house that holds the parish poor,
> Whose walls of mud scarce bear the broken door;
> There, where the putrid vapours, flagging, play,
> And the dull wheel hums doleful through the day.[1]

[1] George Crabbe, *The Village*, Bk. I, 1783.

Let us hope they managed things better in Chester. The parish of St Oswald was one of the 130 who set up a Poor House and a Mr Thompson was in charge. The Dean and Chapter once made use of it:

	s.	d.
1750 Dec. 10. Pd. Thompson for the use of the Poor House	6	0

It is not surprising that such a large parish as St Oswald's found a Poor House necessary, but what is surprising is that in 1751 the Cathedral followed suit with a Poor House of their own, for one would not have thought there would be enough paupers in the Precincts to make it worth their while, especially as some outdoor relief continued to be distributed. As so little has been written about these eighteenth-century workhouses it may not be out of place to give the details of this one.

	£	s.	d.
1751 Jan. 8. To the Master of St. Oswald's poor house for writing out Rules and Bill of Fare for our Poor House		5	6
22. To Mr. Thomas Massey for sheeting cloth for the poor house		16	7
For two chaff beds and Bolsters one pair of bedsocks and a new cord for the Poor house		9	0
23. For a pair of Bedsocks and a cord for Poor house		4	6
24. To Thompson's wife for Treacle, etc.		2	6
To towel cloth for the Poor house		1	4
Feb. 2. To Thompson's wife to buy things for the Poor house		7	2
4. Writing paper for the poor house			6
5. To Mr. Massey for Linnen for the poor house		10	2
To Thompson's wife to buy tow and other things for the poor		10	10
To Mrs. Aldersey for Blew Serge for Do.	1	11	6
To Mr. Orange for a piece of Linen Cloth for Do.	3	5	0
To Mr. Harvie for blankets for Do.	1	7	0
To Stockener for stockens 8 pair		6	10
To 3 pair of Shoes for Do.		2	8
7. To Thompson's wife to buy Meat		2	0
9. To Thompson's wife to buy Corn and Meat		10	6
14. To Thompson's wife to buy knives etc. for poor house		3	0
16. To Thompson's wife		11	0
17. To Ashbrook Taylor for making Cloths for poor		7	10
20. To Thompson's wife to buy coals etc for poor house		8	6
22. Books for poor house		1	9
23. To Edward Davies for 2 wheels for poor house		12	0

THE OLD DEANERY INCORPORATING ST THOMAS' CHAPEL

Chidley, Chester

ABBEY SQUARE,
NORTH SIDE,
BUILT *c.* 1760

The Cathedral Poor House was now well established and Mrs Thompson received a weekly payment varying from 13s. to 15s. for the keep of the paupers committed to her charge. Further purchases were made from time to time:

		£	s.	d.
1751 March 8. To Coy Taylor for poor childrens cloths		1	0	9
14. To Thompson's wife for a Tub			3	0
April 4. To Thompson for a tun of coals			7	0
10. To Thompson's wife for 6 lb. of Tow			3	0
16. Cloths for the poor bought of Mrs. Aldersey			15	0
20. Shoes for two women in the poor house			5	4
May 4. To Ashbrook Taylor for making two gowns for 2 women			5	6

In July there was a change in the management:

	£	s.	d.
July 3. To Thompson's wife at her leaving the Poor house	1	1	0
To Sarah McNairn at her commencing Mistress of the Poor house for two weeks provision	1	0	0
For 2 pair of Bedsocks, 2 Tables, 3 chairs, 1 Form for the poor House		15	0

Other purchases include soap, coals, a frying pan, a chaff bed, a pot, smoothing irons and a tub for the necessary house.

The choice of Sarah McNairn gives us some idea of the status of the Matron of a Poor House, for she had already figured in the Accounts:

	£	s.	d.
1751 Jan 21. To Sarah McNairn on condition the Chapter be no more troubled with her	1	1	0
Feb. 11. To McNairn pauper (being sick)		1	0
April 12. To Sarah McNairn (her child being sick)		1	0
June 29. To Sarah McNairn		1	0

It would appear that the venture was not a success, for in 1752 and the following years nothing more is heard of it and payments are again made to the individuals concerned, namely Margt. Bennett, Widow Davies, Andrew Pugh, Boswell, Mrs Parry, Sarah McNairn, Vernon and (surprisingly) "Thompson's wife".

The amount spent on the poor during the 'fifties was between £40 and £50 a year, but in 1758 and 1759 it rose to £64 and £65 respectively, and it is in the latter year that we find mention of a General Workhouse for the whole City. This united effort on the part of the parishes was allowed for in the Act of 1723, and on 25 April 1759, the Reverend Charles Henchman, Mr Hugh Speed, Mr Charles Boswell, and Mr Robert Taylor were appointed by the Chapter to represent

15*

them on the Board of Guardians. The House, which was built by the Corporation, was situated "on the waste ground lying on the north-west side of their parcel of land called the Roodee". now called Paradise Row.[1] The Accounts for 1759 contain two payments of £7 and £5 to "the General Workhouse" and one item of £12 14s. 2d. for "clothing the poor when they went into the Workhouse". The weekly contribution of the Chapter was about 11s. This arrangement did not last long, for in 1762 an Act was passed for Chester only, setting up a new Board of Guardians who were to take over the Workhouse at a rent of £90 per annum; the sending of all paupers to this House was made compulsory, as was also the rate levied on each parish in proportion to the number of its paupers. Abbey Court was expressly included in the Act. Henceforward the Cathedral Accounts cease to be concerned with the poor, except for the payment to the Workhouse which relieved them of all further responsibility. Payments averaged about £11 a year until 1774 when for some reason they cease altogether for a time. A fitting close to this melancholy subject is to be found in a contemporary statement carved on a stone in Hawarden Park, presumably by the miller of that day or by the Lord of the Manor himself. It runs as follows:

Trust in God for bread and in the King for protection and justice. This mill was erected in 1767 by Sir — Glynne, Lord of the Manor. In this year wheat was 9/- a bushel and barley 5/6. The country was prosperous, charity was abundant, but the poor were starved, riotous and hanged.

9s. a bushel is equivalent to 72s. a quarter. The average price, it will be remembered, up to 1764 was 34s. 11d.

DEAN WILLIAM SMITH 1758-1786

The new Dean was the son of the Reverend Richard Smith, Rector of All Saints', Worcester. Born in 1711 and educated at Worcester Grammar School, he went to New College, Oxford in 1728, where he took his several degrees. On 11 September 1735 he was presented to Holy Trinity, Chester, by the Earl of Derby, to whom he had been Reader since 1732. From 1749 to 1752 he was also Headmaster of Brentwood School, Essex. In 1753 he was nominated Minister of St George's Church, Liverpool and on 28 July 1758 was advanced to the Deanery of Chester through the influence of the Stanley family. To this office he added the Rector of Handley in 1766, but resigned his

---

[1] Quoted from the Act of 1762.

Liverpool benefice the following year. In 1780 he took the Cathedral living of West Kirby, at the same time resigning the Rectory of Holy Trinity which he had held for forty-five years. Four benefices at once seem to have been too much even for those times. William Smith was probably the best scholar that ever held Chester Deanery. His works consisted chiefly in translations of the Greek classics, Longinus in 1739, Thucydides in two volumes in 1758, and Xenophon's *History of the Affairs of Greece* in 1770. He also wrote poetry, and a volume of his poems was published after his death by the Reverend Thomas Crane, Vicar of Over. His memorial by Banks is on the west wall of the North Transept and records that he died on 12 January 1787, and adds that "as a preacher he was admired and esteemed by his respective auditories". His widow, who erected the tablet, is depicted weeping over an urn beside which lie her husband's books and academical cap.

The Chapter over which Dean Smith presided in 1758 was as follows:

William Smith, D.D., Dean	1758–1787
John Mapletoft, M.A.	1719–1761
Samuel Peploe, M.A.	1727–1781
Roger Barnston, M.A.	1739–1782
Abel Ward, M.A.	1744–1781
Richard Jackson, M.A.	1744–1796
Edward Mainwaring, M.A.	1747–1780

The last three of these are new since 1740 when we last looked at them.

Abel Ward, like Richard Milward whose place he took, was a Staffordshire man and also a sizar at Cambridge (Queen's College) where he matriculated in 1736 and took his B.A. in 1740–1, becoming a Fellow of his College the same year. Only three years later he was installed Prebendary of Chester and the following year he was made Chaplain to the Bishop (Peploe) and Rector of St Anne's, Manchester. Archdeacon of Chester in 1751, he was given the Rectory of Dodleston in 1758 but resigned it to Richard Jackson in 1761 when he was preferred to Neston where he died in 1785. His gravestone in the Lady Chapel (not now extant) described him as "a most exemplary man, both in public and private life".

Richard Jackson, also of Queen's College (1731–45), was Vicar of St Oswald's 1739–61. He was collated to a stall in the Cathedral on 27 May 1744. He was also Prebendary of the Cathedrals of York (1750–1796) and Lichfield (1741–96). In addition he was Rector of St Martin's, Chester, from 1738, and in 1761 succeeded Abel Ward at Dodleston. Foster says that he was also Vicar of Trees (? Prees in

Shropshire). He died on 12 November 1796, at what must have been a very advanced age. He must surely take the prize for pluralism.

Edward Mainwaring was the fifth son of James Mainwaring of Bromborough. He went to school at Sedbergh and to St John's, Cambridge, at the early age of sixteen, in 1726. He took his B.A. in 1729–30 and his M.A. the next year. He was ordained Deacon at Lincoln in 1732 and Priest at Chester in 1733. In 1735 he became Vicar of Weaverham and in 1757 Prebendary of Chester, receiving the living of Coddington the next year. In 1755 he exchanged Weaverham for St Bridget's, Chester, and in 1761 exchanged St Bridget's for West Kirby. He died on 30 July 1780, and was buried in the Lady Chapel of the Cathedral, where there used to be a gravestone to his memory on which he was described as

> Polite, learned, ingenious, good
> An honoured ornament
> To the Church of Christ.

THE REBUILDING OF ABBEY SQUARE

Hitherto the date of the fine Georgian square has been a matter of guesswork, but now the Chapter minute book has yielded up its secret and it is possible to give the date, and also the names of the men who built the houses, for there were several of them.

On 25 March 1754, the Dean and Chapter leased to Thomas Prescott, Esq., "part of certain old buildings situate on the north side of Abby Court, and of a parcel of land thereto adjoining on the north and south sides thereof, eastwards adjoining to the dwelling house and premises, now in the occupation of Mrs. Keswick Manley". This property had a frontage of 61 ft. 8 in., "and at the backside thereof 56 ft. and 9 in." and 93 ft. in depth.

At the same time they leased to Robert Taylor, Gent.,[1] "another part of the same old buildings", with land on the north and south sides as above, and the dimensions, measuring westwards from Prescott's building 30 ft. 10 in., "on the backside 32 ft. 4 in." and 93 ft. in depth.

Another part of the same old buildings and adjoining Robert Taylor's portion was leased to Mascie Taylor, with the same length of frontage (32 ft. 10 in.) on the backside 32 ft. 4 in. and in depth 93 ft.

Now this frontage exactly fits the frontage of Nos. 7, 8, 9, and 10, leaving No. 11 (The Retreat Hostel) to represent Mrs Manley's house.

[1] Robert Taylor was the Chapter Clerk; he resigned 25 November 1773, in favour of his son Mascie. The appointment was for life.

It is even possible to get some idea of what these old buildings were, for no less a man than Archbishop Laud described them in his letter to the Dean and Chapter in 1638, and Randle Holme (III) has left us a plan of them. Laud, no doubt quoting Bishop Bridgeman, wrote "the third side hath in it one Prebendes house onlie; and the rest is turned into a malthouse". Randle Holme's plan of uncertain date, but probably later than 1638, shows three houses in the row, two labelled "brewhouse and storehouse" and one (where the Retreat Hostel now stands), "Backhouse with 2 ovens". There can be no doubt that the "old buildings" in 1754 comprised the old monastic brewery and bakery and that Prescott and the two Taylors took a lease of them with the intention of pulling them down and building dwelling-houses in their place. For in 1761 all three are back again in the Chapter office asking for new leases for the houses they had built. Mascie Taylor had built No. 7, Robert had built No. 8, and Prescott had built Nos. 9 and 10. Naturally they were granted very easy terms, as they had so considerably improved the Cathedral property. We may say then with certainty that this side of the Square was built between 1754 and 1761. This is confirmed by a memorandum of the Reverend Wm. Cole (1714–82), who visited his friend, the Rector of Tarporley, in 1755 and went on to Chester, of which, *inter alia*, he wrote:

> On the north-west Corner of the Church, by the Cloysters, the present worthy Bishop is building an entirely new Palace of free Stone, fronting the Abbey Court, where several of the Prebendaries have and are now building very neat and elegant Houses for themselves and when all are completed it will be a most elegant and beautiful Square.

Cole adds a note to say that he dined with the Bishop (Keane) on 6 August 1757, when the Palace was completed. The Bishop told him he had spent £2,200 on it—three years' income.[1] One other point. The old building had land in front of it as well as behind. The new houses must have been brought forward into the Square, so that the block is no longer flush with the end of the west side of the Square as it used to be, and the well shown in the plan outside No. 7 must now be beneath the floor of its front room.

In 1764, which is the date on the spouting, the same architect seems to have built Nos. 5 and 7 Abbey Street. In 1765 in leasing a house next to the Abbey Gateway it was mentioned that there were once "two little rooms which lay under part of the said messuage, whereof one was used for a courthouse and the other had been reputed a place for

---

[1] *L. & C. Hist. Soc.*, n.s., 22 (1913), p. 304.

a gaol belonging to the said Court", and that in 1696 William Coker, cheese factor, took down the building and erected a dwellinghouse in its place.

In the same year an exchange took place which has lasted more or less until today. The Bishop exchanged the old Registry which stood on the site of the present Abbey Chambers for the rooms over the gateway, which henceforward became the Registry, together with two small rooms adjoining the gateway on the south where one of the vergers used to live and which in future were to be offices for the use of the Bishop.

On 26 November 1770, the Dean and Chapter gave their consent to "a navigable canal" to be cut through their lands; it was to run from Chester to Middlewich, "to join the navigation which is now making from the River Trent to the River Mersey".

THE ACCOUNTS

We are now entering upon the period of the Seven Years' War in which as the ally of Frederick the Great and under the leadership of William Pitt we stripped France of her overseas possessions and laid the foundations of our Empire in India and America. The bells of the Cathedral had not been kept so busy since Marlborough's day.

	s.	d.
1758 Augt. 21. To ringing on the taking of Cape Breitton	5	0
1759 Augt. 11. Ringing for the success of prince Ferdinand at Minden Aug. 1	5	0
1759 Sept. 10. Ringing on Admiral Boscawen's success in the Mediterranen	5	0

Actually it was off Lagos in Portugal that Boscawen caught up with and smashed to pieces the Toulon fleet.

	s.	d.
Oct. 20. Ringing on taking Quebeck, Sept. 18	5	0
Dec. 3. Ringing on Admiral Hawke's success over the French Fleet Quiberon Bay, Nov. 20	5	0

This was the wonderful year of which Horace Walpole wrote that: "One is forced to ask every morning what victory there is for fear of missing one."[1] The colours carried by the 22nd Foot (now the Cheshire Regiment) at the taking of Quebec hang in the Cathedral today. The Accounts for 1760 are missing and when they recommence in 1761 the Allies still continue their victorious career.

[1] *Letters to Sir Horace Mann*, No. CCCXIV.

1761 May 16. Paid for taking the citadel of Belisle [a rock fortress   £ s. d.
      off the west coast of France]   5 0
    July 24. Paid ringing for Pondicherry   5 0
        24. Do. for the success of Prince Ferdinand over the
           French army [at Warburg]   5 0
    Dec. 24. Paid Mr. Hart for expenses at the Yacht Inn on the
           Dean and Chapter treating Mr. Comyn   1 0 10

Stephen Comyn Esq. of Lincoln's Inn and Philip Sharpe Esq. of the parish of St James, Westminster, were lessees of the important bailiwick of Chester, for which lease they paid a fine of £1,000 in 1755.

                                     £ s. d.
Paid counsel's fees for the opinion taken by the Chapter
relating to livings in the disposal of the Dean and Chapter   8 10 0
Paid Mr. Lowe for counsel's fees for opinion taken on behalf
of the Dean relating to such presentation   16 17 6

After spending £25 10s. 6d. in this way they arrived at the following agreement: "The present Dean to have the first option of such living as he shall think proper to accept and then the prebendaries to have their option according to seniority till they are all served."

                                     £ s. d.
1762 Jan. 28. Paid Mr. Richardson for mending Mr. Ashbrooke's
        verge   8 0
        Feb. 26. paid John Bulkley, Bookseller, for a Common
        Prayer Book for the Choir   15 0
        July 4. Paid ringing for a victory Prince Ferdinand gained
        over the French army   5 0
        Aug. 7. paid Saml. Bowden for roughcasting Mr. Johnson's
        [Minor Canon] and Mr. Poynton's [Conduct] houses in
        Abby Court   4 4 6
        Oct. 4. Paid for ringing on taking Havannah [from Spain] 5 0
1763 March 6. To paid George Cheatham for his two Journeys
        and Expenses from Manchester being sent over to be tryed
        as a Conduct in the room of Mr. Ely Poynton   1 1 0

Poynton had succeeded Batho as head verger. Cheatham was not appointed.

                                     £ s. d.
1764 Aug. 29. By paid William Jones, Mason for stone and
        mason's work in repairing the pinfold in the further North-
        gate Street belonging to the Dean and Chapter   11 0
1765 Feb. 7. By paid Mr. Baker late organist's burial fee by the
        order of the Dean and Chapter   2 4 6
1766 March 18. Paid Mr. Hall . . . for the expenses of fitting up
        the Rooms over the Cloisters, wh. were thought proper to
        be allowed him on quitting those rooms upon his being
        admitted a Beadsman, as residence there for 40 days wd.
        have gained him a Settlemt.   8 19 8½

This is very obscure. Hall was admitted a Bedesman at Midsummer. It looks as though "those rooms" in which he had previously been living would have gained him a settlement and so made the Dean and Chapter liable for him if he became a pauper, while the rooms over the cloisters (? the old dormitory) would not.

	£	s.	d.
1767 paid Mr. Geo. Hastings, Tinman, a bill for mending lamps		4	0
1769 Feb. 9. Paid Mr. Moody a bill for grates and fenders for the Chapter House	10	8	0
1770 Nov. Paid John Bowden for the whitewashing the Church	28	1	6
1773 Paid Mr. Orme, Subscription to Kent's anthems	1	1	0
1774 Nov. 3. Paid Messrs. Read and Huxley for 300d of Hand Bills in Answr. to a Letter published by Mr. Smith of Nantwich about the Lease of the Linnen Hall		13	6

In the summer of this year the Cathedral received a visit from Dr Samuel Johnson, whose observations, however slight, are always worthy of attention.

> July 27th, 1774. We staid at Chester and saw the Cathedral, which is not of the first rank; the Castle (in one of the rooms the Assizes are held); and the refectory of the old abbey, of which part is a Grammar School. The Master seemed glad to see me. The Cloister is very solemn, over it are chambers in which the singing men live.

We learn from this brief account that the west end of the Refectory had already been cut off and that the dormitory over the cloisters was still in use. We have already seen that one of the bedesmen had been accommodated there and we may take leave to doubt whether the Doctor was accurate in saying that the singing men lived there. The Reverend Robert Vanbrugh was headmaster in 1774 and no wonder he was pleased to welcome such a famous visitor to his school.

	£	s.	d.
1776 April 22. Pd. a voluntary subscription to the relief of the clergy in America	10	10	0

The American War of Independence had begun in the previous year. "Early in 1776 Howe was obliged to evacuate Boston and fall back on Halifax, whither he was followed by streams of loyalists and British officials flying for their lives."[1] No doubt the clergy for whom this subscription was made were among these refugees. And here we may interpolate an extract from the Tarporley accounts:

---

[1] C. R. L. Fletcher, *Introductory History of England*, p. 300.

£ s. d.

1777 May 31. By paid Thos. Eaton a mason's bill for Flaging the
      Broad Isle   51 12   0
      Nov. 24. By paid Do. for flaging part of the South Isle   26 18   0
      By paid Do. for repair'g the steeple and other work   13   3   6
1780 [Jan.] Paid ringing Victory of Sir G. Rodney   5   0

"He captured off Cape Finisterre on Jan. 8, 1780 a valuable fleet of
Spanish merchantmen on their way to Cadiz, and a week later
encountered a powerful Spanish fleet which he totally defeated."[1]

s. d.

1781 March 12. To paid ringing 2 days on taking St. Eustatius   10   6

This was not the famous "Victory of the Saints" which was fought
the following year and was celebrated by another two days' ringing.

£ s. d.

1787 To paid Geo. Bowden for whitewashing the church   25   0   0

The War of American Independence, which included a war with
France and Spain, ended in 1783 with the Treaty of Versailles, which,
thanks to Rodney, was more advantageous to us than might have been
expected. But it did not protect the American loyalists, many of whom
lost all their property. One of these came to Chester and on his death
in 1785 was buried in the South Transept (then St Oswald's Church).
A small stone marks the resting place of the body of Frederick Phillips,
but on the south-west pier of the central tower will be found his
epitaph which breathes the spirit of those times:

> Firmly attached to his Sovereign and the British Constitution, he opposed,
> at the hazard of his life, the late Rebellion in North America; and for this
> faithful discharge of his Duty to his King and Country, he was Proscribed,
> and his Estate, one of the largest in New York, was confiscated by the
> usurped Legislature of that Province. When the British Troops were with-
> drawn from New York in 1783, he quitted a Province to which he had
> always been an Ornament and Benefactor, leaving all his Property behind
> him. . . .

But the interesting thing is this. In 1756 George Washington fell in love
with Phillip's daughter, Mary, and proposed to her. She refused him,
but it is interesting to speculate on what would have been the course
of history if she had accepted him. Married to the daughter of such an
ardent loyalist, would he have been the George Washington that he
afterwards became?[2]

[1] S. J. Low and F. S. Pulling, *Dictionary of English History*.
[2] Paul Leicester Ford, *The True George Washington*, J. B. Lippincott Co.,
Philadelphia, 1902, p. 90. I owe this reference, as so much else, to Canon Baxter.

The Financial Position in 1787

The financial position of the Cathedral in the year that Dean William Smith died was distinctly serious. Ever since 1724 there had been a deficit every year which mounted steadily throughout the century, as the following figures show.

In 1730 the deficit was £21, in 1740 £99, and in 1760 £190. By 1770 it had increased to £565 and by 1780 to £835. It was time that Tarporley came to the rescue. £1,566 had accumulated in that account and in 1785 £600 was transferred to the Cathedral, bringing the deficit down to £280. But this could only be a temporary remedy. By 1787 the deficit had risen again to £482. The reason of course was the Leicester award of 1580 which nailed the Cathedral income down to what it was at the very beginning. Static income and rising prices— need we say more? But as we shall see in the next chapter, the remedy was in the hands of the Dean and Chapter if only they were prepared to take it.

7

FROM 1787 TO 1837

THE end of the eighteenth century and the beginning of the nineteenth was an eventful period in English history. In 1782 the War of American Independence ended in the Declaration of Independence and the loss to Great Britain of what in those days were called the American Colonies. Two years later the younger Pitt became Prime Minister at the age of twenty-four and his term of office was marked by the French Revolution and the long war with France, beginning in 1793 and continuing after Pitt's death right down to 1815.

Just as the first decade of the previous century had been marked by continuous war in which Marlborough faced Louis XIV, so in this one Wellington faced Napoleon. At home the Industrial Revolution was gathering strength, and both riches and poverty were increasing. There were, however, signs that the Church was awakening from her slumber. John Howard was busy at this time (1780) exposing the conditions of the prisons and William Wilberforce had begun his fight for the abolition of slavery. Robert Raikes started the Sunday School Movement in 1791, the Church Missionary Society was founded in 1799 and the British and Foreign Bible Society in 1804. The education of the poor received an impetus by the founding of the British and Foreign Schools Society in 1808 and of the National Society in 1811.

Such was the background at home and abroad against which the history of the Cathedral must be placed, and if the comings and goings of the Cathedral clergy seem very trivial by comparison it must be remembered that it is not the great events of history but the ordinary everyday happenings which give the truer picture of what life was like in days gone by.

DEAN GEORGE COTTON 1787–1805

The new Dean who succeeded William Smith was the third son of Sir Lynch Salusbury Cotton, Bart., of Combermere Abbey. He went to School at Westminster and thence as a Scholar to Trinity, Cambridge in 1761. He took his B.A. in 1765. In 1771 he married Catherine, daughter of James Tomkinson of Dorfold Hall near Nantwich, and was appointed to the living of South Raston (Lincs.) to which in the following year he added Stowe (Bucks.) and Stoke (Staffs.). He resigned the first two in 1775 and 1780 respectively, but remained in possession of Stoke to the end of his life. In 1787 he took his LL.D., was made Dean of Chester and was given the living of Davenham (Ches.) which he exchanged for Dodleston in 1797.

Dean Cotton was the uncle of Sir Stapleton Cotton, who succeeded to the baronetcy in 1809 and became Baron Combermere in 1814 and Viscount in 1827, and whose equestrian statue stands outside the Castle on the Grosvenor Road. It was the Dean's ancestor, Sir Richard Cotton, who more than 200 years before had forcibly obtained the freehold of the bulk of the Cathedral lands and sold it to his friends. There is a certain irony in the fact that his descendant now had to face the consequences.[1] The Chapter over which Dean Cotton presided was constituted as follows:

George Cotton, D.D., Dean	1787–1805
Richard Jackson, D.D.	1744–1796
Thomas Mostyn, M.A.	1776–1808
John Briggs, M.A.	1780–1795
Thomas Ward, M.A.	1781–1827
Thomas Pearce, D.D.	1781–1803
George Travis, M.A.	1782–1797

Jackson has already been dealt with.

Thomas Mostyn was the son of Thomas Mostyn of Whitford, Co. Flint. He was born in 1737 and went, as so many of our prebendaries did, to Christ Church, Oxford. This was in 1755 at the age of eighteen. He took his B.A. in 1759 and after his ordination became in due

---

[1] J. Poole, *History of Chester* (1791), p. 87, has an interesting note on the Deanery: "The Gothic structure of St. Thomas's chapel (the residence of the late Dean Smith) has been very judiciously taken down; and on the site thereof a spacious mansion, more descriptive of the heart of his successor, Dean Cotton, is erected."

Cotton was the Dean who had a way cut through the disused end of the Refectory into the cloisters to provide a short cut from the Deanery to the Cathedral. The alternative was to enter by the slype, for the present entrance from Abbey Square was blocked by the Headmaster's house.

course Canon of St Asaph Cathedral in 1773, Rector of Christleton in 1775, and also Rector of Llanycil, Co. Merioneth. In 1776 he was made Prebendary of Chester and in 1782 Vicar of Northenden. He died on 5 December 1808, aged seventy-one.

John Briggs was a native of Wakefield where he went to school. He went to Trinity College, Cambridge, as a sizar in 1745-6 at the age of seventeen, took his B.A. in 1749-50 and was made a Fellow of his College in 1752, taking Holy Orders in 1758. In 1780 he became Vicar of St Ippolyts, Herts., Rector of Calverton, Bucks., and Prebendary of Chester. In the following year he was made Chancellor of the Diocese and Rector of Methley, Yorks. Although he was such a new-comer he was elected Vice-Dean in 1783 on the death of Roger Barnston. For some reason he resigned his prebend in 1795, though he did not die until 1804, when he was buried at Neston, although he was not the vicar there.

Thomas Ward, youngest son of Archdeacon Abel Ward, was probably born in the precincts, for he was baptized in the Cathedral on 13 January 1757. He went to Queen's College, Cambridge in 1773, took his B.A. in 1777 and was made a Fellow in 1778. In 1781 at the age of twenty-four he succeeded to the stall in the Cathedral which his father had occupied for thirty-seven years and which the son was to hold for another forty-six. His livings were Neston (1783) and Handley (1797)—both of which he held until his death in 1827, aged seventy-one. There is a tablet to his memory in the wall of the Chapel of St Werburgh.

Thomas Pearce was the son of Henry Pearce of Wotton-under-Edge, Co. Glos. He went to Oriel College, Oxford, in 1763 at the age of seventeen, and took his B.A. in 1767. He was installed Prebendary in 1781, having been given the living of Coddington in 1780. In 1786 he was promoted to West Kirby. In 1792 he was made Sub-Dean of the Chapel Royal and took his D.D. in the following year. He died at Lambeth in 1803.

George Travis was a native of Royton near Oldham. Educated at Manchester Grammar School, he went to St John's College, Cambridge, in 1761 and in 1765 appeared as 5th Senior Optime and the Chancellor's Senior Medallist—that is, he was the best classic of his year. Ordained Deacon and Priest in the same year, he married and was made Vicar of Eastham in 1766 and remained there all his life. He also held the Curacy of Bromborough, for which he received £13 a year from the Dean and Chapter. In 1783 he was made a Prebendary by Bishop Porteus and Archdeacon of Chester three years later. To these offices he added the Rectory of Handley in 1787, which he held in plurality. Lest he should be too readily accused of accumulating wealth, it should be pointed out that the living of Eastham when he took it over was worth only £30 a year, and had he not had private means he could not have accepted it. He records that preceding Vicars of Eastham, as far as the memories of parishioners went back, "lived for the greatest part of their lives on charity and died insolvent". Having discovered that the poorness of the living was due to the with-holding of the tithe by the principal landowners in the parish, headed by Sir William Stanley of Hooton, he courageously went to law with them, fought them from court to court and after expending £2,000 of his own money, finally won his case and raised the Eastham tithes from £30 to £100 a year, and this before he was a prebendary and while he was a simple vicar. Some idea of the time it took may be gained from the endorsements on the Cathedral Accounts, which all had to go up to Westminster to be used as evidence. These read: "Travis *v*. Oxton and others 2nd June 1774"; "Travis *v*. Mason *v*. Urmston, Sept. 1775"; "Travis *v*. Stanley, Bart. and another, 17th Dec. 1777". Finally, we have this little bit of information from the Tarporley Accounts which suggests that there were other cases as well:

> 1782 By paid the expence of sending up the Records of the
>   Church to London on the trial of one of the Rev. Mr.
>   Travis's Tithe Causes to support the rights of the Vicarage
>   of Eastham   20 0 0

In 1784 Travis published a volume entitled *Letters to Gibbon*, arguing for the authenticity of the text 1 John 5–7, which drew forth a powerful reply from the famous scholar, Richard Porson. It is no discredit to the Archdeacon that modern criticism has decided in favour of Porson and that that particular verse has been omitted from the revised version of the New Testament.

Travis' memorial tablet may be seen in the north aisle of the Cathe-dral choir. It bears a profile portrait and an inscription which singles out for special mention his "extensive learning, active mind, and generous heart". In 1790 he obtained from the Dean and Chapter a lease of Hillbre Island, and in 1796 he died. His prayer book is still preserved in Eastham Church.[1]

John Cleaver was a Prebendary for only two years (1774–76). He was the son of William Cleaver, a clergyman of Banbury, and was born in 1737, educated at Christ Church, Oxford, where he graduated in 1758

[1] For a fuller account of him see the Rev. F. Sanders in *Wirral Notes and Queries*, I, pp. 21–4.

and eventually became Vicar of Frodsham. He died at the early age of thirty-nine. His brother afterwards became Bishop of Chester (see p. 239).

THE ACCOUNTS

The Accounts in this period are not very informative, for they give merely the name of the tradesman and the amount of his bill and do not specify the nature of the work done. There are therefore few items of this kind worth recording. On the other hand we are always told the occasion for any special ringing of the bells, which in the War years was fairly often. This raises a difficulty. If all the battles are left out the reader will think that the Dean and Chapter were oblivious of the tremendous events which were happening around them. If only some are selected for mention a false impression will be given. If all are mentioned it will suggest that the War was the only thing that mattered. In spite of this I have decided, if only for the sake of uniformity, to follow the practice adopted when dealing with the reign of Queen Anne, and mention them all.

	£	s.	d.
1787 To Geo. Bowden for whitewashing the Church	25	0	0
To ringing for the Bishop of London		5	0

This refers to the translation of Bishop Beilby Porteous to the See of London.

	£	s.	d.
To Great Bell for Lord Lieutenant		12	6
1789 To paid Ringing on the King's Recovery [George III]		5	0
To paid Mr. Rigby of Hawarden towards the expenses of the Iron rails for Abbey Square[1]	26	5	0
1790 To paid advertising Clergy Resolution in the several papers	20	2	0

This was a resolution passed at a meeting of the clergy of the Chester Archdeaconry on 15 February, Archdeacon Travis being in the chair, "to take into consideration the attempts of the Dissenters in various parts of the Kingdom to obtain a repeal of the Corporation and Test Acts, and their assertions that those Acts are acknowledged by many of the established clergy to be a grievance and a common evil". A number of resolutions were then passed to the effect that while they did not wish to deny the dissenters freedom of worship, they did not think they could be entrusted with offices in the State unless they were members of the Established Church. They were suspected of not being

[1] J. Poole, op. cit. "The abbey court is a neat and pleasant square, with an obelisk in the centre, surrounded by a large circle of iron palisades."

loyal supporters of the Constitution. These resolutions were signed by over 250 clergy from all parts of Lancashire and Cheshire headed by the Dean and Chapter who on this occasion attended in full force.[1]

In 1793 war with Revolutionary France broke out and continued with only one year's intermission right down to 1815.

		s.	d.
1794	To paid Ringing all night for Lord Howe's victory	12	6

This was the Battle of the Glorious First of June, in which the Channel fleet defeated the French fleet off Ushant.

			£	s.	d.
1797	Ringing on Admiral Duncan's Victory	1st Acct.		10	0
Do	Do	2nd Acct.	1	0	0

This was the Battle of Camperdown fought on 11 October in which Admiral Duncan routed the Dutch fleet and prevented it uniting with the French. Special importance seems to have been attached to this victory in Chester.

		s.	d.
1798	Ringing on Admiral Nelson's Victory [Battle of the Nile, August 1]	10	0
	Ringing J. Warren's Victory	5	0

A French expedition had landed on the west coast of Ireland and was expecting reinforcements. These were intercepted by Sir John Warren on 11 October and defeated.

		£	s.	d.
1798	Paid to Mr. Walker, a table in the Chapter House and green cloth	1	17	2½
1799	Ringing 25th July and taking Dutch fleet	1	0	0

25 July must have been an anniversary of some kind and had nothing to do with the taking of the Dutch fleet for that occurred on 27 August. A British force under Sir Ralph Abercromby landed at the Helder and threw open the Texel to the British ships. The Dutch seamen, who were loyal to the Prince of Orange, co-operated, and the whole fleet of 13 ships of the line gladly surrendered and were carried off to Yarmouth out of the reach of the French.

		s.	d.
1800	Greswell for matts to cover the organ	5	0
	Cleaning the curtains in the choir	18	0
1801	Ringing Lord Nelson's Victory	10	0

This was the Battle of Copenhagen (2 April) fought to rescue the Danish fleet this time, but unfortunately serious resistance was met

[1] See the *Chester Courant*.

THE REVEREND JOSEPH EATON, CHAPTER CLERK IN 1827

THE ABBEY GATE-
WAY, SHOWING
I ABBEY SQUARE
ON THE RIGHT
AND THE
BISHOP'S GARDEN
WALL ON THE
LEFT

with.[1] This was the famous occasion when Nelson put his telescope to his blind eye and sailed boldly into the harbour in defiance of orders.

	s.	d.
1802 Ringing Ratification of Peace	10	0

This was the Peace of Amiens (25 March), but it did not last more than a year and the war soon began again.

	s.	d.
1803 Ringing 29th July for Volunteers	10	0
Ringing for Prince William of Gloucester	10	0

He was a nephew of George III and "arrived in Chester 1 September. On Sunday, 4 September his Highness inspected the Volunteers on the Roodeye, and accompanied them to the Cathedral, where the Bishop preached".[2]

	£	s.	d.
1804 Ringing presentation of Volunteer Colours		10	0
Mr. Pope an allowance (by order of Chapter) for damage done to his Garden by repairing Free School	2	2	0
1805 Ringing Volunteers returning home		10	0
Messengers to fetch ringers		1	0
Ringing cavalry returning and messenger		11	0
Ringing defeat of combined Fleet by Adml. Calder		10	0
Ringing Adml. Nelson's Victory, Trafalgar		10	0
Ringing Adml. Strachan's Victory		10	0
Illumination		10	0

Admiral Calder on 22 July met the combined French and Spanish fleets on their return from the West Indies where they had given Nelson the slip. Their intention was to join up with the French fleet at Brest and hold the Channel while Napoleon threw his army across. But Calder headed them off from Brest and drove them south into Cadiz—as important and decisive an action as the Battle of Britain in 1940, for it caused Napoleon to give up the idea of invading England. On 4 November Admiral Strachan with three ships-of-the-line captured four French ships which had escaped from Trafalgar, thus rounding off the destruction of the French fleet.

The Volunteers

These had been disbanded on 10 May 1802, after the signing of the Peace, but when war broke out again they had to be reassembled. On

[1] History repeated itself when we had to seize the French fleet in Oran Harbour in 1940.

[2] Pigot, p. 326.

16

27 July there was "a meeting of citizens to raise a Volunteer Corps" and no doubt the ringing of the bells on the twenty-ninth had to do with that. The Colours were presented on 19 March 1804 "by Col. Barnston's lady in the area before his house in Foregate Street; after the ceremony, the regiment marched to the Cathedral, where the colours were consecrated".[1] In 1805 the Volunteers marched to Warrington for 21 days "permanent duty" and presumably were welcomed home by the bells.

The Accounts for this year (1805) show that the two side aisles of the Cathedral were re-slated for £75 18s. 0d., and the King's School (Refectory) roof was replaced at a cost of £448 17s. 8d., the old roof being sold for £40. Hemingway says the old one was "a roof of oak resting on brackets".

DEAN HUGH CHOLMONDELEY 1806–1815

Dean Cotton died on 10 December 1806, while he was at Bath, and was succeeded by Hugh Cholmondeley, B.D., F.S.A., the fourth son of Thomas Cholmondeley of Vale Royal, which the Cholmondeley family had bought in 1616 from the Holcrofts, who in their turn had obtained it at the Dissolution of the Monasteries.[2]

Born in 1772, the new Dean went to Brazenose College, Oxford, of which he was elected a Fellow in 1796 at the early age of twenty-three. The way in which he came to take Holy Orders he has described himself in his letters to Richard Heber, who lived at Hodnet and was half-brother to Reginald Heber, Bishop of Calcutta.[3] He must be judged by the spirit of his age, and his attitude to ordination was probably that of his circle in the beginning of the nineteenth century. He was twenty-six at the time he wrote.

> Stanmore, May 15, 1798.
> After much consideration I have almost resolved to take Orders next Trinity Sunday. It is an object to me to get settled upon some Curacy or other, for living this wandering kind of life will not do for me. And one is more likely by being in Orders to meet with anything than otherwise. I shall, then, too, be able to take Priests Orders at Christmas and get it all over. I am not particularly anxious to go into the Church, but as it must be my profession the sooner I take it up the better.

[1] Pigot, p. 326.
[2] His portrait hangs in the Cathedral parlour.
[3] Author of the hymn "From Greenland's icy mountains" (R. H. Cholmondeley, *The Heber Letters*, pp. 170–2, The Batchworth Press).

Oxford, May 20, 1798.

Harper dissuades me very much from taking Orders and what astonished me very much, the Bishop did the same, when I called on him this morning. I think I shall defer it and become military.

B.N.C. May 26, 1799.

I was ordained last Sunday, so you may direct to the Rev. H. C.

His first living was the Rectory of Harthill. Here he devoted himself to archaeology, a subject in which he was much interested and apparently well fitted for. Was he not an F.S.A.? In 1804 he was given the living of Barrow by Lord Cholmondeley, his cousin.

On 24 February 1806 he succeeded Dr Cotton as Dean of Chester, and once again the story of how he obtained the Deanery is told by himself. What seems to us an unscrupulous rush to get his claim in first was probably not considered in any way peculiar in those days.

To Richard Heber, London, Dec. 14, 1805.

I find you have written to my brother whose letter of application was forwarded to Mr. Pitt at Bath by Lord Chatham last Monday accompanied by one in my favour to Pitt from Lord C. I dare not venture to hope though I certainly have a chance. Pitt will receive the letter the same day the Dean died [i.e. Dec. 10, 1805].

B.N.C. Dec. 18, 1805.

Thank you heartily for all your exertions. Indeed my friends have been wonderfully zealous and Cholmondeley has most fully done his duty. The Dean's death was known to Parker[1] in Chester on Friday last. He instantly sent off an Express to Cholmondeley which on Saturday afternoon found him just returned from a capital run at Belvoir. He instantly set out in a hack-chaise for town where about 12 o'clock on Sunday he arrived at Drummond's. After some consultation about 2 o'clock he started again for Bath from whence I have this morning received the following letter:—

Bath, Monday.

My dear Hugh,

I have this moment left Mr. Pitt, he told me the Grosvenors, J. R. Mill and Leycester had apply'd, but allowed no promise had as yet been given. I spoke to him like a man and a relation [he was second Cousin] not as a petitioner and left him with an assurance that he would do all in his power to arrange matters so as to serve you and not affront them. I may be sanguine but my opinion is you have a good chance. Of this I am certain, had I not seen him, nothing would have been done.   Yrs. affect.

Thomas Cholmondeley.

Thomas Cholmondeley was Hugh's eldest brother, an M.P. and afterwards Lord Delamere. His race to Bath was successful and his

[1] Of Astle in Cheshire. He had married Hugh Cholmondeley's sister.

brother was admitted to the Deanery on 24 February 1806 and took his B.D. in March following. In 1808 he added to his emoluments the living of Tarporley which was in the gift of the Chapter for this turn, and here he spent a good deal of his time. His appointment to Tarporley was characteristic. He wrote to his friend Richard Heber on 16 April 1808:

> You may not perhaps object to a line conveying the information that Mr. Jacson died at Tarporley yesterday evening about five o'clock. You will not be sorry to hear that I think myself secure in succeeding him. But as we know by experience of College Elections nothing can be reckoned upon till it's finally fixed. I expect next Thursday when a Chapter is to be held, will decide the business.

On 24 April he wrote: "I am happy to announce to you that on Thursday I was presented to the Living of Tarporley." It is strange that there is no record of this presentation in the Chapter Book.

> When he first succeeded to the Deanery [writes Ormerod[1]] many nuisances existed in the Cathedral, from long indiscriminate access; the substantial parts were on the verge of decay, and many beautiful specimens of architecture as early as that of the original Norman foundation were obscured by piles of rubbish; these nuisances were almost instantaniously [sic] done away with, the material parts of the fabric were restored as substantially as the slender funds of the Chaper admitted; and many ornamental repairs and decorations were effected, which reflect the highest credit on his science and taste.

Ormerod was writing an obituary notice of a personal friend and his encomiums must be checked by other documentary evidence.

Hanshall in his *History of Cheshire* (1823) writes:

> This valuable man set on foot the reparation of the Cathedral, opened the different avenues in the cloisters, and other parts long before blocked up and erected iron palisadoes in front of the Cathedral.

A footnote to page 223, headed *Itinerary of the County*, says:

> In 1812 under the superintendence of the late Dean Cholmondeley the site of the southern angle of the Cloisters was cleared, and it was then that the Saxon arches were discovered.

These three accounts seem to agree that the Dean cleared away rubbish from the South Walk of the Cloisters. It is common knowledge that this South Walk had entirely disappeared long before 1870 when Sir Gilbert Scott rebuilt it in order to support the vaulting of the

[1] II, p. 156.

north aisle of the nave, and it is natural to suppose that the rubbish the Dean cleared away was the fallen roof of the Cloister. But the second earliest guide book we possess, dated 1793,[1] says that the South Walk was already in ruins and the rubbish removed. "Three walks of the cloisters are entire: that to the South was in ruins, but at the time of repairing the Chapter house, the rubbish was taken away and the court made level." And there we must leave it.

The Dormitory

In 1815 Dr Pigot says: "The Dormitory and the stone steps leading to it are in existence, though in a very ruinous state".

The Stranger's Companion (4th edition, p. 39) dated 1828, as far as can be ascertained from internal evidence, says: "Above these may still be seen the remnants of the ancient dormitory."

In 1831 J. Hemingway says: "Over the east cloister was a dormitory, which has either been destroyed, or suffered to fall into decay, much to the injury of the appearance of these venerable conventual buildings".[2] This fixes the disappearing of the dormitory between 1815 and 1831.

The Chapter who welcomed Dean Cholmondeley on 28 March 1806 was constituted as follows:

Thomas Mostyn, M.A.	1766–1808
Thomas Ward, M.A.	1781–1827
Thomas Trevor, D.C.L.	1795–1827
Unwin Clarke, M.A.	1801–1847
Charles Sawkins, M.A.	1801–1818
Thomas Maddock, M.A.	1803–1825

Since 1787 there had also been

Thomas Braithwaite	1797–1801

of whom nothing is known, and

William Page, M.A.	1796–1801

William Page, whose father lived at Oporto, Portugal, was educated at Christ Church, Oxford, took his B.A. in 1759 and returned to Oporto after ordination as chaplain to the factory there. In 1776 he became Rector of Frodsham and was installed at the Cathedral in 1796 where he remained until his death in 1801 at the age of sixty-four.

[1] *The History of the Cathedral Church at Chester from its Foundation to the Present Time*, p. 105. London. Printed for T. and J. Egerton, Whitehall, and sold by R. Broster, Chester, MDCCXCIII.

[2] p. 48.

Unwin Clarke was the son of Stockdell Clarke, gentleman, of Sudbury, Suffolk. He went to Wadham College, Oxford in 1782 and took his B.A. and M.A. in 1792. He was made a prebendary of Chester Cathedral in 1801 and was given the living of Dodleston in 1806 on the death of its Rector, Dean Cotton. His other livings were Eastham (1827) and Neston (1828). He was also Archdeacon of Chester. He died in 1847 at the great age of eighty-three.

Thomas Trevor was the eldest son of the Reverend Evan Humphreys of Eastham, who was Rector of Montgomery. Thomas, who changed his name in 1784, went to school at Harrow and from there proceeded to St John's College, Cambridge, in 1788. He took the degree of LL.B. in 1795 and of D.C.L. at Oxford in 1816. He was ordained deacon in 1793 and two years later was ordained priest and immediately made prebendary of Chester with the living of Coddington added to his stall. In 1797 he went to Eastham, and in 1803 he gave up Coddington for West Kirby, which he held with Eastham until his death in 1827. While he lived at Eastham he also held the curacy of Bromborough.

Charles Sawkins, son of James Sawkins of Lyminge, Kent, gent., went to Christ Church in 1774, aged sixteen, took his B.A. in 1778 and his M.A. in 1781 and started his ordained life as perpetual curate of Binsey, Oxon, in 1797. In 1801 he was made Prebendary and also Vicar of Frodsham, a living in the gift of his old college, where he remained until his death in 1818.

Thomas Maddock was the son of the Reverend Thomas Maddock of Liverpool. He went to B.N.C., Oxford in 1780 at the age of seventeen, took his B.A. in 1783, M.A. in 1786. He was made Prebendary of Chester in 1783 and in 1786 was appointed by Lord Derby to Holy Trinity, Chester, to which was added by the Dean and Chapter the Rectory of Coddington in 1806. The latter benefice he relinquished in 1809 for the living of Northenden, where he died in 1825.

Trouble in the Chapter

In November 1812 an unfortunate difference of opinion arose in the Chapter over the appointment of a new Chapter Clerk in the place of Mascie Taylor who had resigned. Four of the Prebendaries voted for the Sacrist, the Reverend Joseph Eaton, while the other two and the Dean voted for Mr Ward, the Deputy Registrar. The office carried with it that of Steward, Auditor, and Registrar. The appointment of the Reverend Joseph Eaton was entered in the Chapter Book and signed by the four Prebendaries, Thomas Ward (Vice-Dean), Thomas

Trevor, Unwin Clarke (Archdeacon) and Thomas Maddock. Beneath this entry is written: "I refuse to admit the Revd. Joseph Eaton to any of the above offices—Hugh Cholmondeley, Dean". And beneath that again is written in another hand: "The Dean, in refusing to admit the Reverend Joseph Eaton to any of the above offices, has acted in perfect agreement with our wishes.—Charles Sawkins, Richard Godley."

The battle was now joined and it is mentioned here because there was more in it than a petty quarrel; the real point at issue was whether the Dean had a right of veto over Chapter proceedings as he claimed to have. For the moment he had the whip hand, for in those days the Dean held one half (either the obverse or the reverse) of the Chapter Seal without which no appointment could be made. Both sides appealed, the Dean to the Archbishop of York and the four prebendaries to their own Bishop, who was also their Visitor. Fortunately, but not unnaturally, the decision was the same in both cases. Both agreed that a Minor Canon could not be a Chapter Clerk, Auditor and Steward without breaking the Cathedral statutes. As to the Dean's claim to a right of veto, the Archbishop declined to give an opinion, but the Bishop pronounced against it. The Dean wrote a protest against this latter decision and inserted it himself in the Chapter Book, an action which called forth a protest from the four prebendaries. Meanwhile Joseph Eaton resigned, William Ward was appointed by the whole Chapter and peace reigned once more.

A FINANCIAL CRISIS

There was however one outcome of it which was important. The four prebendaries in their appeal to the Bishop raised the question of their finances. For a long time now—since 1724—there had been a deficit every year on the working of the Cathedral, which the Dean and Chapter had tried to meet by borrowing under the Chapter seal. But the debt grew steadily and the time came when the security of the Chapter no longer sufficed and the money had to be borrowed on the security of the individual members of the Chapter. That too had now come to an end through the unwillingness of the prebendaries to sign any further securities, and the last £500 had to be borrowed by the Dean alone. The total debt was now £4,260. It is true that they had also been borrowing on the security of their Tarporley property, but Counsel's opinion, taken in October 1811, warned them that they could not legally do this. What was to be done, they asked the Bishop, and referred him "to the 38th section of our Statutes which

places them [their finances] under the jurisdiction of the Visitor".
Their income, they said, came from three sources:

1. Annual rents.
2. An estate at Tarporley left to them by Dean Arderne.
3. Fines on the renewal of leases.

The first of these has been appropriated for the discharge of the salaries
of the officers of the church and repairs of the ffabrick.

The second has been applied according to the will of the Donor in
defending the rights of the church and occasionally in aid of the first
fund. . . .

*The third ffund is divided into 8 shares amongst the members of the body, the
Dean taking 2 shares.*

So there we have it in black and white! No wonder the Cathedral
finances were in a poor way. The Chapter book shows that the property
in the hands of the Dean and Chapter was let at ridiculously low rents
and that the real income from it arose from the fines imposed every
time a lease was renewed, which was generally every seven years. *And
these fines went into the pockets of the Dean and Chapter.* For example,
the rent of the Bailiwick of Chester, which was the most valuable
property they possessed, was only £73 p.a.; but the fine for a 21-years'
lease was £2,920. That this was a very wasteful way of dealing with
Cathedral property was admitted by the Chapter themselves when
they put their case up to Counsel about the Tarporley estate. For they
wrote:

The profits of this estate amounting at present to no more than £800
have been applied in aid of the funds of the Church, but *as the system
of leasing for lives or a term of years, or a fine, being very wisely abandoned,
the property whenever it becomes clear may be worth* £1,500 *per annum.*

This strange method of dealing with Cathedral property was common to all ecclesiastical corporations and was only brought to an end
in 1852–6 with much difficulty, the difficulties being due to the lawyers
and not to the clergy. In justice to the latter it has been said that "it
was practically impossible for them in the absence of powers of sale and
purchase, to bring the wasteful process to a close".[1]

We are in a position now to appreciate the Bishop's answers to their
cry for help. He was George Henry Law.

The third point to which my attention has been requested is the embar-
rassed state of the Finances of the Dean and Chapter. And here, Reverend

[1] R. T. Davidson and Wm. Benham, *Life of Archbishop Tait*, vol. I, p. 175.

Brethren, I must declare my honest opinion. That some degree of blame attaches to you all. The expenses incurred by the Body should, in part at least, have been defrayed by the same body and at the time that they were incurred . . . if all other ffunds unfortunately prove insufficient, the fines in aid of them must be had resource to. . . . I hope that I only discharge the duty which the Statutes upon this head impose upon me as Visitor by ordering that an eighth part of the ffines be set apart and applied each year at the November audit to the discharge of all the debts of the Dean and Chapter as a body till the whole of them are paid off.

The effect of this very sensible order is to be seen—if we may anticipate a little—in a memorandum preserved in the Muniment Room headed:

Fine Money carried to the Church Account:

			£	s.	d.
$\frac{1}{8}$ to audit	1814		335	16	11
$\frac{1}{8}$,,	1815		24	11	2
$\frac{1}{8}$,,	1816		54	11	$4\frac{1}{2}$
$\frac{1}{8}$,,	1817		51	16	1
$\frac{1}{2}$ Bailiwick Fine	1818		406	5	0
$\frac{1}{8}$ to audit	1818		6	10	0
$\frac{1}{4}$,,	1819		362	15	0
$\frac{1}{4}$,,	1820		27	5	0
$\frac{1}{4}$,,	1821		55	5	0
$\frac{1}{4}$,,	1822		3	15	0
$\frac{1}{8}$,,	1823		43	7	$6\frac{1}{2}$
$\frac{1}{8}$,,	1824		47	7	10
$\frac{1}{8}$ Bailiwick	1825		485	0	0
$\frac{1}{8}$ to audit	1825		6	11	3
$\frac{1}{8}$,,	1826		148	0	0
12 years —			£2059	7	2	(£158 p.a.)

THE BISHOPS OF CHESTER (1788–1837)

It may be well to put on record the occupants of the See of Chester during this period although only one or two of them had much to do with the Cathedral.

William Cleaver (1788–1800) was Principal of B.N.C., Oxon, 1785–1809, and owed his bishopric to having once been tutor to the Marquess of Buckingham. He was translated to Bangor and thence to St Asaph.

Henry William Majendie (1800–10) was Prebendary of St Paul's Cathedral before being consecrated bishop. Like his predecessor he was translated to Bangor.

Bowyer Edward Sparke (1810–12) was Dean of Bristol. He was translated to Ely after having been in Chester only two years.

George Henry Law (1812–24) was the son of a Bishop of Carlisle and himself a prebendary of that Cathedral. One of his brothers he made Prebendary of Chester and another one was Lord Ellenborough, Lord Chief Justice. Bishop Law was translated to Bath and Wells.

Charles James Blomfield (1824–8), the son of a Norfolk schoolmaster, was Archdeacon of Colchester before he was made Bishop of Chester. He was translated to London.

John Bird Sumner (1828–48) was Canon of Durham, was appointed Bishop of Chester by Robert Peel and translated to Canterbury by Lord John Russell.

It is supposed that it was the small income of the See which led to these constant translations, which in turn gave rise to the saying: "The Bishop of Chester never dies".

THE ACCOUNTS 1806–12

Ringing for victories in the long-drawn-out war inevitably provides most of the extracts from the Accounts, but it is interesting to see how the war was viewed in England and which engagement was thought worthy of the ringing of the bells and for how long.

	s.	d.
1806 Ringing Admiral Duckworth's victory	10	0
Ringing Admiral Warren's victory	10	0

"In February the French force at St. Domingo surrendered to Sir James Duckworth: Admiral Warren in March closed the career of the adventurous Linois."[1]

	£	s.	d.
Paid Boden for cleaning and colouring the Cathedral	46	5	0
William Hall Cleaning the Cathedral after colouring	2	12	6
Mr. Humbertson Solicitor	53	7	3

These legal expenses arose from the Dean and Chapter taking Counsel's opinion as to the legality of appointments to livings while the Deanery was vacant. Counsel was doubtful and advised that any such appointments should be made over again. So Unwin Clarke was re-instituted to Dodleston and Thomas Maddock to Coddington.

	s.	d.
1807 Bill for parchmt, vergers, seal and ingrossing the address to his Majesty respecting the Catholic Bill	15	0

[1] J. Holland Rose, *The Life of Napoleon*, II, 81. Linois is described as "the terror of our merchantmen in Eastern Seas". Ibid. I, 376.

This was a bill to remove some of the disabilities of Roman Catholics who served in the Army and Navy. The King stopped it by dismissing his ministers.

	s.	d.
Ringing the defeat of the French by Russia in May[1]	10	0
Ringing the taking of Copenhagen [Sept 7th by Ld. Cathcart]	10	0
1808 Ringing the taking of the French fleet at Cadiz	10	0

The fleet consisted of five ships which had been in Cadiz harbour since Trafalgar and were now captured by the Spanish insurgents.[2]

	s.	d.
Ringing the defeat of the French by the Spanish patriots	10	0

This was little more than a skirmish in which the French fled before the insurgents right back to Barcelona on 12 June.[3]

	£	s.	d.
Ringing the Surrender of the French army commanded by Genl. Dupont to the Spanish Patriots [at Baylen]		10	0
Ringing on the 29th of Aug. for the glorious news from Portugal [Battle of Rovica, Aug. 17]		7	6
Ringing on the defeat of Junot in Portugal by the British commanded by Sir Arthur Wellesley [Vimiero, Aug. 21]		10	0
Ringing on the surrender of the French troops in Portugal [Convention of Cintra]		10	0
Mr. Eaton [Sacrist] in lieu of perquisites formerly taken by the Sacrist out of the offerings—½ year at Mich'as.		4	0	0

		£	s.	d.
The Vergers the like—½ year due Mich'as.	1	11	6	
Do an allowance on Good Friday (by order of Mr. Trevor)	1	0	6	
			2	2	0
Do their fees on tolling the bell for Mr. Mostyn			12	6

This is explained by the following resolution passed by the Chapter on 21 April 1808:

It was also ordered that the sum of eight pounds be annually paid to the Sacrist in lieu of perquisites formerly paid him out of the Offering money given whenever the holy sacrament of the Lord's Supper is administered. And that from the date hereof the Treasurer do pay all expenses for bread and wine. And that the sum of one guinea be paid annually to each of the Vergers, and to the Sweeper, in lieu of their perquisites on the same occasion.

[1] J. H. Rose, op. cit., II, 109: "The fighting in the open also went against the allies, though at Puttusk, a town north of Warsaw, the Russians claimed that the contest had been drawn in their favour."
[2] Camb. Mod. History, IX, p. 238.
[3] Napier's Peninsula War, ch. 6, p. 77.

Prebendary Mostyn for whom they tolled the bell was the doyen of the Chapter, having joined it in 1776—thirty-two years ago.

		£	s.	d.
1809	Ringing the defeat of the French Fleet in Basque Roads by Adm'l. Gambier and Lord Cockrane [April 11th]		10	0
	Do the taking of Flushing		10	0
	Finney, Cross Foxes for a Dinner for part of the Members of the Church on the Jubilee	3	7	0
1810	Ringing for Lord Wellington's Victory, Buscao [Sept. 27]		10	0

	T. Hodkinson, The balance of cash paid the workmen employed about the Cloisters and other places	154	8	10
	Cash from the Prebendaries	12	12	0

————141 16 10

1810	Tolling the Great Bell for Princess Amelia [favourite daughter of George III who had died]		12	6
1812	Ringing the good news from Lord Wellington [Ciudad Rodrigo and Badajoz, Jan. 19 and Ap. 6]		7	6
	Ringing the Battle of Salamanca [July 22]		15	0
	Ringing the taking of Madrid		15	0
	Ringing the complete overthrow of the French by the Russians [Retreat from Moscow began Oct. 18th]		7	6
1813	Great Bell for the Duchess of Brunswick		12	6
	Ringing the 4th June and the Battle of Vittoria	1	2	6
	Ringing the taking of the Pyrenees and 12th August	1	2	6
	Ringing the Victory gained by the Austrians [Kulm]		15	0
	Ringing the Victory gained by the Allied Armies [Leipzig, Oct. 16–19]		15	0
	Ringing the Defeat of Suchett [The French Commander in Catalonia]		15	0
1814	Mr. Leatherbarrow's bill for the Illumination	8	0	0
	4th June a Peace [Treaty of Paris—May 30]		15	0
	Weeding the Sprice		8	0
	Illumination		15	0
	Thanksgiving		15	0
	August. Cleaning the Chandeliers		16	0

DEAN ROBERT HODGSON 1816–1820

Robert Hodgson, D.D., was instituted to the Deanery on 25 January 1816, on the death of Dean Cholmondeley. He was a Cheshire man, the son of Robert Hodgson of Congleton and Mildren, daughter of the Reverend Robert Porteous. He went to school at Macclesfield and from there proceeded to Peterhouse, Cambridge where he took his B.A. (14th Wrangler) in 1795 and the following year was elected a

Fellow of his College. Ordained in 1796, he served as Chaplain to the Bishop of London, Beilby Porteus, who was his great uncle and a former Bishop of Chester (1777–87). Promotion was therefore easy and assured. He was Rector of St George's, Hanover Square, 1803–14; Chaplain to the King; Vicar of Hillingdon with Valridge, 1810–14; Archdeacon of St Albans, 1814–16. He left Chester in 1820 to become Dean of Carlisle (1820–40) and also Chaplain-General to the Forces (1824).

THE ACCOUNTS

		£	s.	d.
1818	Rev. George Pearson Lecturer at St. Peter's, a donation	10	0	0
	Clothier's bill (Mr. Francis) for hanging the stalls and pulpit	37	16	6
	Iron Chest for the Registers	2	3	6
1819	Laying the gas pipes in the Cathedral	68	18	11½
	Enlarging and altering the swell organ	30	0	0
	Bill for ornaments in the Choir	3	0	0
1820	Gass bill for lighting the Cathedral	3	0	0
	Mr. Holland, a new clock for the Broad Aisle	2	10	0
	A damask table cloth for the Altar	2	10	0
1821	Police for paving Church Yard	4	12	6
	Kelley's Balance of Bill for the late repairs	200	0	0
	Martin and Ingram, Balance of their Bill for the late repairs	29	19	5
1821	A piece of plate presented to the Chapter Clerk [Rev. J. Eaton]	20	0	0
	Martin and Ingram, Balance of their Bill for the late repairs	29	19	5
	Gas Bill for lighting up the Choir	4	0	0
	Expenses on a Parliamentary Petition		17	10
1822	Martin and Ingram, Carpenter's Bill for 1821 and 1822	263	1	9½
1824	Christian Knowledge Society donation	5	5	0
	Do do. do Subscription	5	5	0
	Mr. Morgan assisting at the organ (paid to the Bishop)	10	0	0

The Restoration of 1818–19

One would never guess from the meagre details given in the Accounts that a considerable restoration of the Cathedral was undertaken in 1818 and 1819, but fortunately the details of Martin and Ingram's bill for work done in 1819 have been preserved and give us some idea of the nature of this restoration. It seems to have been very much over-due. In an appeal issued to the clergy of the diocese on 1

July 1818, the Bishop (George Henry Law) asked for contributions from each parish "for the repair of our Cathedral".

> It may perhaps be unnecessary for me to apprize you [he wrote] that the funds of the Capitular Body are unequal even to the annual expences of the Cathedral, much more to the repair of it. From this cause, and from an anxious wish on the part of the Dean and Chapter to leave nothing undone that they could accomplish, they have become involved in a considerable degree of debt. An accurate Survey and Estimate have been made by Mr. Harrison, the Architect, and from these it appears, that at least £7000 are required for the decent repair of our ancient and venerable fabric. Unless something be done, and done soon, the building must inevitably fall into a state of disgraceful dilapidation.[1]

Further evidence about this restoration can be obtained from *The Stranger's Companion*, the guide-book of that day, first published in 1823. There it is stated:

> The exterior had, from neglect, or the low state of revenue, fallen into the most abject and fearful decay, till it was taken under repair by public subscription; much has been done to strengthen it, and many parts are renewed; the exterior has likewise been much improved and beautified.

This account appeared annually until 1828, when a new editor rewrote it and added a "History of the Cathedral" in which he stated:

> It is greatly to be lamented that owing to the low state of the Cathedral revenues the whole building was suffered to fall into a serious state of dilapidation before it was attended to. . . . A subscription was therefore set on foot throughout the Diocese, and a handsome sum was collected, though not sufficient it was thought to restore the grandeur of its former architectural dignity. Accordingly, the repairs as they now stand were completed at the least possible expense.

This is borne out by details from the carpenter's bill alluded to above. Extracts from a bill of Martin and Ingram, Chester, 1819:

				£	s.	d.
March 27	176 ft. of ¾ in. red deal for Coir [*sic*]			2	6	5½
	Thos. Ingram at Tabernacle work		4d		16	8
	Thos. Edge at do do		5d	1	0	10
April 3	100 feet of 1 in Red Deal for Doors and Tabernacle work			2	1	8
	Thos. Ingram at Tabernacle work		4d		16	8
	Thos. Edge at "		6d	1	5	0
April 17	Thos. Edge at "		5½d	1	2	11
May 15	Thos. Edge at do		5½d	1	1	10
" 22	9½ ft. of ¾ in. for Tabernacle				2	4½

[1] Ormerod, I, 252.

				£	s.	d.
May	22	Thos. Ingram at Tabernacle wk	2d		8	4
		Thos. Edge do do	6 days	1	5	0
,,	29	33 feet of 1½ inch deal for East window		1	0	7½
June	5	37½ feet of 1 in. Deal for Catofiles under window			15	7½
		Thos. Ingram at Tabernacle	6d	1	5	0
		John Snelson at Catofiles	6d	1	5	0
,,	12	Thos. Edge at Tabernacle and Porch	6d	1	5	0
		228 feet of 2½ plank for Bell floor		10	9	0
		172 Treads up Tower as pr. Contract		1	16	4

The purchase of red deal and the many days spent on the tabernacle work in the Choir—49½ in all—rouse our apprehensions. What damage, we wonder, was being done. The answer is given by the firm which repaired the woodwork in the Choir in 1870. They wrote:

> All the old stalls and canopies were in a very bad state, and had been to a large extent repaired in deal . . . no less than 35 of the large topmost finials were either altogether missing or in deal. . . . The canopies at the west end were all new, as also six of the canopies to the side stalls, which were found to be all in deal.[1]

The Stranger's Companion[2] gives these further details about this restoration. The walls of the Choir were found "to be too much decayed to support a new stone roof", and "an artificial one of lath and plaster has been suggested to supply the deficiency . . . anything would be preferable to its present uncouth ceiling". "The tower of the church", we read, "has five unequal bells, which we cannot commend for their melody." That this restoration did not pass off without any friction is clear from the correspondence between the Dean and Chapter and the architect, the famous Thomas Harrison. Harrison had rebuilt the Castle and erected the monument on Moel Fammau, and in his eighty-first year was going to be asked to design the Grosvenor Bridge, his greatest work, which he did not live to see completed. Dean Hodgson wrote to him on 30 November 1818, asking him to advise on getting tenders for the work, "and for that purpose it will be necessary to state by public advertisement, as near as may be, what is to be done, and what part of it is to be undertaken *first*". Harrison did what he was asked to do, but on 5 March 1819, he wrote to Prebendary Slade, "despairing that any professional skill of mine can be of use under the present interference of the individual I mentioned to you". Slade replied courteously but firmly: "We are truly obliged to your

---

[1] *C.A.J.*, IX, p. 48.
[2] 4th ed., c. 1828, p. 46.

important advice, but at the same time feel ourselves to be alone responsible." Harrison replied with some asperity:

> Altho' the restoration of a building like the Cathedral cannot be considered as the most agreeable employment in which an architect can be engaged; yet from the high respect I have for the worthy Lord Bishop of Chester, who first employed me to examine this Church, and for the very Revd. the Dean and other members of the Chapter, I willingly entered upon the business, however I might be remunerated, and made the necessary drawings, specifications, estimates etc preparatory to commencing the operations, little suspecting that any person would so soon interfere in what I conceived essentially necessary for the benefit of the work.

He added that as an architect of "this almost ruinous church" he must be allowed to superintend the repairs in order to guard against accidents, "whereas I learnt from your self I am to be restrained from visiting the works whenever I may think proper". In consequence he begged to be excused having anything further to do with the work and—parting shot—he would take his foreman with him. On the face of it he seems to have been rather badly treated, but we have not got the Dean and Chapter's side of the story.

DEAN PETER VAUGHAN 1820–1826

Peter Vaughan was the son of a doctor in Leicester. He went to Merton College, Oxford in 1787 at the age of seventeen and had an unbroken career there—except for one year as assistant master at Rugby School in 1792—ending up as Warden of his College, an office which he held from 1810 to 1825. During that time he seems to have been Vicar of High Offley (Staffs.) and Minister of St John the Baptist, Oxford. When he came to Chester as Dean in 1820 he received the Chapter living of Northenden, which he held till his death on 25 April 1825. Half the Chapter at this time had changed from what it was under Dean Cholmondeley, and was now constituted as follows:

Thomas Ward, M.A.	1781–1827
Thomas Trevor Trevor, D.C.L.	1795–1827
Unwin Clarke, M.A.	1811–1847
James Slade, M.A.	1816–1860
James Thomas Law, M.A.	1818–1828
Francis Wrangham, M.A.	1825–1843

James Slade was the son of a clergyman of Northamptonshire who had educated his boy himself, and evidently found it difficult to pay for him at Cambridge, for James went to Emmanuel College in 1800 as a sizar. However, he repaid his father's self-denial by being placed 9th Wrangler in 1804 and being made Fellow and Tutor of his College in 1806, in which year he was ordained. From 1807 to 1811 he managed to hold two curacies at once, Willingham (Camb.) and Dodford (Northants.). Then he got the living of Teversham (Camb.) and married on the strength of it, adding to it in 1813 the Vicarage of Milton in the same county. He resigned the latter benefice on being made Prebendary of Chester in 1816, but received instead the Vicarage of Bolton-le-Moors (Lancs.) in 1817, and the Rectory of Tattenhall (Ches.) in 1818. He resigned the latter and Teversham in 1826 when the Dean and Chapter presented him to Northenden, which he exchanged for West Kirby in 1829, and here at last he remained until his death in 1860, aged seventy-seven. For the last four years of his long life he ceased to be a pluralist, for he resigned Bolton in 1856. He attained a great reputation as a preacher and as an advocate of Church reform—(including the abolition of pluralism?)—and the Bolton Parish Sunday School became famous under his care. He also wrote several books on the Bible.

James Thomas Law, eldest son of a Carlisle clergyman, was educated at the Grammar School there and went to Christ's College, Cambridge in 1807. He took his B.A. in 1812, was made Fellow of his College in 1814 and was ordained priest in 1815. His first living was Tattenhall which he held for only two years (1816–18) and then was made Prebendary of both Lichfield and Chester Cathedrals—this at the early age of twenty-eight and in the third year of his priesthood. This rapid promotion was due to shameless nepotism on the part of the Bishop of Chester, George Henry Law, who was his brother. To his two pre-bends Law the younger added the livings of Childwall (Lancs.) and Bowdon (Ches.) (1818–21), and while at Bowdon he married Lady Henrietta Charlotte Gray, eldest daughter of the Earl of Stamford. In 1821 he was made Chancellor of Lichfield and in 1825 Vicar of Harborne (Staffs.), a living he resigned in 1845 on being given the sinecure office of Master of St John's Hospital, Lichfield,[1] where he died in 1876. In the meantime he had been obliged to resign his Chester prebend (1828) for reasons which will be given later. Besides some ecclesiastical works he was the author of *The Poor Man's Garden or a few brief rules regulating allotments of land to the poor for potato gardens.*

Francis Wrangham, who was admitted a sizar at the age of sixteen to Magdalene College, Camb., in 1785, was the son of a Yorkshire farmer,

[1] Cf. *The Warden* (1855), by Anthony Trollope.

and went to school in Hull. He took his B.A. in 1790 (3rd Wrangler). Ordained in 1794 he was made Vicar of Hunmanby with Muston, Yorks., a benefice which he held for the rest of his life. He was made F.R.S. in 1804, Archdeacon of Cleveland in 1820 and Prebendary of York in 1823. In 1827 he came to Chester as Prebendary of the Cathedral and was given the living of Dodleston. He resigned his other cures except Hunmanby, but in 1828 was made Archdeacon of the East Riding. He was an ardent book collector and a friend of William Wordsworth. He died on 27 December 1842.

DEAN COPLESTON 1826–28

The new Dean was a Devon man and managed to combine his duties as Dean with those of Provost of Oriel College, Oxford. His career was wholly academic, for he was made Fellow of Oriel as soon as he had graduated. From 1802 to 1812 he was Professor of Poetry. He went on from Chester to become Bishop of Llandaff in 1826 and Dean of St Paul's in 1828.

RESTORATION OF ST OSWALD'S CHURCH

It must have been shortly before his departure in 1824 that Bishop Law ordered the parishioners of St Oswald's (the South Transept of the Cathedral) to put their church into complete repair. According to *The Stranger's Companion* of 1825 it was separated from the rest of the Cathedral by a screen and contained nothing worthy of remark: "From the nature of the building it is very heavy and gloomy". The details of the restoration are given in the 1833 edition, which records that:

> The whole was new flagged and pewed,[1] a new pulpit and reading desk added; and the old gallery, which was at the west side, taken down, and a new one erected at the south end; the walls were cleaned, and the whole as far as possible, renewed; so that it is now the neatest Church in the City.

In that period to call a building "neat" was the highest praise you could give it. The 1849 edition adds this paragraph:

> In the following year (1828) several other improvements were added by the munificence of Dean Copleston. Hitherto the screen, which divided the parish church from the side aisles of the nave and choir, was com-

---

[1] *The Ecclesiologist* for April 1846 wrote: "One of the first improvements should be the *unpewing* of the spacious and beautiful South Transept" (quoted in *History of Chester Cathedral*, J. Hicklin, p. 99).

paratively low, but this he raised to the roof; a handsome throne for the bishop was also placed against the screen inside the church, on each side of which is an elevated seat, one for the dean and the other for the precentor. Under the superintendence of Dr. Copleston also, the ground within the Cloisters and the Churchyard was lowered to its level, and a trench dug round the building from south to north, in order to preserve the interior from dampness.

So that although this Dean was only in Chester for two years he made a valuable contribution to the fabric of the Cathedral. There is some difference of opinion about the screen, for Winkles (1842) calls it a wall,[1] but this seems hardly likely. There were two doors in it, leading into the two aisles of the parish church.

The south window seems to have been included in the restoration ordered by Bishop Law, for the editor of *The Stranger's Companion* (1833) writes:

> The south window, from its newness and modern appearance certainly does not tend to increase our veneration, though it must be admitted that it was not placed there before something of the kind was required. The former window was unquestionably one of the most magnificent of its kind, and was the wonder and praise of every scientific admirer. Just before it was taken down, several draughts were made of it by artists of the city, so that its beautiful form may still be contemplated with delight.

Would that some of these "draughts" had survived.[2]

ST THOMAS' COURT 1783–1815

The minutes of this Court, if they may be so called, have survived for the above years. They are headed "The View of Frank Pledge with the Court Baron of the Reverend the Dean and Chapter", but in the Steward's order to the Bailiff to summon the court it is styled "The Court Leet and Court Baron". All three titles take us back to Norman times. The frank pledge was originally an association of ten men who were to be standing securities for one another and bound to report any offenders within their ranks. They met twice a year to be "viewed", and this "view" became associated with the Court Leet or private police court held by the Lord of the Manor for his tenants. "Twice a year", says S. R. Maitland, "the villagers, bond or free, had to report themselves and tell tales of one another".[3] After the passage

---

[1] *Cathedrals in Great Britain*, III, p. 62.
[2] The present window was put in in 1887.
[3] Pollock and Maitland, *History of English Law*, I, 581.

of seven centuries we find them still doing so, albeit with considerable reluctance. In this court the bailiff was the judge. The Court Baron was originally for the free tenants of the manor and they themselves were the judges, but the distinction between the two courts had long ago been given up since there was no longer any distinction between servile and free tenure of land. In the Court Leet in Norman times the fines were "affeered"—that is to say the amount to be paid by each person who had been found guilty was fixed by two or more of the suitors who were sworn to do the work justly.[1] Strange though it may seem, this practice still continued right down to the nineteenth century. In 1814 for example we find:

Affeerers
We Edward Bailey and Thomas Millington Inhabitants within the View of Frank pledge chosen and sworn affeerers by the Court having heard the several amerciaments before mentioned read do adjudge the same to be reasonable.
                                        E. Bailey
                                        T. Millington.

We come now to the constitution of the Court at the end of the eighteenth century. It used to be held in the room north of and adjoining the Abbey gateway, according to Randle Holmes' plan, but from 1808 it seems to have been held in different inns, whose names are scribbled on the outside of the Minutes as, e.g., in 1808 and 1814 The Ram in Boughton, in 1809 The Castle and Falcon in Watergate St, and the Red Lion in Boughton; in 1810 The Stag's Head, "behind the Exchange", in 1811 The Bull's Head and The Wheatsheaf in Boughton. There were 83 tenants distributed as follows:

Outside Chester	5	Parsons Lane	2	Boughton	36
Abbey Square	5	Watergate Street	1	Bridge Trafford	8
Northgate Street	25	Cuppins Lane	1	Total——83	

A Jury of 18 was summoned (and its members were fined if they did not appear)—9 from Chester and the other 9 from Boughton and Trafford in proportion to the number of tenants in those places. All the "suitors" or tenants were summoned, and the chief and often the only business of the Court was fining those who did not attend. Once a year, however, a constable and a burleyman were elected.[2] The duties of the latter were to

[1] Pollock and Maitland, *History of English Law*, I, 560.
[2] The burleyman—a word described as obsolete in the *English Dialect Dictionary* (1888)—is still in use at Antrobus, a village a few miles from Northwich. He is

Present defaulters—and other Presentments. You shall well and truly
affeer and affirm (?) the several amerciaments here made and now to you
read over; you shall spare no one out of Love, Fear, or Affection, nor raise
or enhance [the fine of] anyone out of malice or hatred, but impartially
shall do your duty herein. So help it.

A letter of apology for non-attendance has been preserved among
the records of the Court and is here reproduced in its original spelling:

gentlemen,

As I am on the King's duty and cannot atend on your Court this Day I
hope youl be so good to excuse me and I shall be glad to wett any other
time with Pliuser in your Company.

I am gentilmen your very
Humbel Servint

Chester 31 Octbr. 1796   Davd. Melvill.

The word is certainly "wett", but there is no mention in the Accounts
of a dinner in connection with the Court. However, another loose
paper without heading or date suggests that the word is justified!

	£	s.	d.
24 Dinners at 2/-		2	8	0
1 Bottle Brandy			10	0
2 Do of Rum			16	0
2 Do of Wine			11	0
3 Do of Gin			12	0
3 Bowles of Sugar			1	6
4 Lemons			1	0
Tobacco				8
		5	0	2
Ale and Porter			19	4
		£5	19	6

The presentments made to the Court were few and far between.
Many years passed without any being made at all, except for non-
attendance at the Court. Such presentments as there were are usually
of persons who have not scoured their water course, but in 1801 we
have a complaint that in Great Boughton a "certain garden place,
adjoining that of Mr. George Lowe, is become a place of resort for
many idle and disorderly persons who assemble there upon the Lord's

appointed by the parish council to assess damage done by straying cattle. "The
word is derived from the 'bye-law man', who carried out the local customs of a
manor or township." (Boyd, p. 79.)

Day and practise gaming and create great disturbance to the neigh-
bourhood by quarrelling and profane language".

Also in 1803 there was a pigstye in Sandy Lane that was deemed a
nuisance and the owner was given a month in which to move it. John
Healey Butcher was presented "for not ditching his ditch and repairing
the plott adjoining the Hoole Lane Field and along the Green Lane in
Boughton", Thomas Taylor and Edwd. Mainwaring Esqs. were
presented for not repairing a garden wall.

The right to hold a private court was one which was jealously
guarded, for the fines went to the Lord of the Manor. One would
have thought that they were not worth very much in these later days
but in 1769 the Dean and Chapter paid the Chapter Clerk's "Bill of
costs in the dispute between the Dean and Chapter and Trafford
Barnston Esq. as to the right of the suit and service of the inhabitants
of Bridge Trafford to the Court Leet and Court Baron of the Manor
of St Thomas", amounting to £43 18s. 9d. So they must have thought
it a privilege worth fighting for.

To complete the picture let us glance at the Manor Court of Tarporley which came into the hands of the Dean and Chapter as a result
of the Arderne legacy in c. 1740. In 1815 three persons were presented
"for leaving pigs going at large in the public street of Tarporley" and
five persons "for leaving dunghills" in the same street. But the most
interesting presentment is that of Dean Cholmondeley himself "for
stopping the way to a public well called the Church Well and taking
away the water from the same and we amerce him in the sum of ten
pounds". This is an interesting example of the rights of the Manor
Court to punish the Lord of the Manor himself if he transgressed the
custom of the manor, a right which goes back to Saxon times. "The
custom of the manor" was superior to private rights.

We notice in conclusion that in 1810 "it is agreed by the jury of this
meeting that all Pigs found in the street at Tarporley shall be taken to
the pinfold and fined".

THE BUILDING OF NOS. 2-8 ABBEY STREET

No one can view the Cathedral from the north without regretting
the row of four houses in Abbey Street, which have no architectural
merit in themselves and completely block the view of the Refectory
and the Cathedral behind it, and the question is often asked why they
were ever allowed to be built. The answer is that they were built by
one of the prebendaries in opposition to the Dean and the rest of the

Chapter, as a result of which the offender was suspended by the Bishop, who suffered an action in the King's Bench in consequence. This is how it happened.

In 1821 Prebendary James Thomas Law persuaded a Chapter meeting consisting of only two others beside himself to give him a lease of his prebendal property, consisting of Nos. 1 and 2 Abbey Square[1] and a stable and garden in Abbey Street, We can let him tell his own story in a letter to Dean Copleston, at Oriel College, Oxford, dated 28 September 1826:

> I succeeded to a most dilapidated prebendal property. Being engaged at the time building etc at Bowdon I put off any expenses of bricks and mortar at Chester. But my Father . . . informed the Chapter that he considered my houses in Abbey Square, as left by Mr. Preby. Sawkins, a nuisance. The Chapter of course would do nothing, but put the whole onus upon me. I laid out in consequence £800 to £1000 on my property there. But I told the Chapter my predecessors had a lease for 40 years as an encouragement to them, and I claimed the same indulgence, which was granted to me. When I had finished my House, I turned to my Stables, and told Dean Vaughan they were in a shocking state, and must be taken down. [He asked the Chapter to take them over and give him something in exchange, but they declined.] Whilst I was yet doubtful what my next step should be, a respectable man named Thomas offered to take a Building Lease of the Land. As the Dean and Chapter seemed so totally indifferent what was done, I accepted his offer, first sending him to Mr. Eaton, the Chapter Clerk, to see that all was correct. That is my case.

The Dean's case may be read in a memorial he presented to the Bishop dated 26 April 1827, requesting him to "Visit" the Cathedral.

> Soon after my Installation in September last my attention was drawn to a row of brick houses then building in Abbey Street on a narrow strip of ground between the Street and the Cloisters, which all the neighbours regarded as a nuisance, the houses being of an inferior order and likely to introduce a low population within the precincts of the Church. They were besides objectionable as darkening the School windows, confining the air, hiding the ancient architecture of the Abbey, and carrying back their offices within a few feet of the School window.

The Dean also said that the lease which Law had obtained was not a valid one, as it contravened the Statutes, and in any case it expressly stipulated that the stables should be maintained and kept in a state of

[1] See p. 231.

repair, and he had pulled them down. Law met these arguments by a counter-attack.

> I consider [he wrote in his letter to the Dean quoted above] the Archdeacon's stables, *blocking-up* the East Window of the School as a *much greater* nuisance. Perhaps you would begin by having them removed? Again, the house immediately opposite the Deanery, I mean Mr. Rowland's surgery etc., and also the houses to your right as you go along the passage[1] from the Deanery to the Cathedral surely are worse. They too should be previously removed.

So the correspondence went on, Law sitting securely in his Lichfield prebendal house and only once coming to Chester to attend a Chapter meeting called expressly to settle this dispute. The Dean's patience began to be exhausted. In January 1827, he arrived in Chester from Oxford and received a note from Prebendary Trevor, Vicar of Eastham, asking him to put his views before the Chapter, as he was too ill to attend himself. In reply the Dean gave vent to his feelings.

> I am come [he wrote] resolved as to the course it becomes me to take. We have been too lenient and forbearing already. It seems to have encouraged Mr. Law to act towards us, not as a person who has fallen into a material error, which he regrets and would willingly amend, but as a party who sets us at defiance, who sneers at our efforts of kindness, and who presumes to treat on a footing of offensive familiarity the body whose statutes he has violated for his own benefit.

What the Chapter wanted was that Law should surrender his lease and remove the half-built houses and they were prepared to meet him half-way if he would consent to do this.

Then on 13 February 1827, Mr Thomas intervened. Writing from King Street, he said he was called upon either to complete the houses forthwith or "pay the Contractor for the building of them agreeably to a measurement price *as they now are*". As he thought the latter would cost almost as much as the former he proposed to finish them, and finish them he did, and that is how they are with us to this day.

The rest of the story is soon told. In July 1827 Bishop Blomfield was called in as Visitor, with the result that he suspended Law. The latter refused to resign and hung on until towards the end of 1829, though without salary. During 1828 he applied in the Court of King's Bench for "a Rule to show cause why a Writ of Prohibition should not issue

---

[1] A picture of the passage is in the *The Stranger's Companion*, 1833.

against Dr. Blomfield", but the Judges returned a vague and indeterminate decision, and as the Bishop was just then translated to London, the case was dropped.

We learn from this unhappy dispute two hitherto unknown dates of buildings in the precincts. The date of Nos. 2–8 Abbey Street is 1828 and the date of 1 and 2 Abbey Square is 1821–6. A glance at these two houses will reveal to the most unobservant eye the difference in style between them and the rest of the houses on that side of the Square. We miss especially the Georgian front doorways.

In the Accounts for 1829 the name of James Thomas Law is superseded by Richard Vanbrugh Law, who is in turn superseded in 1834 by William Barlow. Meanwhile Dean Copleston in 1828 had been promoted to the Deanery of St Paul's and the Bishopric of Llandaff, and his place was taken at Chester by Henry Phillpotts, D.D., who had been Prebendary of Durham. He was also Rector of Stanhope and continued to hold that benefice in addition to his Deanery. In 1831 he was made Bishop of Exeter and George Davys took his place as Dean. Davys had been Fellow of Christ's College, Cambridge (1806–14), Vicar of Willoughby-on-the-Wolds, Notts. (1811–29) and in 1827 was appointed tutor to Princess Victoria. Perhaps it is not too fanciful to see a connection between this appointment and the opening of Grosvenor Bridge by the Princess in 1832.

EPILOGUE

We conclude with a general view of the Cathedral as it was in the year Queen Victoria ascended the throne.[1]

Starting at the west end of the nave, which of course was devoid of chairs or pews, we should find the Norman arches of the present bapistery blocked up in order to provide a wine cellar for the Bishop's palace. A flat wooden ceiling obscured the stone work above the arches of the central tower. The choir was divided from the nave by the pulpitum, a mediaeval stone wall adorned with the eighteenth-century arms of Earls of Chester, which are now to be found affixed to the south wall of the refectory. The pulpitum had a projecting porch in the middle of it on which was placed the organ—"a full-toned organ, newly erected by Messrs. Bewcher and Fleetwood".[2] The choir itself was cluttered up with ugly box pews and galleries, from which the Bishop's throne must have stood out in marked contrast, built as it

[1] Based on Hemingway, op. cit. and *The Stranger's Companion*, 1833 edition.
[2] A view of the nave at this time is given in Ormerod, I, 254.

was out of parts of St Werburgh's shrine. A pulpit stood opposite to it.
The arch behind the high altar was blocked by a stone screen, and it was
probably on this that the tapestry now on the west wall of the refectory
was displayed to form a reredos. The Lady Chapel was open on both
sides to take in both St Werburgh's Chapel on the north and the
corresponding chapel (destroyed by Gilbert Scott) on the south.

APPENDIX I

CHRONOLOGICAL LIST OF BISHOPS AND DEANS

BISHOPS OF CHESTER

Succession of the Bishops over the Diocese of Chester founded out of the Diocese of Lichfield, 1541:

1541   John Bird, D.D., Oxon. Deprived by Queen Mary, 1554. Buried at Great Dunmow, Essex, 1558.

1554   George Cotes, D.D., Oxon. Died at Chester, 1555.

1556   Cuthbert Scott, D.D., Camb. Deprived, and died at Louvain, 1565.

1561   William Downham, D.D., Oxon. Died in Nov., 1577. Buried in Chester Cathedral.

1579   William Chaderton, D.D., Camb. Translated to Lincoln, 1595.

1595   Hugh Billet or Bellot, D.D., Camb. Buried at Wrexham.

1597   Richard Vaughan, D.D., Camb. Translated to London, 1604.

1605   George Lloyd, D.D., Camb. Buried in Chester Cathedral.

1616   Thomas Morton, D.D., Camb. Translated to Lichfield and Coventry, 1619.

1619   John Bridgeman, D.D., Camb. Held the See until Episcopacy was suspended by the Commonwealth. Died about 1652, and was buried at Kinnerley, Shropshire.

1660   Brian Walton, D.D., Camb. Died at London. Buried in St Paul's Cathedral, 1661.

1662   Henry Ferne, D.D., Camb. Died at London before he took possession of the See.

1662   George Hall, D.D., Oxon. Died at Wigan, and was buried in the Parish Church there, 1668.

1668   John Wilkins, D.D., F.R.S., Oxon. Died at London, and was buried at St Lawrence Jewry.

1673   John Pearson, D.D., F.R.S., Camb. Died at Chester. Buried in the Cathedral.

1686   Thomas Cartwright, D.D., Oxon. Died in Ireland and was buried in Christ Church, Dublin, 1689.

1689   Nicholas Stratford, D.D., Oxon. Died in 1707 and was buried in Chester Cathedral.

1708   Sir William Dawes, Bart., D.D., Camb. Translated to York.

1714   Francis Gastrell, D.D., Oxon. Died 1725. Buried in Christ Church, Oxford.

1726   Samuel Peploe, D.D., Oxon. Died 1752. Buried in Chester Cathedral.

1752   Edmund Keene, D.D., Camb. Translated to Ely, 1771.

1771   William Markham, D.C.L., Oxon. Translated to York, 1777.

1777   Beilby Porteus, D.D., Camb., Translated to London, 1787.

1788   William Cleaver, D.D., Oxon. Translated to Bangor, 1800.

1800   Henry William Majendie, D.D., Camb. Translated to Bangor, 1809.

1810   Bowyer Edwd. Sparke, D.D., Camb. Translated to Ely, 1812.

1812   George Henry Law, D.D., Camb. Translated to Bath and Wells, 1824.

1824   Charles J. Blomfield, D.D., Camb. Translated to London, 1828.

1828   John Bird Sumner, D.D., Camb. Translated to Canterbury, 1848.

1848   John Graham, D.D., Camb. Died at Chester, 1865. Buried in the Cemetery, Chester.

1865   William Jacobson, D.D., Oxon. Died at Chester, 1884. Buried in the Cemetery, Chester.

1884   William Stubbs, D.D., LL.D., Oxon. Translated to Oxford, 1888.

1889   Francis John Jayne, D.D., Oxon. Resigned 1919. Died at Oswestry, 1921. Buried at Bowdon.

1919   Henry Luke Paget, D.D., Oxon. Resigned 1932. Died at London, 1937. Buried at Kingsbury.

1932   Geoffrey Francis Fisher, D.D., Oxon. Translated to London, 1939; translated to Canterbury, 1945.

1939   Douglas Henry Crick, D.D., Lambeth. Resigned 1955.

1955   Gerald Alexander Ellison, D.D., Lambeth

DEANS OF CHESTER

1541   Thomas Clark. The last Abbot of St Werburgh's.

1541   Henry Mann, D.D., Oxon. Afterwards Bishop of Sodor and Man.

1547   William Cliffe, D.D., LL.D., Oxon.

1558   Richard Walker, M.A. The last Dean of St John's, Chester.

1567   John Piers, D.D., Oxon. Afterwards Bishop of Rochester and Salisbury, and Archbishop of York.

1572   Richard Longworth, D.D., Camb.

1579   Richard Dorset, D.D.

1580   Thomas Modesley, B.D.

1589   John Nutter, B.D.

1603   William Barlow, D.D., Camb. Afterwards Bishop of Rochester and Lincoln.

1605   Henry Parry, D.D., Oxon. Successively Bishop of Rochester, Gloucester and Worcester.

1606   Thomas Mallory, B.D., Camb.

1644   William Nicholls, D.D., Camb.

1660 Henry Bridgeman, D.D., Oxon. Also Bishop of Sodor and Man.
1682 James Arderne, D.D., Camb.
1692 Laurence Fogge, D.D., Camb.
1718 Walter Offley, Oxon.
1722 Thomas Allen, LL.D., Camb.
1732 Thomas Brooke, LL.D., Oxon.
1758 William Smith, D.D., Oxon.
1786 George Cotton, D.D., L.L.D.
1806 Hugh Cholmondeley, B.D., F.S.A.
1816 Robert Hodgson, D.D.
1820 Peter Vaughan, D.D.
1826 Edward Copleston, D.D., Oxon. Later Bishop of Llandaff.
1828 Henry Phillpots, D.D., Oxon. Later Bishop of Exeter.
1831 George Davys, D.D., Camb. Later Bishop of Peterborough.
1839 Frederick Anson, D.D., Oxon. Died 1867.
1867 John Saul Howson, D.D., Camb. Died 1885. Buried in the Cathedral Garth Garden.
1886 John Lionel Darby, D.D., Dublin. Died 1919.
1920 Frank Selwyn Macauley Bennett, M.A., Oxon., D.D. Resigned 1937. Died 1947.
1937 Norman Henry Tubbs, M.A., D.D., Camb. Formerly Bishop of Rangoon. Resigned 1953.
1954 Michael McCausland Gibbs, M.A.

APPENDIX II

A FULL RENTAL OF THE REVENUE BELONGING TO THE CATHEDRAL CHURCH OF CHRIST AND THE BLESSED VIRGIN MARY IN CHESTER PERFECTED BY ELLIS RYECROFT, 1663.[1]

	£	s.	d.
Bailywick of Chester			
From Wm Jollife Esq. for ye revenue issueing out of ye premises	73	00	00
Rectory of St Oswalds			
From Edward Russell for Boughton Barne	15	00	00
From John Hurlston Esq. for Wirvin barn	7	16	00
From George Manley Esq. for Chester barn	24	01	00
From Edward Russell for ye green churchyard		11	4
From Roger Mostyn & Alice Barnston for 2 gardens & a highway		04	04
From Henry Harpur for a garden etc. near ye Wolfs head		02	00
Tollage of Dee Mills			
From John Brerewood Esq. Thomas Weston cum aliis	5	00	00
St Oswald's Altarages			
From John Case for ye Altarages issueing out of ye premises	5	00	00
Saughton tythes			
From ye heires of Alderman Charles Walley	2	00	00
Huntingdon tythes			
From ye heires of Sr George Beverly	1	00	00
Brewhouse			
From John Ratcliffe Esq. for his rent of ye brewhouse wth its appurtences	2	4	0
Pensions from ye Rectories			
Chrisleton	1	3	0
Dodleston		18	0
Codington		3	0
Warton		4	0
Tattenhall		3	0
Hanley		13	4
Astbury		12	0
Northenden		4	0
Bebington	1	6	8

[1] Written at the end of a small calf-bound volume of the Statutes in the Cathedral Library.

		£	s.	d.
Eastham		1	13	4
Wallazey		2	0	
Thurstaston		5	0	
St Peter's Chester		2	0	0
West Kirby		2	13	4
St Maries Chester		2	13	4

14 16 0

Whitbie, Lea & Overpoole
From Thomas Glaseor Esq.   40 2 2
ex Manerio de Lea £10 11s. 4d.
de Whitby & Overpool £29 10s. 10d.
[to be paid at West door twice a year: penalties for non-payment]
Whitbie
John Frogge   2 8 6
James Halewood   1 12 0
John Pye   1 4 0

5 4 6

Sutton, Elton, Avernley, Ince, etc.
From Thomas Cholmondeley Esq. for his rent issueing out of yᵉ
premises   168 19 0
Eastham Plymyard Ferryboat etc.
From Sir Willm. Stanley for Eastham   24
Eastham wood & Ferrie boat   1 13 6
Plymyard   5 5 11   30 19 5
The Mannʳ of Saughton
From yᵉ heires of Alderman Charles Walley for yᵉ rent issueing
out of ye premises   51 12 02
Stanford Mill & tenemᵗ
From Peter Venables Esq. Baron of Kinderton for his rent
issueing out of yᵉ premises etc.   25 13 8
Huntingdon, Cheveley & Crewe
From — ¹Cotton Esq. for his rent etc.   29 11 00
Rectory of Presbury
From Thomas Legh Esq. for his rent etc.   113 11 04
Rectory of Neston
From Henry Harpur Esq. for his rent of yᵉ tyth issueing etc. 41 12 09
Rufford in Comᵈ Lane
From — Hesketh Esq. a Fee farm rent issueing out of yᵉ same
mannʳ of Rufford   2 0 0
Castle rent
From yᵉ Kˢ Maᵗⁱᵉ for a Fee farm rent issueing out of yᵉ Earledom
of Chester   19 10 00

¹ In this and in a few other places a hiatus occurs in the original document.

				£	s.	d.
Long Meadow in Moston						
John Cowles 2 pts	2	0	5			
Geo. Legh Esq. a 3^d part	1	0	0	3	0	5
Northerden [*sic*]						
From Sam: Vaudrey Esq. a fee farm rent etc.				1	2	9
Irebi, Gresby, Frankby, Wallazey, Knoctorum						
Edw. Glege Esq. for Irby hall	4	10	2½			
[24 other names]				31	13	4
Barnshawe						
From Hen: Mainwaring Esq. for his rent etc.				54	00	10
Newton, Wirvin Croughton & Idenshawe						
From John Hurlston Esq. & Sir Peter Pyndar Knight for ye rent etc.				52	8	2
Bromborough, Childerthornton & Nether Bebington						
James Green Esq. for Bromb. hall	21	15	3			
[13 other names]				32	11	3
Tilston Fernall						
From Sir Thomas Wilbraham Bart. for his rent etc.				5	13	2
Chisleton						
From Raph Cotgrave for his rent etc.					15	10
Brumbrough Glebe land & wood						
From Sir Thomas Powell for his rent issueing out of ye premises, one capital messuage & water mill				10	4	4
Upton						
[6 names]				31	7	0
Moston						
Raph Morgell for Moston demesne	5	16	6			
Willm Brock Esq.		13	2			
— Moston & — Barnston for Alderseys l^{ds}	2	5	4			
Geo. Chamberlain for H. Birkinheads l^{ds}		3	4			
G. Chamberlain more for p^t of Mr Moston's l^{ds}		3	4			
				9	1	8
Chorleton						
John Hatton		7	0			
Robert Ashton	2	12	8			
Geo. Chamberlain for Mary Forshawe's l^{ds}	1	18	10			
Geo. Legh for Mr Margell's lands	1	12	5			
Hen: Margell for Mr Robinson's lands	1	18	10	8	9	6
Boughton [18 names]				40	0	2
Saughall & Shotwick						
Robert Leicesters heires		11	4			
— Johnson	1	14	10			

£ s. d.

Robert Mason for Geo. Barkleys lds.	1 10 2½	
Doe	19 10	
Tho. Jackson for Edw. Cowens lds.	1 1 2	
Richard Clark	8 6	
Willm Clark	6 3	
Thomas Chamberlain	16 0	
Joseph Hocknell Esq.	1 11 1½	

8 19 3

Chorleton Mill
From ye heires of Thomas Whitfeild for a rent etc.   1 14 8
Boughton Mill
From ye heires of John Hankie for a rent etc.   2 12 10
Abbey Court
From Raph Morgell for ye rent of a house adjoining the Bp's
Registry   2 10 0
From Mr John Oldfeild for ye rent of an house due   1 0 0
From Mrs Elizabeth Bridgeman for ye rent of a house due   6 8
Northgate Street, Chester
From John Grimsdich for his rente issueing out of a parcell of
land lyeing near ye North gate streete   1 14 8
Rectory of Shotwick   23 7 0
Hilbree Island & Boardland tythe West Kirby
From — for Hilbre & the Boardland tyths ye old
reserved rent viz ye Boardland tyths £2 13s. 4d. & for Hilbree
2s. 9d.   2 16 1
Totall of ye Revenue of the Cathedral of Chester   984 12 8

[Note. £40 0s. 2d. for Boughton has been counted twice over!]

Whereof Decayed rents
Huntingdon tythe Mr H. Harpur   1 0 0
Rufford Mr Hesketh now payeth   2 0 0
Boughton Mill Thos Hankeys heirs   2 13 10
Chorlton mill Tho. Whitfeilds heires   1 14 8
S. Peter's pension   2 0 0

Wch makes   £9 7 6

The gross income of the Monastery at the Dissolution was £1,080 16s. 10½d.
In 1607 it was £970 8s. 4d., of which £910 5s. 11½d. was received (from
Receiver books).
In 1663 it was £984 12s. 8d., but actually only £934 0s. 6d. (see p. 135).
18+

BIBLIOGRAPHY AND ABBREVIATIONS

Acts of the Privy Council, 1575–7. Rolls Series, 163.

Anon.	*A History of Chester Cathedral*, by a member of the Chester Archaeological Society, between 1850 and 1867.
Barber	Ven. E. Barber, *Handbook to Chester Cathedral*, 1920.
Boyd	A. W. Boyd, *A Country Parish*, 1951.
Bridgeman	Rev. J. T. O. Bridgeman, *History of Wigan Church*.
C.A.J.	*Chester Archaeological Journal*.
Calamy	A. G. Matthews, *Calamy Revised*.
Ches. Hist.	*Cheshire Historian*.
Chetham	Chetham Society.
Cowper	Cowper MSS. collected by Dr William Cowper, M.D., F.S.A. (1701–67), now housed in the County Record Office, Chester Castle.

Durham Account Rolls, Surtees Society, CIII.

Earwaker	J. P. Earwaker, *The History of the Church and Parish of St Mary-on-the-Hill*, Chester, 1898.
Foster	J. Foster, *Alumni Oxonienses*.
Hanshall	J. H. Hanshall, *History of the City and County Palatine of Chester*, 1823.
Harl.	Harleian MSS. in the British Museum.
Hemingway	J. Hemingway, *A History of the City of Chester*, 2 vols., 1831.
Ledger	Bishop Bridgeman's *Ledger* in the Diocesan Registry.
L. and C. Ant. Soc.	Lancashire and Cheshire Antiquarian Society.
L. and C. Hist. Soc.	Lancashire and Cheshire Historic Society.
L. and C. Record Soc.	Lancashire and Cheshire Record Society.
L. and P. Dom.	Calendar of Letters and Papers, Domestic.
Lysons	D. and S. Lysons, *Magna Britannia*, vol. II, Part II.

Moore   The Rev. P. C. Moore, Ph.D., *Cathedral Worship in England since the Reformation.*

Morris   P. H. Morris, *Chester during the Plantagenet and Tudor Periods,* undated, but later than 1881.

Notitia Cestriensis, Bishop Gastrell, Chetham Soc., Vol. VIII.

Ormerod   G. Ormerod, *History of the County Palatine and City of Chester,* 2nd edition, ed. T. Helsby, 1882.

Palatine Note Book

Parker   J. H. Parker, *The Mediaeval Architecture of Chester,* 1858.

Phillips   C. S. Phillips, *Canterbury Cathedral in the Middle Ages,* S.P.C.K.

Piccope   G. J. Piccope, ed. *Wills and inventories from the Ecclesiastical Courts, Chester,* Chetham Soc. Vol. XXXIII.

P.R.O.   Public Record Office.

Pigot   [J. N. Pigot.] *History of the City of Chester,* 1815.

Registers   *Registers of Chester Cathedral,* 1687–1812, Parish Register Society, 1904.

Richards   R. Richards, *Old Cheshire Churches,* 1947.

Rites of Durham, Surtees Society, CVII.

Scott   S. Cooper Scott, *Lectures on the History of St John Baptist Church and Parish, Chester,* 1899.

Sheaf   *The Cheshire Sheaf,* a weekly column in the *Chester Courant* begun in 1880 and forming an invaluable collection of local history.

Simpson   F. A. Simpson, *History of the Church of St Peter,* 1909.

Stow   John Stow, *Chronicles.*

Stranger's Companion, from *c.* 1823. G. Bateman, Chester.

Tatham   G. B. Tatham, *The Puritans in Power,* C.U.P., 1913.

Vale Royal   King's *Vale Royal,* 1656.

Venn   John and J. A. Venn, *Alumni Cantabrigienses.*

Walker   A. G. Matthews, *Walker Revised* (Walker's *Sufferings of the Clergy*).

Westlake   G. Westlake, *History of Westminster Abbey,* 2 vols., 1923.

Winkles   Winkles' *Cathedral Churches*, 3 vols., 1836.

Wirral Notes and Queries, 2 vols., 1892, 1893, ed. F. Sanders and W. Fergusson Irvine.

Wood   Anthony à Wood, *Athenae Oxonienses*.

The names of other books consulted will be found in the footnotes.

INDEX OF PERSONS AND PLACES

All places are in Cheshire except where otherwise stated

18*

INDEX OF TRADES

PAINTER
Hodges, 136

PLUMBER
Painter, 202
Plimmer, John, 52
Salt, Geo., 92

SHOEMAKER
Pulleyn, 31

SLATER
Coppach, Thos., 213
Sconce, 89

SMITH
Eaton, Thos., 93
Hulme, Thos., 52–3
Huntingdon, Wm., 14
Johnson, 94
Jones, Wm., 221
Sprag, John, 14

TAYLOR
Ashbrook, 214–5

UPHOLSTERER
Bingley, 182, 189
Hervey, 214
Parker, 186–7

VERGER
Ashbrooke, 202, 221
Davis, John, 189, 202
Evans, James, 170, 172–7, 180, 181
Fletcher, John, 158
Hughes, Chas., 187
Hughes, Henry, 123–5, 148, 150–1, 162
Parry, Peter, 187, 193, 201
Tailour, Wm., 189

WATER CARRIER
Hey, Hugh, 5

WHITESMITH
Hastings, Geo, 222
Totty, 176, 203

INDEX OF SUBJECTS

ANTHEMS, 194–5

BIBLE, 9, 14, 94
Bonfire, 38–9, 90
Brief, 168–70
Burleyman, 250

COINAGE, DEPRECIATION OF, 22–3
"Concealed Lands", 77
Correction, House of, 175, 212–3
Cock money, 209
Curfew, 188

DEODAND, 53

GABLE RENTS, 38
Gowrie conspiracy, 90–1

LIGHT HORSE, 94, 124–5

HAWARDEN PARK, 216
Horse pond, 14, 33, 62

MIDSUMMER SHOW, 38–9
Mortuary, 110

POOR RELIEF, 210–16
Pinfold, 221
Plague, The, 86, 186
Players, The, 61, 68

REGISTRY, THE, 220
Rowton Moor, Battle of, 126

ST THOMAS' COURT, 249
Ship money, 121
Singing bread, 16
S.P.C.K., 177, 243

VOLUNTEERS, THE, 231

WAITS, THE, 111
Water-leaders, 68
Wallasey Races, 153
Whitsun Plays, 43